IN THEIR OWN WORDS

Previous titles

A Canadian Shame: The Indian Act and Residential Schools

In Their Own Words

Testimony from the Students of Canada's Indigenous Residential School Program

By Darren Grimes

© 2022 by Darren Grimes
All rights reserved.

1. Indigenous History   2. Indigenous Studies   I. Title: In Their Own Words
II. Title: Testimony from the Students of Canada's Indigenous Residential School Program

Cover Art: Henry Hablak
Book Design: Natascha van Tonder
Editing: Natascha van Tonder

Special Thanks:
Natascha van Tonder
Graham Dunlop
Henry Hablak
Kyle Delisle
Ryan Gideon

Other Titles by Darren Grimes
A Canadian Shame: The Indian Act and Residential Schools
Acanadianshame.ca

Table of Contents

Table of Contents 5
Preface 7
Introduction 9
Before the Schools 12
Kidnapped by Institutions 27
Places of Refuge? 37
The Journey 42
Arriving at School 56
Day to Day Life in a Residential School 101
Chores 138
Religious Indoctrination 148
Breaking up Siblings 159
Student Gender Relations 167
Contact with Parents 175
Trauma, Emotional Neglect, and Despair 194
Truancy, Learning to Lie, or Worse 208
Harsh Discipline 218
Outright Abuse 241
Student vs Student 260
Warm memories 277
Graduation Days 285

TABLE OF CONTENTS

To conclude 290
Acknowledgements 292
Appendix 293
Bibliography 309

Preface

On June 11th, 2008, then Prime Minister Stephen Harper would formally apologize for the federal government's role in the Residential School Program initiating a 7 year "Truth and Reconciliation Commission". While far from perfect, it was the first attempt of any real substance to right the wrongs of the past, or at least to properly understand them. It also resulted in tens of thousands of hours of research and testimony, without which this book would not be possible.

"Mr. Speaker, I stand before you today to offer an apology to former students of Indian residential schools. The treatment of children in Indian residential schools is a sad chapter in our history. In the 1870's, the federal government, partly in order to meet its obligation to educate Aboriginal children, began to play a role in the development and administration of these schools.

Two primary objectives of the residential schools system were to remove and isolate children from the influence of their homes, families, traditions and cultures, and to assimilate them into the dominant culture. These objectives were based on the assumption Aboriginal cultures and spiritual beliefs were inferior and unequal. Indeed, some sought, as it was infamously said, "to kill the Indian in the child."

Today, we recognize that this policy of assimilation was wrong, has caused great harm, and has no place in our country. Most schools were operated as "joint ventures" with Anglican, Catholic, Presbyterian or United churches. The government of Canada built an educational system in which very young children were often forcibly removed from their homes, often taken far from their communities. Many were inadequately fed, clothed, and housed. All were deprived of the care and nurturing of their parents, grandparents, and communities.

First Nations, Inuit and Métis languages and cultural practices were prohibited in these schools. Tragically, some of these children died while attending residential schools and others never returned home.

The government now recognizes that the consequences of the Indian residential schools policy were profoundly negative and that this policy has had a lasting and damaging impact on Aboriginal culture, heritage, and language. While some former students have spoken positively about their experiences at residential schools, these stories are far overshadowed by tragic accounts of the emotional, physical, and sexual abuse and neglect of helpless children, and their separation from powerless families and communities.

The legacy of Indian residential schools has contributed to social problems that continue to exist in many communities today. It has taken extraordinary courage for the thousands of survivors that have come forward to speak publicly about the abuse they suffered. It is a testament to their resilience as individuals and to the strength of their cultures. Regrettably, many former students are not with us today and died never having received a full apology from the government of Canada. The government recognizes that the absence of an apology has been an impediment to healing and reconciliation.

PREFACE

> Therefore, on behalf of the government of Canada and all Canadians, I stand before you, in this chamber so central to our life as a country, to apologize to Aboriginal peoples for Canada's role in the Indian residential schools system.
>
> To the approximately 80,000 living former students, and all family members and communities, the government of Canada now recognizes that it was wrong to forcibly remove children from their homes and we apologize for having done this.
>
> We now recognize that it was wrong to separate children from rich and vibrant cultures and traditions, that it created a void in many lives and communities, and we apologize for having done this.
>
> We now recognize that, in separating children from their families, we undermined the ability of many to adequately parent their own children and sowed the seeds for generations to follow, and we apologize for having done this.
>
> We now recognize that, far too often, these institutions gave rise to abuse or neglect and were inadequately controlled, and we apologize for failing to protect you.
>
> Not only did you suffer these abuses as children, but as you became parents, you were powerless to protect your own children from suffering the same experience, and for this we are sorry.
>
> The burden of this experience has been on your shoulders for far too long. The burden is properly ours as a government, and as a country. There is no place in Canada for the attitudes that inspired the Indian residential schools system to ever again prevail. You have been working on recovering from this experience for a long time and in a very real sense, we are now joining you on this journey.
>
> The government of Canada sincerely apologizes and asks the forgiveness of the Aboriginal peoples of this country for failing them so profoundly. We are sorry.
>
> In moving towards healing, reconciliation, and resolution of the sad legacy of Indian residential schools, implementation of the Indian Residential Schools Settlement agreement began on September 19, 2007. Years of work by survivors, communities, and aboriginal organizations culminated in an agreement that gives us a new beginning and an opportunity to move forward together in partnership. A cornerstone of the settlement agreement is the Indian Residential Schools Truth and Reconciliation Commission.
>
> This commission presents a unique opportunity to educate all Canadians on the Indian residential schools system. It will be a positive step in forging a new relationship between Aboriginal peoples and other Canadians, a relationship based on the knowledge of our shared history, a respect for each other and a desire to move forward together with a renewed understanding that strong families, strong communities, and vibrant cultures and traditions will contribute to a stronger Canada for all of us. [1]

---

[1] Harper, *Apology*, 2008

Introduction

In Canada, the Indian residential school system was a network of mandatory boarding schools for Indigenous peoples. The network was funded by the Canadian government's Department of Indian Affairs and administered by Christian churches. The school system was created to remove Indigenous children from the influence of their own culture and assimilate them into the dominant European-Canadian culture. Over the course of the system's more than hundred-year existence, at least 150,000 children were placed in residential schools nationally. By the 1930s about 30 percent of Indigenous children were believed to be attending residential schools. The number of school-related deaths remains unknown due to incomplete records. Estimates range from 3,200 to over 30,000.

Over the last few years, the history of the relationship between Canada's Indigenous peoples, the Government of Canada, and the church has come to the forefront of public discourse. A darker shade has been applied to the colonial history of the country which has had mixed results in acceptance from average Canadians. In the era of "wokeness", these topics can become even more incendiary than they have been historically, and even more careful attention must be made to how they are reported and discussed. Let me be clear that the point of this book is not to throw fuel on an already raging fire, but to make sure that in the discussion the voices of the students that attended these institutions is not lost in the political noise that frequents our reality in early 2022.

Governments and Institutions have historically been the largest purveyors of human suffering and the case of the Canadian Residential School System fits the mold. The relationship between Canadians and First Nations is one that would be better served by open dialogue than with legislation. We cannot move into a better or more unified future until the mistakes of the past are, at a minimum, realized. First Nations communities find themselves still to this day reeling and recovering from a culturally traumatic experience that is less than a generation past. Poverty, substance abuse, and suicide plague many Indigenous communities to this day and unless we learn the why of the situation correcting it for future generations seems impossible.

This book will avoid policy and solutions and focus more on storytelling, though not by the author, by the testimony of hundreds of Indigenous people that attended the schools over the last 50-60 years as recounted to the Truth and Reconciliation Commission of Canada between 2008 and 2015. In their own words we can hope to come to learn the pain they experienced daily. What it was like to be taken away from your family and community and raised in the schools, sometimes not seeing your family for months or years and in still more sad and extreme cases, never again. While painful, reading these accounts offer us all a brighter future, less affected by judgement and misunderstanding, and more favourable to empathy.

Introduction

It's time to move beyond blaming and shaming and into an era of understanding and compassion between Canada and First Nations communities. The point of this book is not to lay blame, but instead to start a conversation about our tumultuous past and how, with that past in mind, we can move forward, together. Before jumping into the stories from the courageous survivors of Canada's Residential School program, revisit their timeline (Appendix), as written by John Edmond.[2]

---

[2] Edmond, "Indian Residential Schools: A Chronology."

Before the Schools

In this chapter, students reminisce on happier and simpler times before the forced attendance of Residential Schools. Canada's Indigenous populations existed for thousands of years off the land and were still in a period of adjustment to the onset of Europeans and the creation of Reserves. In the mid 1880's the Residential School system would come into being and by 1920 amendments to the Indian Act would make attendance mandatory and made attendance at any other institution illegal.

The system was brought in by Prime Minister John A. MacDonald, after sending Nicholas Flood Davin to study industrial schools for Indigenous children in the United States. Davin's recommendation to follow the U.S. example of "aggressive civilization" led to public funding for the Canadian residential school system. "If anything is to be done with the Indian, we must catch him very young. The children must be kept constantly within the circle of civilized conditions," Davin wrote in his 1879 *Report on Industrial Schools for Indians and Half-Breeds*.[3]

While these students would have already been living under the reserve system for several years, mandatory attendance was to catch them off guard. Taking children once raised by the extended family and greater community into institutions to be raised by

---

[3] Davin Nicholas Flood, *Report*, 12.

Before the Schools

Government and Church officials who had little to no regard for their culture and it extreme cases, even their safety. In this first Chapter we will hear some accounts from life before being taken to the schools to live for months and even years at a time.

"When I think back to my childhood, it brings back memories, really nice memories of how life was as Anishinaabe, as you know, how we, how we lived before, before we were sent to school. And the things that I remember, the legends at night that my dad used to tell us, stories, and how he used to show us how to trap and funny things that happened. You know there's a lot of things that are really, that are still in my thoughts of how we were loved by our parents. They really cared for us. And it was such a good life, you know. It, it's doing the things, like, it was free, we were free I guess is the word I'm looking for, is a real free environment of us. I'm not saying that we didn't get disciplined if we got, if we did something wrong, we, you know. There was that, but not, but it was a friendly, friendly, like a loving discipline, if you will." — **Bob Baxter**.[4]

"I'm come from a long way, I came a long way. I'm from Great Lake Mistissini. That's where I was born in the bush. It was a pride for me to say that because I was born in the bush in a tent. It's something that remains in my heart going to the woods, living in the woods. It's in my heart. Before going to the boarding school, my parents often told

---
[4] TRC, *Statement*, 01-ON-24NOV10-012.

me what they were doing in the woods when I was born. What they were doing, we were in camp with other families. The stories my father told us, my mother, too." — **Louise Bossum**.[5]

Before she was enrolled in residential school in Québec in the 1960s, **Thérèse Niquay** lived on what she described as "the family territory." She had very positive memories of that part of her life.

"I remember especially the winter landscapes, fall landscapes too. I remember very well I often looked at my father, hunting beaver especially. I admired my father a lot. And I remember at one point I was looking at him, I think I was on the small hill, and he was below, he had made a hole in the ice, and he was hunting beaver with a, with a harpoon, and I was there, I was looking at him and I was singing. And I remember when I was kid I sang a lot, very often. And I also remember that we lived or my, my paternal grandmother was most often with us, my, my father's mother, and we lived in a large family also, an extended family in the bush. Those are great memories."[6]

Jeannette Coo Coo, who attended the La Tuque, Québec, school in the 1960s, said she was a member of what might be the last generation of Aboriginal people who were raised in the forest. "In the forest, what I remember of my childhood was bearskin, which I liked. I was there, and it was the

---

[5] TRC, *Statement*, SP105.
[6] TRC, *Statement*, SP105.

bearskin that my father put for us to sit on, that was it. That is why I'm pleased to see that here. And what I remember in my childhood also was the, my mother's songs, because we lived in tents, and there was young children, and my mother sang for the youngest, and at the same time this helped us to fall asleep. It was beneficial to everyone, my mother's songs, and that is what I remember, that is what I am happy to say that it was what was, I was raised with what was instilled in me, so to speak."[6]

Albert Elias grew up in the Northwest Territories near the community of Tuktoyaktuk. "Yeah, when I first opened, like, when I first saw the world, I guess, we were outdoors and when I opened my eyes and started to, you know, and I was just a baby, I guess, and I, we were out in the land. The land was all around me, the snow, the sky, the sun, and I had my parents. And we had a dog team. We were travelling, I think it was on Banks Island, and I was amazed at what I saw, just the environment, the peace, the strength, the love, the smile on my dad's face. And when I wake up he's singing a short song to me of love."[7]

Bob Baxter was born on the Albany River in northern Ontario. "So, that's how I, that's how I grew up, you know, and knowing all that stuff where listening to the familiar sounds of my dad's snowshoes in the winter when he came to, when he came back from trapping late in the afternoon,

---

[7] TRC, *Statement*, SC092.

towards, when it's already dark, and waiting for him to come home and tell us the legends, because no tv back then. So, it was great. My mom was great, too. She really looked after us, made sure that we were clothed and fed. That was good times. I remember eating wild game all the time. And 'cause we had our grandparents that really looked after us, too, that I have good memories of, until, 'til that day that we were taken from there, taken away to school."[8]

Prior to attending the Roman Catholic school in Kenora, Ontario, **Lynda Pahpasay McDonald** lived with her family near Sydney Lake in northwestern Ontario in the 1950s. "We spent most of our time in the trapline, in the cabin, and we'd play outside and it was really good. There was no drinking. There was, it was, like, it was a small sized cabin, and my parents took good care of us. And they were really, I remember those happy days, like there was no violence. We had a little bit of food, but we always had a meal, like we ate, the beaver meat or moose meat if my dad got a moose, and deer meat, and, and fish." She could not recall being physically disciplined during this time. "They more or less just told me, you know, don't do this, you know you'll hurt yourself and what not, but it was all in Ojibway, all spoken in Ojibway. And I spoke Ojibway when I was a child, and there was a lot of fun." Her mother would harvest plants to be used as medicine. "And we would, my parents would take us out blueberry picking, and my grandparents would always take us

---

[8] TRC, *Statement*, 01-ON-24NOV10-012.

blueberry picking, or we'd go in the canoe, and we'd go, you know, or my grandmother would always be gathering traditional medicines. She had picked the wild ginger, and I would go with her, and we'd go pick all the medicines that we needed. And I also remember my mom picking up this medicine. It would, like, if we had any cut, or open wound, she would use this, like a ball, like, sort of a fungus ball, and she would open it, and she would put it on our wounds and whatever, and would heal, you know, real fast. And, and she knew all her traditional medicines. And at the time, I remember my, my grandpa and my dad, they used to have a drum, and they would, you know, drum and they would sing, during certain times of the year."[9]

Mabel Brown had similar memories of her life growing up in the Northwest Territories. "You know life in the bush is really good. And when, when we were growing up we went, when my dad was alive, him and my mom brought us out into the bush. And we, we went as a family together. They taught us, when they'd teach us they taught us how to do things. They'd tell us first, they'd show us, and then we'd do it and then that's how we learned that. And that's how so many people now know when, when we see a snare or how to set it or set traps because my grandmother showed me how to set traps. And how to tell what kind of trees are what and what the different kind of things you take off the gum, and things like that; what it's used for and you know,

---

[9] TRC, *Statement*, 02-MB-16JU10-130.

chew and my mom and dad used to dig up roots from the ground and I used to just love that roots. Chew on it and all those things are medicine for our bodies too. And I still, I still, can't eat just store-bought foods. I have to have caribou or fish or moose meat or something like that and to, to feel full; to feel satisfied."[10]

Emily Kematch was born in 1953 in York Factory, Manitoba, and grew up in York Landing. "My family is Cree in origin. My mom and dad spoke Cree and that's my Native language is Cree and that's the only language I spoke at home. And when I was six years old, I only understood basic, really like from my brothers and sisters when they came back from residential school. Like, 'What is your name?' And I knew to say, 'Emily' and not very much English. And I was very close to my mother. Her and I were, I was just attached to her like, I loved my mother and I knew she loved me. Same with my father, he showed it in different ways. He was a very quiet man, but his actions spoke volumes. He hunted, he was a hunter, a trapper, a fisherman and that's how we survived, my family because he didn't work, he didn't have a job and my father was a, what they call a lay reader in the Anglican faith. He led church services in my community and my family was Anglican in faith. My father ran the services in my hometown of York Landing. He did the services in Cree and that's what I

---

[10] TRC, *Statement*, 2011-0325.

miss about our community right now, is that aspect is the Cree singing, 'cause it's not around anymore."[11]

Piita Irniq was born near Repulse Bay, in what is now Nunavut. "I lived in an igloo in the wintertime. A very happy upbringing with my family, and both my mother and father were very good storytellers, and they would tell legends, and they would sing songs, traditional, sing traditional Inuit songs. They would, my father in particular, would talk about hunting stories. My mother would sew all of the clothes that we had, you know, caribou clothing and things like that, sealskin clothing. I still wear sealskin clothing today, particularly my boots, you know, when I'm, I'm dancing, for example. So, my mother would sew, teaching my sister how to sew, so that she could become a very good seamstress when she grows up, or older. And in the meantime, I was apparently being trained to be a good Inuk, and be able to hunt animals for survival, caribou, seals, a square flipper, bearded seal, Arctic char, you know, these kinds of things, including birds. And I was also being told, or being taught how to build an igloo, a snow house. When I was a little boy, growing up to be a young boy at that time, my other memories included walking on the land with my father. My father was my mentor. He, he was a great hunter. So, I would go out with him on the land, walking in search of caribou, and I would watch him each time he caught a caribou, and I would learn by observing. As Inuit, I learned a long, long time ago

---

[11] TRC, *Statement*, 02-MB-18JU10-063.

that you learn by observation, and that's what I was doing as a little boy becoming a young man at that particular period of time. So, in the wintertime, we would travel by dog team. I remember travelling by dog team as early as three or four years old. Hunting, again, you know, hunting is a way of life that I remember when I was growing up for survival, and caribou hunting, and seal hunting, and fishing. And, and my, my father also did some trapping, foxes."[12]

Anthony Henry was born in Swan Lake, Ontario. "I was born in a tent in the woods so I was brought to the world in a very harsh environment, which I guess is a good thing because it made me the tough guy I am." He said he was raised in a traditional lifestyle based on trapping, hunting, fishing and harvesting of edible plants, such as wild rice and other edible materials. "Total, total traditional style is what I call it. My parents were extraordinary people. They prepared me to be an independent individual. They taught me a lot of things that I've used throughout my life as a traditional person. They taught me how to survive."[13]

As **Albert Fiddler** was growing up in Saskatchewan, his father taught him how to live off the land. "I remember my dad teaching me how to hunt, and learn how to snare rabbits, learn how to take care of horses. I was riding horses already on, four years old, and I'm riding with a bareback, and I

---

[12] TRC, *Statement*, 2011-2905.
[13] TRC, *Statement*, 02-MB-17JU10-086.

enjoy that thing. I still remember that because I was a fairly decent cowboy, you know, like Little Beaver, as they used to call him in the comic books. I used to hang on onto just the mane. I didn't, I didn't even have a bridle." His father also taught him to hunt. "And it's funny sometimes, you know, and some of it was fun. Some of it was kind of patience, and pretty chilly sometimes when he was telling me when, how to snare chickens out of the, out of the willows. We're using this, a little wire, and a long stick, and standing on the dark side of, and waiting for the chickens to come and feed on the willows, and now we'd snare them down, yeah."[14]

Doris Young attended residential schools in Manitoba and Saskatchewan. Her early childhood was spent in northern Manitoba. "The family that I had, my mother and father, and my brothers and sisters, and my grandparents, and my aunties and uncles. The community that I lived in was a safe one. It was a place where we were cared for, and loved by our parents, and our grandparents, and that community that I lived at we were safe. We were, we were well taken care of. We lived on the land, and on the water, meaning by fishing. My dad was a chief, but he was also what we would call a labourer in those days, but he was also a hunter, trapper, and fisherman, and that's how he supported us. And my mother spoke only Cree, and that's the language that we spoke in our household, and she thought it was very important for us to, to have that language

---

[14] TRC, *Statement*, 2011-1760.

because, it was the basis of our culture, as I came to understand it later in life. And she was the one that enforced that, that language that we spoke in our house."[15]

Delores Adolph was born in 1951 and grew up in a self-sufficient Aboriginal family in British Columbia. "Before I came to residential school, our, our families fished and hunted for our food. Our mother, she grew our own vegetables, because we were quite a ways from the stores, and because we lived in the remote area where, where there is no stores. And you know there was, our means of travel was canoes, so that's how we travelled. And our, our home life, it was not the greatest, but what our parents were trying to teach us how to, how to be, to keep busy, and then, and for us not to say there's nothing to do. So, we, we packed water, and we packed, we packed our wood. Sometimes we had to roll our wood up, up the dike, and then roll it down the other side, and, and we had to learn how to cut our, our wood, and make kindling for the fire, and that was our way of life. And, and my grandfather was busy trying to teach us how to build canoes. Build, make paddles. Build a bailer, to bail water out of our canoe. And, and then they were trying to teach us how to, how to race on those old fishing canoes, and we always beat the boys. And they didn't like that, because we, we beat them all the time. So, that meant that we were, that we were strong at that point, before we came to residential

---
[15] TRC, *Statement*, 2011-3517.

school. And my life has been upside down since I came to residential school."[16]

Rosalie Webber, who later attended a boarding school in Newfoundland, spent her early childhood with her parents in Labrador in the 1940s. "My father was a fisherman and my mother also worked with him and they worked together. He was a trapper and my mom trapped with him. Also my mom made all of our clothes and all of his clothing. And they knitted and they cooked and my mom was a midwife. It was very happy. We were always busy with the family. Everything was a family thing, you know. I remember gathering water from the one little brook that ran through Spotted Islands, where I was born. I remember, you know, the dogs. I remember my brothers and I had one sister and, I had another sister, a step-sister, but she lived in Newfoundland and I didn't know her. We were quite happy, you know, and my mother was a hunter like my dad. They'd go out in partridge season and, and always in competition and with a single .22 she'd come in with about 150 and he'd be lucky to make the 100. [laughter] And then the community would take it and it would be bottled and canned for winter provisions, 'cause being, being a trapper in the winter time, they all had their own trapping areas. So they, many of them went in their own traplines and as we did and my father trapped in Porcupine Bay. And so we would journey there when fishing season

---

[16] TRC, *Statement*, 2011-3458.

was over. I was just a small child so I remember happy days."[17]

Martha Loon was born in 1972 in northwestern Ontario and attended the Poplar Hill, Ontario, school in the 1980s. Stories were a large part of the education she received from her parents. "They were stories that, you know, they, they taught us how, how to behave. You know they taught us our values. We even just, you know how, you know you hear stories about the beaver, and I always used to wonder why my mom would every time she was skinning beaver, she'd always set aside the, the kneecaps separately. She'd put those aside. And then afterwards she'd go, she'd go, either paddle out to the water somewhere, like a deep part, and that's where she threw them in. And, and I always know, wondered why she would do that. I've never questioned. It wasn't until I was older I asked her, like, 'Why do you do that?' She says, you know, 'This is what we're supposed to do, to respect and honour the beaver, to thank the beaver for giving its life so that we could eat it, use its pelt. This is what the beaver wants us to do.' The same thing as you treat a duck, a duck, the duck bones a certain way. You know all that's got, got purpose and a reason for it."[18]

Grandparents played an important role in raising children in many communities. **Richard Hall**,

---

[17] TRC, *Statement*, 2011-2891.
[18] TRC, *Statement*, 01-ON-24NOV10-021.

who went to the Alberni, British Columbia school, recalled with deep affection his pre-residential school upbringing and the role that his grandparents played.

"And my grandmother she taught us to be orderly. She taught us to go to church. She dressed us to go to church. She loved the church. My playground was my friends, with my friends was the mountains, streams, the ocean, and we're raised in the ocean because we went fishing all summer long and we travelled to the communities, the fishing grounds because at the mountains where … the places where we spend our days, times, the rivers, from in playing in the river, no fear and that was normal. With my grandfather, he took me with him at the young age, he took me, he taught me to work in the boats with him. He taught me how to repair boats. He will take me to talk to his friends and all I did was to speak their language and speak their Native tongue while they prepared fish around the fire. He took me wherever he went and I later learned that he was my lifeline. He helped me and guided me the best he could."[19]

Patrick James Hall was born in 1960 and grew up in what is now called the Dakota Tipi First Nation. "And, I remember, I remember a lot of times, I guess, with my grandfather, my grandmother. One of them in my mind, I remember. My grandfather used to haul wood on a sleigh. He had horses. And, so, my older brothers would go with him, too, and

---

[19] TRC, *Statement*, 2011-1852.

we just, he'd take us for horse rides. And, he used to talk with us all the time in Dakota. I mean, we used to, we used to remember what he said because we'd always be laughing, having fun, and.... My grandpa was very, very active guy. He, he always made sure, you know, he made sure that we had everything for the family. We used to go hunting, deer hunting and fishing, trapping. And, my mother, too, she was a very hard worker 'cause she used to be hauling water, cutting wood. And that was just during the winters. It was very hard 'cause we have to cut wood, and break the ice for water, and heat it up for the stove."[20]

One former student, who attended residential school in the Northwest Territories, recalled that her home life was violent and frightening. "There was a lot of violence. There was a lot of, we were very afraid of my father. He was a very angry man. And, and my mother used to run away on him and he used to come home to us kids and then, just really verbally abuse us and make us really scared of him. We used to be, I, I used to run to the neighbours and hide behind their door because I was so scared of him."[21]

---

[20] TRC, *Statement*, 03-001-10-036.
[21] TRC, *Statement*, 2011-2689.

Kidnapped by Institutions

Imagine if you can, back to your earliest childhood memories. The safety most of us felt around our loved ones, having our mothers, fathers, grandparents, and siblings in our lives to help lighten the load and comfort us in hard times. Or perhaps you're a parent. Imagine the church or the state showing up at your door, and under threat of violence via incarceration, demanding your children as young as six be taken by them to an institution of their choosing to be properly educated and/or "re-educated'. This was the reality faced by many Indigenous parents and grandparents in the late nineteenth and early twentieth century in Canada, and several other countries such as the United States, Australia, and New Zealand to name a few. In this chapter the focus will be that moment of departure. How did it feel to be ripped away from your family when you were only a child and brought someplace where you couldn't understand the culture or the language? Through the stories of those that were there we can try and imagine ourselves in their shoes, as uncomfortable as that may be.

When **Josephine Eshkibok** was eight years old, a priest came to her home in northern Ontario and presented her mother with a letter. "My mother opened the letter, and I could see her face; I could see her face, it was kind of sad but mad too. She said to me, 'I have to let you go,' she told us. So we had to, go to, go to school at Spanish Residential School."²²

Isaac Daniels recalled one dramatic evening in 1945, when the Indian agent came to his father's home on the James Smith Reserve in Saskatchewan. "I didn't understand a word, 'cause I spoke Cree. Cree was the main language in our family. So, so my dad was kind of angry. I kept seeing him pointing to that Indian agent. So that night we were going to bed, it was just a one-room shack we all lived in, and I heard my dad talking to my mom there, and he was kind of crying, but he was talking in Cree now. He said that, 'It's either residential school for my boys, or I go to jail.' He said that in Cree. So, I overheard him. So I said the next morning, we all got up, and I said, 'Well, I'm going to residential school,' 'cause I didn't want my dad to go to jail."²³

Donna Antoine was enrolled in a British Columbia residential school after a visit from a government official to her family. "It must have been in the summer, the, the Indian agent came to, to see my father. I imagine it must have been the Indian agent because it looked pretty serious. He was talking to him for some time, and because we couldn't understand, we, we couldn't even eavesdrop what they were talking about. So after some time spent there, father sat, sat us down, and told us that this Indian agent came to tell us, tell him

---

²² TRC, *Statement*, 2011-2014.
²³ TRC, *Statement*, 2011-1779.

that we had to go to school, to a boarding school, one that is not close to our home, but far away."

The official had told her father that he would be sent to jail if he did not send Antoine to residential school. "We were sort of caught in, in wanting to stay home, and seeing our parents go to jail, and we thought, we must have thought who's gonna look after us if our parents go to jail?"[24]

In the late 1940s, **Vitaline Elsie Jenner** was living with her family in northern Alberta. "My, my mom and dad loved me, loved all of us a lot. They took care of us the best that they knew how, and I felt so comfortable being at home." This came to an end in the fall of 1951. "My parents were told that we had to go to the residential school. And prior to that, at times, my dad didn't make very much money, so sometimes he would go to the welfare to get, to get ration, or get some monies to support twelve of us. And my parents were told that if they didn't put us in the residential school that all that would be cut off. So, my parents felt forced to put us in the residential school, eight of us, eight out of, of twelve." [25]

Many parents sent their children to residential school for one reason: they had been told they would be sent to jail if they kept their children at home. **Ken A. Littledeer's** father told him that "if I didn't go to school, he'd go to jail, that's what he told

---

[24] TRC, *Statement*, 2011-3287.
[25] TRC, *Statement*, 02-MB-16JU10-131.

me." As a result, he was enrolled in the Sioux Lookout, Ontario, school.[26]

Andrew Bull Calf was raised by his grandfather, Herbert Bull Calf. When he was enrolled in residential school in Cardston, Alberta, his grandfather was told "that if he didn't bring me, my grandfather would be ... would go to jail and be charged."[27]

When **Martha Minoose** told her mother she did not wish to return to the Roman Catholic school in Cardston, her mother explained, "If you don't go to school, your dad is going to go to jail. We are going to get a letter written in red that's very serious."[28]

Maureen Gloria Johnson went to the Lower Post school in northern British Columbia in 1959.
"I went there with a bus. They load us all up on a bus, and took us. And I remember my, my mom had a really hard time letting us kids go, and she had, she had a really hard time. She begged the priest, and the priest said it was law that we had to go, and if we didn't go, then my parents would be in trouble." [29]

In the face of such coercion, parents often felt helpless and ashamed. **Paul Dixon** attended residential schools in Ontario and Québec. Once he

---

[26] TRC, *Statement*, 01-ON-24-NOV10-028.
[27] TRC, *Statement*, 2011-0273.
[28] TRC, *Statement*, 2011-1748.
[29] TRC, *Statement*, 2011-1126.

spoke to his father about his experience at the schools. According to Dixon, "He got angry and said, 'I had no choice, you know.' It really, it really hit me hard. I wasn't accusing him of anything, you know, I just wanted some explanations. He said, 'I, I will, I will go, I would go in jail, I will go in jail if I didn't let you go.'"[30]

When she was four or five, **Lynda Pahpasay McDonald** was taken by plane from her parents' home on Sydney Lake, Ontario. "I looked outside, my mom was, you know, flailing her arms, and, and I, and she must have been crying, and I see my dad grabbing her, and, I was wondering why, why my mom was, you know, she was struggling. She told me many years later what happened, and she explained to me why we had to be sent away to, to residential school. And, and I just couldn't get that memory out of my head, and I still remember to this day what, what happened that day. And she told me, like, she was so hurt, and, and I used to ask her, 'Why did you let us go, like, why didn't you stop them, you know? Why didn't you, you know, come and get us?' And she told me, 'We couldn't, because they told us if we tried to do anything, like, get you guys back, we'd be thrown into jail.' So, they didn't want to end up in jail, 'cause they still had babies at, at the cabin."[31]

Dorothy Ross recalled how unhappy her father was about sending his children to residential

---

[30] TRC, *Statement*, SP101.
[31] TRC, *Statement*, 02-MB-16JU10-130.

school. "As we got older, I remember Dad, I knew Dad was already angry. He was angry at the school for taking us away, for taking myself and my siblings. He couldn't, couldn't do, he couldn't do anything to help us. Either, same thing with my mom, 'there's nothing I can do to help you.'"[32]

Albert Marshall hated his parents for sending him to the Shubenacadie, Nova Scotia, school. Many years later, he asked his brother what the family reaction had been to his being sent to school. He didn't answer me for a while, a long time. He says, "Nobody said anything for days, because my father was crying every day. Finally my father told the family, 'I failed as a father. I couldn't protect my child, but I just couldn't because you know what the Mounties, the priest, the Indian agents told me? They told me, if I don't, if I resist too much then they would take the other younger, younger brother and younger, younger children.' Then he says, 'It was not a choice. I could not say, take them or take the three of them. But I couldn't say nothing and I know I have to live with that.'"[33]

Jaco Anaviapik's parents opposed his being sent to the Pond Inlet hostel in what is now Nunavut. "When they started taking kids on the land to attend school the RCMP boat would pick us up. There is no doubt that our parents were intimidated by the police into letting us go. They were put in a position

---

[32] TRC, *Statement*, 01-ON-24NOV10-014.
[33] TRC, *Statement*, 02-MB-17JU10-050.

where they could not say no. Even though they did not want us to go they were too afraid of the police, too afraid to stand up to the police. I am one of the lucky ones because my father did say no when they wanted to take me. He told them he would bring me himself once the ice had formed. I was brought here after the children who had been rounded up by boat had already started. That first year my parents came several times to take me home but they were refused by the area administrator. My sister told me that my parents were very sad at that time." Rather than be separated from their children, his parents moved to Pond Inlet. "After two years had passed my family decided to move to Pond because they knew I had to go to school." [34]

In some cases, parents reluctantly sent their children because the residential school represented their only educational option. **Ellen Smith's** father attended the Anglican residential school at Hay River in the Northwest Territories. She believes that his experiences at the school led him to oppose her being sent to residential school. However, her grandfather believed it was necessary that she get an education. "My dad reluctantly let me go to school because my grandpa said that "in the future she will help our people; she needs to go there." And that struggle occurred with my dad over the years. For eleven years, that I went to residential school. But my grandpa was the one that said, "They have to go. She has to go." She was sent to the Anglican school in

---

[34] TRC, *Statement*, SP044.

Aklavik in 1953. She eventually attended three other residential schools. Some parents wanted their children to gain the knowledge they believed was needed to protect their community and culture. [35]

When **Shirley Williams's** father took her to catch the bus to the Spanish, Ontario, girls' school, he bought her an ice cream and gave her four instructions: "One was remember who you are. Do not forget your language. Whatever they do to you in there, be strong. And the fourth one, learn about the Indian Act, and come back and teach me. So with those four things, he said that 'you don't know why I'm telling you this, but some day you will understand.'"[36]

One student, who attended the Gordon's, Saskatchewan, school, recalled the ways in which the churches competed against one another to recruit students. "But when we look at the residential schools, you know, and the churches we recognize, you know, at least I've seen it, you know, that we've had these two competing religions, the Anglican and the Catholic churches both competing for our souls it seemed. You know, I remember growing up on the reserve here when they were looking for students. They were competing against each other. We were the prizes, you know, that they would gain if they won. I remember they, the Catholic priests coming out with, you know, used hockey equipment and

---

[35] TRC, *Statement*, 2011-0346.
[36] TRC, *Statement*, 2011-5040.

telling us, you know, 'Come and come to our school. Come and play hockey for us. Come and play in our band. We got all kinds of bands here; we got trombones and trumpets and drums,' and all that kind of stuff. They use all this stuff to encourage us or entice us to come to the Catholic school. And then on the other hand, the Anglicans, they would come out with what they called 'bale clothes.' They bring out bunch of clothes in a bale, like, a big bale. It was all used clothing and they'd give it to the women on the reserve here, and the women made blankets and stuff like that out of these old clothes. But that's the way they, they competed for us as people."[37]

Some children wanted to go to school, at least initially. **Leon Wyallon**, who attended the Roman Catholic residence in Fort Smith in the 1960s, said he looked forward to residential school "because I wanted to learn; learn to talk English and learn, so I can learn both languages at the same time." He hated his first year at the residence, particularly the restrictions on speaking his own language. But he said, "My mom and dad didn't listen to me; but they still sent me back."[38]

In other cases, missionaries convinced students of the benefits of going to school. **Anthony Henry** said that a priest named Father LaSalle convinced him to come to residential school at Kenora. According to Henry, his mother did not want

---

[37] TRC, *Statement,* SP039.
[38] TRC, *Statement,* 2011-0244.

him to go to residential school, but LaSalle, who spoke fluent Ojibway, convinced him it would be beneficial.[39]

---

[39] TRC, *Statement,* 02-MB-17JU10-086.

Places of Refuge?

While many of the students hated the idea of leaving their families, in some cases the schools could be looked upon as a refuge. The Indigenous culture at this time had already been largely affected and First Nation people in Canada had already been put onto reserves. Most of these reserves were affected largely by poverty, trauma, and alcoholism and were often in geographical locations where life off the land, which had been the norm for hundreds of generations proved difficult to impossible. This resulted in an Indigenous population largely dependent on the Canadian government for sustenance, a problem which in many areas continues to this day. The effects of the schools themselves were muti-generational as a parent that had spent their childhood in a residential school had little to no experience in raising children of their own and were in many cases dealing with extreme trauma. In this sense the schools could be viewed as a means of escape from poverty, or worse. When stuck between a rock and a hard place often a change of scenery, no matter the pretext, can be a welcome change and open new opportunities. Regardless, the traumatic effects of the schools would prove to be extreme in most cases.

Poverty and the inability to feed and clothe their children forced some parents to send their children to residential school. When **Ivan George** was enrolled in the Mission, British Columbia, school, his father was a single parent with six children under the age of fourteen. When the time came to return to the school after his first summer holiday, Ivan told his father he did not wish to return. "He says, 'You have to. I can't provide for you, or nothing to feed you, clothes on your back, education.' So, I went back, and I said, 'Oh, I better,' because you know where, what, what's going on, all that. So, I stayed the whole year without running away."[40]

Cecilia Whitefield-Big George said her mother was not able to support her family when they lived in Big Grassy in northwestern Ontario. "She would go and clean, work for people, eh, like do their laundry and clean their floors and clean the house for them and that's how she fed us. They'd give her food, eh. And then when the priest arrived he told her, you know they'd be in a good place if they went to school. And so that's how that happened. I, my little sister, she was only four years old. So that's how we first got picked up."[41]

One former student, whose grandparents had also attended residential school, placed his daughter in residential school when she was thirteen. "I didn't have a wife at the time and I felt that was a good place for her, so I wasn't really fully aware of the, you know, the negative parts of, the parts, negative, negativity of residential school 'cause really, I guess, when I look at the residential school

---

[40] TRC, *Statement,* 2011-3472.
[41] TRC, *Statement,* 02-MB-17JU10-030.

issue, you know, I saw, you know, physically, I guess, better than what I experienced at the reserve. On the reserve I had a very abusive dad, my dad was abusive, physically abusive, and we lived in a little log cabin and we didn't have regular meals."[42]

Ethel Johnson said she and her siblings were sent to the Shubenacadie school when her mother was diagnosed with tuberculosis. "My father couldn't look after us. I was ten years old, there was another one, there was five of us, and the three of us were old enough to go to residential school; I never even heard about it 'til then. 'Cause my father had to work and he had to maintain a house, fix our meals, he just couldn't do it. So I don't know where he found out or how this was possible, but we ended up going over there anyway. This was in '46."[43]

Dorothy Jane Beaulieu attended the Fort Resolution, Northwest Territories, school after the death of her father. "And they seemed to pick on orphans, you know. My father, I lost my father when I was, in 1949 we lost him. And I stayed here in a mission eleven and a half years, and I never went home for seven years. I had no, no, nowhere to go, you know. My sisters were living in Yellowknife, but they were all, you know, they were all married, and had children of their own. So you know I would, my sister Nora and I, we just stayed there, you know."[44]

---

[42] TRC, *Statement*, SP039.
[43] TRC, *Statement*, 2011-2680.
[44] TRC, *Statement*, 2011-0379.

Illness and family breakup meant that in some cases, children were raised by their grandparents. After **Hazel Mary Anderson's** parents separated in 1972, her grandmother took care of her and her two siblings. They lived on the Piapot Reserve in Saskatchewan until her grandmother was in her early seventies. At that time, the children were sent to residential school.[45]

Prior to going to the Shubenacadie school, one student was being cared for by his grandparents. "I went there basically because I felt sorry for my grandparents who were trying to look after me and trying to keep, maintain, and they were struggling."[46]

One former Blue Quills, Alberta, student said: "We have, at that time, there was six of us who are older, who were living at the house, but there was three others, younger ones, who were from another father, but they lived with us. So, now in our family currently, we had twelve. But the oldest ones, the six of us, had to see and witness a lot of, a lot of violence, especially abuse with my mom and dad. We had two sisters, and four, or three brothers, and myself, that's six. I was the youngest of the siblings of that bunch. But there was times when, you know, drinking would be to excess, so, so my moshum and my kokum would take us in to protect us from, from the fighting, and the pain and the struggles. There was, as far as I can recall, one day there was some

---

[45] TRC, *Statement*, 02-MB-18JU10-034.
[46] TRC, *Statement*, 2011-2681.

lady or social worker that just came to our house at my kokum's place, Jenny's, and they told us we were just going for a ride in a big, fancy car. And of course, you know, we were poor, we didn't have any of that stuff, so we thought it would be kind of nice, but nobody told us where we were going. So all I could remember was my auntie, my kokum, we are at the, the house, and waving goodbye, and all I remember was just peeking out the window in the back, and not understanding why, you know, Grandma was crying. But we went, and they brought us to a big school, just out by the Saddle Lake Reserve. It was the Blue Quills school. And I was only five, so you know I was youngest of the six."[47]

In some cases, parents placed their children in the school to protect them from violence in the community. Both of **Dorene Bernard's** parents had attended the Shubenacadie school. "My father spent eleven years in a residential school, from 1929 to 1940. My mom spent around seven years there during the 1940s. Whatever would have made them think that it had changed, that it was better in 1960s than it was when they were there? I don't know. But I could tell you that our lives outside the residential school was bad enough that she felt she was alone to make those decisions, that it was better for us to be there than with other family members, with our extended family. We were safer in her eyes to be there than at home."[48]

---

[47] TRC, *Statement*, 2011-3279.
[48] TRC, *Statement*, SP029.

The Journey

At its peak the Canadian residential school system consisted of 139 schools spread from British Columbia to eastern Quebec. Canada is an immense country, over 9,000 km wide and 4,000km high, with over 600 First Nations, and because of this the distance travelled to school could be extreme. Bearing in mind this started in and around the turn of the 20th century, travelling great distances was far from comfortable or even safe. When we consider that these journeys were made by children as young as 6 years old, often with extremely limited supervision, we can start to get a feel for the magnitude of the undertaking from both an emotional and a physical perspective.

Frederick Ernest Koe recalled that one morning, there was a knock at his parents' door in Aklavik, Northwest Territories. "Anglican Minister Donna Webster and RCMP officers at the door, and they're asking for me and telling me to pack up because I had to go. Well pack up, a few little things, no suitcases, my hunting bag is still kind of dirty, throw whatever stuff you had in it and you go. And I didn't get to say goodbye to my dad or my brother Allan, didn't get to pet my dogs or nothing, you know, we're going. Marched over to Frankie's house which was just half a block away and picked him up and then we were marched to the plane, just like we're criminals, you know marching to this policeman to get on the plane. And that was my experience leaving Aklavik. And it was a pretty monumental point in my life, very dramatic, I guess. You don't realize this until after, because those times, you just did what the people in charge told you to do."[49]

Howard Stacy Jones said he was taken without his parents' knowledge from a public school in Port Renfrew, British Columbia, to the Kuper Island school. "I was kidnapped from Port Renfrew's elementary school when I was around six years old, and this happened right in the elementary schoolyard. And my auntie witnessed this and another non-Native witnessed this, and they are still alive as I speak. These are two witnesses trying, saw me fighting, trying to get away with, from the two RCMP officers that threw me in the back seat of the car and drove off with me. And my mom didn't know where I was for three days, frantically stressed out and worried about where I was, and she finally found out that I was in Kuper Island residential school."[50]

For many residential school students, the school year started in a long ride in the back of a school-owned farm truck. **Shirley Leon** attended the Kamloops, British Columbia, school in the 1940s. She described her first memory of residential school as "seeing the cattle trucks come onto the reserve, and scoop up the kids to go, and seeing my cousins cry, and then, and they were put on these trucks, and

---

[49] TRC, *Statement*, SC091.
[50] TRC, *Statement*, 01-BC-03DE10-001.

hauled off, and we didn't know where, and my grandmother and mother hiding us under the bed. And when the, the federal health nurse or the Indian agent would try to come into the house, my grandmother would club them with her cane."[51]

The day she left for the Lestock, Saskatchewan, school, **Marlene Kayseas's** parents drove her into the town of Wadena. "There was a big truck there. It had a back door and that truck was full of kids and there was no windows on that truck, it was dark in there. And that's where we were put. There was a bunch of kids there from up north, Yellowquill, Kenaston, and my reserve. And all you hear was yelling and kids were fighting in there and some were crying. And we were falling down on the floor because there was no place to sit, we were standing up. And it seemed like such a long time to get there."[52]

Rick Gilbert's first experience with residential schooling came when his older siblings were sent away to school. "And I remember just directly outside of the house there was a cattle truck parked there and they were loading kids on the back of this cattle truck. And that's how they were taking my, well I am going to call them my brother and sister, they were taking my brother and sister away in this cattle truck to the mission. I didn't know then

---

[51] TRC, *Statement*, 2011-5048.
[52] TRC, *Statement*, SP035.

that that's what they were doing, but that's what happened."[53]

Alma Scott was taken to the Fort Alexander, Manitoba, school when she was five years old. "We got taken away by a big truck. I can still remember my mom and dad looking at us, and they were really, really sad looking. My dad's shoulders were just hunched, and he, to me, it looked like his spirit was broken. I didn't have the words at five for that, but I do now. I just remember feeling really sad, and I was in this truck full of other kids who were crying, and so I cried with them."[54]

Leona Bird was six when she was sent to the Prince Albert, Saskatchewan, school. "And then we seen this army covered wagon truck, army truck outside the place. And as we were walking towards it, kids were herded into there like cattle, into the army truck. Then in the far distance I seen my mother with my little sister. I went running to her, and she says, 'Leona,' she was crying, and I was so scared. I didn't know what was going on, I didn't know what was happening. My sister didn't cry because she didn't understand what we, we were, what's gonna happen to us. Anyway, it was time for me and her to go, and she, when we got in that truck, she just held me, pinched me, and held me on my skirt. 'Momma, Momma, Momma.' And then my mother couldn't do nothing, she just stood there,

---

[53] TRC, *Statement*, 2011-2389.
[54] TRC, *Statement*, 02-MB-16JU10-016.

weeping. And then I took my little sister, and tried to make her calm down, I just told her, 'We're going bye-bye, we're going somewhere for a little while.' Well, nobody told us how long we were gonna be gone. It's just, like, we were gonna go into this big truck, and that's how, that's how it started."[55]

Sam Ross recalled putting up a fight when the Indian agent came to his family's home in northern Manitoba to take him to residential school in Prince Albert, Saskatchewan. "I remember hiding under the bed there; they pulled us out from under the bed, me and my younger brother. We ran, you know, we cried a lot and but that didn't help better; they took us out. They took us out to the truck; all four of us. My other two brothers walked to the truck. But me and my late, younger brother, we fought all the way, right up, right to the station, train station, CNR station."[56]

As in Sam Ross's case, the truck ride was sometimes followed by a train ride. In the 1950s, **Benjamin Joseph** travelled by bus and train to the Shubenacadie school. "And I don't know who were there, anyway, there was a police officer and two people, told my father that 'we're going to take your children to the better place.' And my dad didn't understand because, my dad was getting sick, he had asthma. He didn't understand, then, and he agreed with them, anyway, he agreed with the people that

---

[55] TRC, *Statement*, 2011-4415.
[56] TRC, *Statement*, 2011-0294.

would take us, all my brothers and my sisters to the place that I don't know. So about a couple days later, a bus came in to our home, and told us, 'Get on the bus,' I don't know, could be an Indian agent, and the RCMP. Told us, 'Go on the bus, go on the bus, we take you to a better place.' So we had to agree with them because I didn't understand as a young boy. I had to listen to what they said because we listened to our dad, we listened to him because he knows what's best for us. So we went on the bus, so they picked every child in our community, in my reserve. Picked every child, put them on the bus, send us to a train station at Grand Narrows, that morning, about, around 7:30, around there I think. And every child they put on, didn't say anything. They put them on the bus and through Grand Narrows, then we waited there. We didn't have no food, we didn't have no clothes to take with us. We just get on the bus and go. So, that morning, we heard the, told my brothers we had to sit over here and wait for the train to come. So we heard a train, we heard a whistle and we said, and my brother said, 'Oh, that's the train coming to pick us up, pick us up.' I said, 'Okay,' you know. So when the train came, they put us on, Indian agents put us on, the RCMP put us on the train. Told us to sit over here. So it doesn't matter, so we left from Grand Narrows. Every station we stopped at, there was children, Native children, that had long hair when I looked out the window. And I went, 'Wow, there's more children going on the train, probably they're going the same way as I'm going.' So at that time it didn't matter to me, so every station we stopped, there was Native children, girls and boys. And there was RCMP and an Indian agent lining them up, put them on the train, put them on the seats. No one's talking about anything, I didn't know them. Every station, and by the time we got to Truro, there was full of Native people, Native children on the train. Wow, there was a whole bunch of us. Had long hair, you know, had no clothes to take with them. So we didn't know, we didn't understand. So we got to Truro, so we changed trains and then the conductor, he says, when we got to the point where we went, the conductor said, 'Last stop for Shubenacadie. Last stop, get ready.' So we were driving and we wouldn't take that long. So we got all the children, all the girls on one side and all the boys on one side. And we didn't understand nothing. And when the train came so far, I think it would be around 12:00, or between 12:00 or 12:30, we got to our destination and the conductor was saying, 'Shubenacadie, Shubenacadie, next stop.' So he was saying that, so we all stop and the Indian agent was sitting in the front there. He said, 'Okay guys, get ready.'"[57]

Larry Beardy had a strong memory of the first train trip that took him from Churchill, Manitoba, to the Anglican residential school in Dauphin, Manitoba—a journey of 1,200 km. "I think it was two days and one whole day of travel on the train to Dauphin. So, it was quite a, it was quite a ride. And when we boarded the train, I was very excited. It's like going on a journey, going for a, a

---

[57] TRC, *Statement*, SC075.

travel. It's not my first time going on a train, but I was going alone. I was going with my sister and my other older siblings. And, and the train ride was okay for the first half hour or so, then I realized I was alone. My mother was not there. And like the rest of the children, there was a lot of crying on that train. At every stop if you understand the Canadian National Railway, families lived in sections every twenty, fifteen miles, and children will get on the train, and then there'd be more crying, and everybody started crying, all the way to Dauphin, that's how it was. So, there was a lot of tears. That train, I want to call that train of tears, and a lot of anger, a lot of frustration. I did that for several years."[58]

Emily Kematch was sent from York Landing in northern Manitoba to the Gordon's school in Saskatchewan. When she was put on the train that was to take her there, she did not know she was being sent to school. "I didn't know I was going away to school. I thought I was just going for a train ride and I was just excited to go. My sisters and my brothers were on the train too and I felt like, I have family with me, but I didn't understand why my parents didn't come on with us. They were just on the side of the railway there and they were waving at us as the train was moving away. And I remember asking one of the kids from back home, 'How come our parents aren't coming?' and then she said, that girl said, 'They can't come 'cause we're going to

---

[58] TRC, *Statement*, SP082.

school.' And I was talking to her in Cree and I said, 'Well, I don't want to go to school, I'd rather stay home and stay with my parents.' And she said, she told me, 'No, we can't, we have to go and get our education,' and then at night as we were travelling along, I got really lonesome." Because her siblings were going to the Anglican school in Dauphin, they got off there. Emily stayed on the train. "We were on the train, I'd say, like, three days to get to Saskatchewan and when we got there, three of my cousins were with me, those were the only ones I knew. Three boys, there's Billy, Gordon, and Nelson and I was the only girl from my hometown."[59]

Many students whose parents belonged to the United Church were sent from northern British Columbia to residential school in Edmonton because there was no United Church residential school closer to where they lived. **Sphenia Jones's** journey to residential school started from Haida Gwaii (also known as the Queen Charlotte Islands), off the coast of British Columbia. "And I went on a boat first from Haida Gwaii. There was really lots of Haidas that were going to Edmonton at that time, and some Skidegate, as well as Masset, and we got on a really big boat. They used to have a, they used to call it a steamer. It used to bring groceries and stuff like that maybe once a year, twice a year to Haida Gwaii, that's what they put us on, and then we got off the boat in Prince Rupert, and then they started hauling us on a train there. The train station building is still

---

[59] TRC *Statement*, 02-MB-18JU10-063.

there in Rupert, where we all had to wait. There was really lots of us. And I don't remember what month it was, or anything like that. But we used to have to do stops along the way, and pick up more Native children. And we were on the train, gee, for about four days, I think, something like that. And the more people they picked up, the more squished we all became in, inside the train, and we were packed in like a bunch of sardines. There was kids laying around on the floor, all along in, in where the walkway was supposed to be. And I could hear really lots of crying all the time, crying, crying, crying." She recalled that at one stop, the train picked up an infant. "I could hear a baby crying about the second day, so I start looking, and I found this little one in the corner. There was a whole bunch of kids around. I don't know if they were alive or whatever, you know. I picked him up, anyway, and I remember packing him around. I lost the space that I was sitting at. So, I was walking around. I was lucky I had a coat. I took my coat off, I remember holding him, sitting, holding him, looking at his face. Nothing to eat, nothing to drink. I couldn't give him anything."[60]

Students from remote communities often were taken to residential school by small airplanes. At the end of the summer in 1957, a plane that was normally used to transport fish landed on the water at Co-op Point on Reindeer Lake, in northern Saskatchewan. **John B. Custer** recalled the roundup: "And all of a sudden I seen this priest coming, and

---

[60] TRC, *Statement*, 2011-3300.

this RCMP, and they told me let's go for a walk. So, I went, walked down to the fish plane, and this is where they, they threw me in without the consent of my grandparents. And there was already a bunch of kids there. There was about at least twenty-five to thirty kids. And that's at the young age of seven years old, I remember this very well. This, the fish, the fish plane was, it had a very strong smell of fish, and he half-assed washed that plane, and it was, there was still slime fish in there, in that plane. And there was a whole bunch of kids there, and I was just wondering what am I doing in this plane? Most of the kids were crying, and I could see their parents on the shoreline, waving goodbye, and most of them were crying."[61]

Florence Horassi was taken to the Fort Providence, Northwest Territories school in a small airplane. "On its way to the school, the plane stopped at a number of small communities to pick up students. And then we got to, there's another place that we stop at, there's another, this one young boy got on the plane there. Had a lot, a lot of crying. There's ... a lot of kids in the plane. Some of them were sitting on the floor of the plane. It was just full. When the plane took off, there's about six or seven older ones, didn't cry, but I saw tears come right out of their eyes. Everybody else was crying. There's a whole plane crying. I wanted to cry, too, 'cause my brother was crying, but I held my tears back and held him." She and her brother were separated once they reached the school. "When we got to Providence, my

---

[61] TRC, *Statement*, 02-MB-19JU10-057.

brother was scared. We got off the plane. There was nuns waiting for us on the shore, brothers, Father, priests. He, he was scared, so he grabbed hold of my hand, he was holding my hand. We don't have no luggage, or no, no clothes, just what we had on, just what we had on. And we walk up the hill, to the top of the hill, and my brother was so scared. He was just holding onto my hand so tight. And then top of the hill, the priest came, and he told me he's got to go this way, and, and then the Sister came over to me, told me you got to go this way. They're trying to break our hands apart, but he wouldn't let go of my hand, holding. And the priest was holding his hand, and the sister was holding my hand. They broke our hands apart like that."[62]

Joe Krimmerdjuar was taken to the Chesterfield Inlet school in the Northwest Territories in 1957. "And my mother was on the beach when I was boarding the plane. With few clothes I had, maybe one pair of pants, maybe a sock that my mother had put into her flour sack. And I know that she started walking home not even bothering to look at me. And today I think maybe she had tears in her eyes. Maybe she was crying."[63]

In the Northwest Territories, students often were taken to school by boat. **Albert Elias** was sent to the Anglican school in Aklavik in 1952. "So in 1952 we were sent away. In those days there's, you know,

---

[62] TRC, *Statement*, 2011-0394.
[63] TRC, *Statement*, SC091.

there's no airplanes like we have now. So the Anglican Mission schooner, a small boat, came down to Tuk and we were boarded, we were, you know, we got on the boat, and all excited and waving and, and we left Tuk. And then we travelled a ways along the, along the way to Aklavik was camps, hunting camps, fishing camps, and we stopped at those places and picked up students as we went along. At one stop, all the children got off the boat. When it was time to get back on the boat, the boy walking ahead of Albert decided to run away. Just before he stepped on the walk plank he dashed to one side and he ran away. He ran away. And the Anglican missionary there, he ran after him and caught him and, and I saw for the first time how somebody could be so rough to a small child and carry that boy like a rag doll up to the boat. And I asked myself there, the fear, fear came to my being, you know, and I sensed fear, like, I never felt it before, and I said, 'What have I got myself into?' you know. Before I even reached Aklavik I start seeing violence, you know, which I really never saw before. And that was, to me, it always, you know, it was always in my memory. So the first trauma, I guess."[64]

Sam Kautainuk was twelve years old when he was taken to the Pond Inlet school in what is now Nunavut. "The boat they used to bring us here is still there down by Ulayuk School. That's the boat that picked me up from our outpost camp. It was the RMCP, the Area Administrator and two women. The

---

[64] TRC, *Statement*, SC092.

The Journey

special constable lifted me by my shoulders and put me in the boat so that I could go to school. They ignored my cries for my mother. I remember as the boat took us away I kept my eyes on my parents' tent until I couldn't see it anymore. That moment was the most painful thing I ever experienced in my life."[65]

---

[65] TRC, *Statement*, SP044.

Arriving at School

The first day of school can be a stressful and overwhelming day for a child. Even if you don't have children of your own that you've seen a little stressed or upset about heading back to school after the summer break, you can probably remember sometime in the not-so-distant past that you had these feeling of apprehension towards school life yourself. I was certainly no fan of school. I hated the early mornings and how it stole away the best hours of the day. The best hours of the day seem somewhat paltry in comparison to the best years of a child's life. What bonds are interrupted when a young child is taken from the family home and settled into government and/or religious institutions?

While first nations children in Canada are not the first, nor the last in history to be raised out of the family home, the fact that they did so in places that had little to no knowledge of their cultures, history, or languages was especially destructive. In most cases, what little was known about Indigenous culture and spirituality was looked down upon as heathenistic devil worship. This is evidenced by the banning of indigenous religious ceremonies like the *Potlach* and the *Sun Dance* and the refusal to allow students in Residential schools to communicate with one another in their native languages.

Nellie Ningewance was raised in Hudson, Ontario, and went to the Sioux Lookout, Ontario, school in the 1950s and 1960s. Her parents enrolled her in the school at the government's insistence. She told her mother she did not want to go. "But the day came where we, we were all bussed out from Hudson. My mother told me to pack my stuff; a little bit of what I needed, what I wanted. I remember I had a little doll that my dad had given me for a Christmas present. And I had a little trunk where I made my own doll clothes. I started sewing when I was nine years old. My mom taught us all this though, sewing. So I used to make my own doll clothes; I packed those up, what I wanted. I guess I had mixed feelings. I was kind of excited to go away to go to school. My mom tried to make it feel comfortable for me and I know it was hard for her and hard for me. But when the time we were ready to leave, they had a bus; and there was lots of people with their kids waiting to leave. And I made sure I, I was the last one to board the bus, 'cause I didn't want to go. I remember hugging my mom, begging her, getting on the bus; waving at them as they were going, pulling away. I don't remember how long the ride was from Hudson to Pelican at the time, but it seemed like a long ride.... When we arrived there, again I was, I made sure I was the last one to get on the bus. And when I arrived there, a guy standing at the bottom there helping all the students to get on the bus, reaching out his hand like this; I didn't even want to touch him. I didn't even want to get off. I'm hanging to the bar; I didn't want to get off. To me he looked so ugly. He was dark, short, and he was trying to coax me to come down the stairs and to help me get off the bus. I hang onto the bus and they had to force me and pull me down to get off the bus. The next three days I guess was sort of, like it was like floating.... I remember crying then calming down for a while, then crying again.... When we arrived we had to register that we had arrived then they took us to cut our hair. The next thing was to get our clothes. They gave us two pairs of jeans, two pairs of tee-shirts, two church dresses, they were beautiful dresses; two pairs of shoes, two pairs of socks, two pairs of everything. And we had a number; they gave us a number and that number was tied in our, in all our clothes; our garments, our jackets, everything was numbered. After that we were told to be in the, go in the shower; at least fifteen of us girls all in one shower. We were told to strip down and, with all the other girls; and that was not a comfortable feeling. And for me I guess it was violating my privacy. I didn't even want to look at anybody else. It was hard. After that, they gave us our toothbrushes to brush our teeth. And they asked us to put our hands out and they put some white dry powder stuff on our hands. I didn't know what it was. I smelt it, but now today I know it was baking soda. I didn't realize what it was then."[66]

Campbell Papequash had been raised by his grandfather. When his grandfather died in 1946, Papequash "was apprehended by the missionaries and taken to residential school. When I was taken to this residential school you know I experienced a foreign way of life that I really didn't understand. I was taken into this big building that would become the detention of my life and the fear of life. When I was taken to that residential school you know I see these ladies, you know so stoical looking, passionate-less and they wore these robes that I've never seen women wear before, they only showed their forehead and their eyes and the bottom of their face and their hands. Now to me that is very fearful because you know there wasn't any kind of passion and I could see, you know, I could see it in their eyes. When I was taken to this residential school, I was taken into the infirmary but before I entered the infirmary, you know, I

---

[66] TRC, *Statement*, 2011-0305.

Arriving at School

looked around this big, huge building, and I see all these crosses all over the walls. I look at those crosses and I see a man hanging on that cross and I didn't recognize who this man was. And this man seemed dead and passionate-less on that cross. I didn't know who this man was on that cross. And then I was taken to the infirmary and there, you know, I was stripped of my clothes, the clothes that I came to residential school with, you know, my moccasins, and I had nice, beautiful long hair and they were neatly braided by mother before I went to residential school, before I was apprehended by the residential school missionaries. And after I was taken there, they took off my clothes and then they deloused me. I didn't know what was happening, but I learned about it later, that they were delousing me; 'the dirty, no-good-for-nothing savages, lousy.' And then they cut off my beautiful hair. You know and my hair, my hair represents such a spiritual significance of my life and my spirit. And they did not know, you know, what they were doing to me. You know and I cried, and I see them throw my hair into a garbage can, my long, beautiful braids. And then after they deloused me then I was thrown into the shower, you know, to go wash all that kerosene on my body and on my head. And I was shaved, bald-headed. And then after I had the shower, they gave me these clothes that didn't fit, and they gave me these shoes that didn't fit, and they all had numbers on them. And after the shower then I was taken up to the dormitory. And when I went to, when I was taken up to this dormitory, I seen many beds up there, all lined up so neatly and the beds made so neatly. And then they gave me a pillow, they gave me blankets, they gave me sheets to make up my bed. And lo and behold, you know, I did not know how to make that bed because I came from a place of buffalo robes and deer hides and rabbit skins to cover with, no such thing as a pillow."[67]

Marthe Basile-Coocoo recalled feeling a chill on first seeing the Pointe Bleue, Québec, school. "It was something like a grey day, it was a day without sunshine. It was, it was the impression that I had, that I was only six years old, then, well, the nuns separated us, my brothers, and then my uncles, then I no longer understood. Then that, that was a period there, of suffering, nights of crying, we all gathered in a corner, meaning that we came together, and there we cried. Our nights were like that."[68]

Louise Large could not speak any English when her grandmother took her to the Blue Quills, Alberta, school in the early 1960s. "My grandma and I got into this black car, and I was kind of excited, and I was looking at the window and look. I'd never rode in a car before, or I might have, but this was a strange person. I went to, we drove into Blue Quills, and it was a big building, and I was in awe with the way it looked, and I was okay 'cause I had my grandma with me, and we got off, and we went up the stairs. And that was okay, I was hanging onto my grandma, I was going into this strange place. And, and we walked up the stairs into the building, and down the hallway, going to the left, and there was a room there, and two nuns came."

As was often the case, she was not used to seeing nuns dressed in religious habits. "I didn't know they were nuns. I don't know why they were dressed the way they were. They had long black skirts, dresses, and at that time

---

[67] TRC, *Statement*, SP038.
[68] TRC, *Statement*, 2011-6103.

they looked weird 'cause they had these little weird hats and a veil, kind of like a black bridesmaid or something, and they were all smiling at me." She was shocked to discover she was going to be left at the school. The nuns had to hold Louise tight to stop her from trying to leave with her grandmother. "And I wasn't aware at that time that my grandma was gonna leave me there. I'm not ever sure how she told me, but they started holding me and my grandma left and I started fighting them because I didn't want my grandma to leave me, and, and I started screaming, and crying and crying, and it must have been about, I don't know, when I look back, probably long enough to know that my grandma was long gone. They let me go, and they started yelling at me to shut up, or I don't know, they had a real mean tone of voice. It must have been about, when I think about it, it was in the morning, and I just screamed and screamed for hours. It seemed like for hours. They all ran down to the water's edge to get on the float plane that would take them to school. On their arrival, they were taken to the school by the same truck that was used to haul garbage to the local refuse site. From that point on, the experience was much more somber. And I can still recall today the, the quiet, the quiet, and all the sadness, the atmosphere, as we entered that big stone building. The excitement in the morning was gone, and everybody was quiet because the … senior students that had been there before knew the rules, and us newcomers were just beginning to see, and we were little, we were young. I remember how they took our clothes, the clothes that we wore when we left, and they also cut our hair. We had short hair from there on. And they put a chemical on our hair, which was some kind of a white powder."[69]

---

[69] TRC, *Statement*, 01-AB-06JA11-012.

Arriving at School

Linda Head was initially excited about the prospect of a plane trip that would take her to the Prince Albert, Saskatchewan school. "My dad kissed me, and up I went, I didn't care [laughs] 'cause this was something new for me." The plane landed on the Saskatchewan River. "There was a, a car waiting for us, or the truck. But I got into the car, and the boys were in the truck, like an army, an army truck. They stood outside the, outside, you know, at the back, not inside. They gave us, told us which dorm to go, and, and there was a person standing, but the kids were, you know, lining up, and this person took me to the line. And when the line was full, I guess when we were, they took us to the dorm…. We had our numbers, and a bed number. And she told us to settle down. Well, I wasn't understanding this 'cause it was English, but I followed, you know, watch, watch everybody, and … she took my hand, and guided me to the bed, and the number showed me what number I was, number four, and we had to find number four. So that's how it was then. My stuff, I had to set it down, then I, I was under, under the bed, not the higher up, I had the lower bed. So, I was just lying around there … the music was loud, the radio. Everybody was talking in Cree, some of them in Cree, some of them in English, well a little bit of English. And my cousins … we were in together some of them, some of us at the same age, so they came over and talked to me. I said, 'Well, here we are.' Here I was missing home already."[70]

Gilles Petiquay, who attended the Pointe Bleue, Québec, school, was shocked by the numbering system at the school. "I remember that the first number that I had at the

---

[70] TRC, *Statement*, 2011-4442.

Arriving at School

residential school was 95. I had that number—95—for a year. The second number was number 4. I had it for a longer period of time. The third number was 56. I also kept it for a long time. We walked with the numbers on us."[71]

Mary Courchene grew up on the Fort Alexander Reserve in Manitoba. Her parents' home was just a five-minute walk away from the Fort Alexander boarding school. "One morning my mom woke us up and said we were going to school that day and then she takes out new clothes that she had bought us and I was just so happy, so over the moon. And, she was very, very quiet. And she was dressing us up and she didn't say too much. She didn't say, "Oh I'll see you," and all of that. She just said, she just dressed us up with, with no comment. And then we left; we left for the school." When the family reached the school, they were greeted by a nun. Mary's brother became frightened. Mary told him to behave himself. She then turned around to say goodbye to her mother, but she was gone. Her mother had gone to residential school as a child. "And she could not bear to talk to her children and prepare her children to go to residential school. It was just too, too much for her." Courchene said that on that day, her life changed. "It began ten years of the most miserable part of my life, here on, here, in the world."[72]

Roy Denny was perplexed and frightened by the clothing that the priests and sisters wore at the Shubenacadie school. "And we were greeted by this man dressed in black with a long gown. That was the priest, come to find later. And the nuns with their black, black outfits with

---

[71] TRC, *Statement*, 2011-6001.
[72] TRC, Statement, 2011-2515.

the white collar and a white, white collar and, like a breast plate of white. And their freaky looking hats that were, I don't, I couldn't, know what they remind me of. And I didn't see, first time I ever seen nuns and priests. And they, and they were speaking to me, and I couldn't understand them." He had not fully understood that his father was going to be leaving him at the school. "So when my father left I tried to stop him; I tried, I tried to go, you know, tried to go with him, but he said, 'No, you got to stay.' That was real hard."[73]

Archie Hyacinthe said he was unprepared for life in the Catholic school in Kenora. "It was almost like we were, you know, captured, or taken to another form of home. Like I said, nobody really explained to us, as if we were just being taken away from our home, and our parents. We were detached I guess from our home and our parents, and it's scary when you, when you first think, think about it as a child, because you never had that separation in your lifetime before that. So that was the, I think that's when the trauma started for me, being separated from my sister, from my parents, and from our, our home. We were no longer free. It was like being, you know, taken to a strange land, even though it was our, our, our land, as I understood later on."[74]

Dorene Bernard was only four and a half years old when she was enrolled in the Shubenacadie residential school. She had thought that the family was simply taking her older siblings back to the school after a holiday. "I remember that day. We went down there to take my sister and brother back. My father and mom went in to talk to the priest, but

---

[73] TRC, *Statement*, 2011-2678.
[74] TRC, *Statement*, 2011-2678.

they were making plans to leave me behind. But I didn't know that, so I went on the girls' side with my sister and she told me after couple hours went by that they had already left. I would say it was pretty difficult to feel that abandoned at four and a half years old. But I had my sister, my older sister Karen, she took care of me the best way she could."[75]

When parents brought their children to the school themselves, the moment of departure was often heartbreaking. **Ida Ralph Quisess** could recall her father "crying in the chapel" when she and her siblings were sent to residential school. "He was crying, and that, one of the, these women in black dresses, I later learned they were sisters, they called them, nuns, the Oblate nuns, later, many years after I learned what their title was, and the one that spoke our language told him, 'We'll keep your little girls, we'll raise them,' and then my father started to cry."[76]

Vitaline Elsie Jenner resisted being sent to school. "And I didn't want to go to the residential school. I didn't realize what I was going to come up against upon being there. I resisted. I cried and I fought with my mom. My mom was the one that took us there and dragged, actually just about dragged me there, because of my resistance, not wanting, I hung onto everything that was in the way, resisting." The separation at the Fort Chipewyan school in northern Alberta was traumatic. "And so when I went upon, when we went into the residential school, it was in the parlour, and there was a nun that was receiving the students that were going into the residential school, and I, you know,

---

[75] TRC, *Statement*, SP029.
[76] TRC, *Statement*, 01-ON-24NOV10-002.

like I hung onto my mom as tight as I can. And what I remember was she had taken my hand, and what she did, what my mom did, I, I don't remember the rest of my siblings, it's just like I kind of blocked out, because that was traumatic already for me as it was, being taken there, you know, and this great big building looked so strange and foreign to me, and so she took my hand, and forcefully put my hand in the nun's hand, and the nun grabbed it, so I wouldn't run away. So, she grabbed it, and I was screaming and hollering. And in my language I said, 'Mama, Mama, kâya nakasin' and in English it was, 'Mom, Mom, don't leave me.' 'Cause that's all I knew was to speak Cree. And so the nun took us, and Mom, I, I turned around, and Mom was walking away. And I didn't realize, I guess, that she was also crying."[77]

Lily Bruce's parents were in tears when they left her and her brother at the Alert Bay, British Columbia, school. "And our parents talked to the principal, and, and then Mom was in tears, and I remember the last time she was in tears was when my brother Jimmy was put in that school. And her and Dad went through those double doors in the front, and the principal and his wife were saying that they were gonna take good care of us, that they were gonna treat us like they were our new parents, and not to worry about us, and just bringing our hopes up, and so Mom and Dad left. And I grabbed my brother, and my brother held me, we just started crying. [audible crying] We were hurt because Mom and Dad left us there."[78]

---

[77] TRC, *Statement*, 02-MB-16JU10-131.
[78] TRC, *Statement*, 2011-3285.

ARRIVING AT SCHOOL

Margaret Simpson attended the Fort Chipewyan school in the 1950s. She was initially excited to be going to residential school because she would be going with her brother George. "I was happy I was going with him, and my dad took us and there we're walking to the, to this big orange building. It was in, and we got there, and I was so happy 'cause I was going to go in here with George and I was going to be with him but you know this was far as it was going to go once we made it in there. He went one way, and I was calling him and this other nun took me the other way, so we separated right there. Right from there I was wondering what is happening here? I was so lost, I was so lost. And they brought me downstairs and then I looked and all of a sudden, I seen my dad passing on the other side of the fence, he was walking. I just went running, I seen the door over there and I went running I was going to go see my dad over there. But they stopped me, and I was crying and I was telling my dad to come and he didn't hear me and I was wondering what is happening, I don't even know."[79]

The rest of a new student's first day is often remembered as being invasive, humiliating, and dehumanizing. Her first day at the Catholic school in Kenora left **Lynda Pahpasay McDonald** frightened and distressed. "And I had, I must have had long hair, like long, long hair, like, and my brothers, even my brother had long hair, and he looked like a little girl. Then they took us into this, it was like a greeting area, we went in there, and they kind of counted us, me and my siblings. And I was hanging onto my sister, and she told me not to cry, so don't cry, you know, you just, you listen. She was trying to tell me, and I was crying, and of

---

[79] TRC, *Statement*, 02-MB-18JU10-051.

ARRIVING AT SCHOOL

course me and my sister were crying, there's three of us, we're just a year apart. Me, Barbara, and Sandy were standing there, crying. She was telling us not to cry, and, and just do what we had to do. And, and I remember having, watching my brother being, like, taken away, my older brother, Marcel. They took him, and he had long hair also. And we were taken upstairs, and they gave us some clothing, and they put numbers on our clothes. I remember there's little tags in the back, they put numbers, and they told us that was your number. Well, I can't remember my number. And, and we seen the nuns. They had these big black outfits, and they were scary looking, I remember. And of course they weren't really, they looked really, I don't know, mean, I guess. And, and we, they took us upstairs, I remember that, and they gave us these clothes, different clothes, and they took us to another room, then they kind of, like, and they took our old clothes, they took that, and they made us take a bath or a shower. I think it was a bath at that time. After we came out, and they washed our hair, and I don't know, they kind of put some kind of thing on our hair, like, you know, our heads, and they're checking our hair and stuff like that. And then they took us to this chair, and they put a white cloth over our shoulders, and they started cutting our hair. And you know they cut real straight bangs, and real short hair, like, it was real straight haircuts. I didn't like the fact that they cut off all our hair. And same with my brother, they had, they cut off all of, most of his hair. They had a, he had a brush cut, like."[80]

When **Emily Kematch** arrived at the Gordon's, Saskatchewan school from York Landing in northern

---

[80] TRC, *Statement*, 02-MB-16JU10-130.

Manitoba, her hair was treated with a white powder and then cut. "And we had our clothes that we went there with even though we didn't have much. We had our own clothes but they took those away from us and we had to wear the clothes that they gave us, same sort of clothes that we had to wear."[81]

Verna Kirkness attended the Dauphin, Manitoba, residential school. On arrival at that school after a lengthy train trip, she said she was stripped of all her clothing. "They didn't tell me that they were gonna do that. And they poured something on my head, I don't know what it was, but it didn't smell too good. To this day, I don't know what it is. But from my understanding, from people explaining it to me, it was coal oil, or some, some kind of oil, and they poured that on my head, and then they cut my hair really, really short. And then, and when we, we sat, I remember sitting, I don't know it's, it looked like a picnic table. It was in the corner, I think it was in the corner, and I sat there. I was looking around, and I was looking for my sister. And then I, and then I think we were given a doughnut, or some kind of pastry, and then we were sent to bed. And I remember my first bed. It was right by the door. And then as when you walk in, it was on your right-hand side, and I was on the top bunk, the first bunk bed, I was on the top bunk, and that's my first, my very first night there."[82]

At the Blue Quills school, **Alice Quinney** and the other recently arrived students were told they were to be given a bath. "I had never been naked in front of anybody

---

[81] TRC, *Statement*, 02-MB-18JU10-063.
[82] TRC, *Statement*, 02-MB-18JU10-033.

ever before, except my mom, who would give us a bath in, in the bathtub at home, in a, in a round tub, you know the old round tubs that they had, the steel tubs, that's the kind of, you know. And so that was hard too, they told us before, when we went down to the bathroom, we all had to strip, and they put this nasty smelling stuff in our hair, for bugs, they said, if we had brought any bugs with us. So, they put all that stuff, and some kind of powder that smelled really bad. And then we were, we had to take off all our clothes, and, and go in, in the showers together."[83]

On her arrival at the Alberni, British Columbia school, **Lily Bruce** was separated from her brother and taken to the girls' dormitory. "I had to take a bath, and it was late at night, and I kept crying, and she was calling me a crybaby, and just kept yelling at me, and said if I woke up anybody, I was in deep trouble. 'And if your mother and dad really cared about you, they wouldn't have left you here.' [audible crying] And then she started pulling my long hair, checking for lice. [audible crying] After she checked my hair and shampooed my hair, I had to have vinegar put in there, and being yanked around in that tub, too, had to wash every part of my body or else they were gonna do it, and I didn't want, I didn't want them to touch me."[84]

Helen Harry's hair was cut on her arrival at the Williams Lake, British Columbia, school. "And I remember not wanting to cut my hair, because I remember my mom had really long hair, down to her waist. And she never ever cut it, and she never cut our hair either. All the girls had really long

---

[83] TRC, *Statement*, 02-MB-18JU10-049.
[84] TRC, *Statement*, 2011-3285.

Arriving at School

hair in our family. And I kept saying that I didn't want to cut my hair, but they just sat me on the chair and they just got scissors and they just grabbed my hair, and they just cut it. And they had this big bucket there, and they just threw everybody's hair in that bucket. I remember going back to the dorm and there was other girls that were upset about their hair. They were mad and crying that they had to get their hair cut. And then when that was all done, we were made to wash our hair out with some kind of shampoo. And I just remember it smelling really awful. The smell was bad. And this is, I think it had something to do with delousing people, I'm not sure."[85]

In 1985, **Ricky Kakekagumick** was one of a group of children who were own to the Poplar Hill, Ontario school. On arrival, the boys and girls were separated and marched to their dormitories. "When we got there, there's staff people there, Mennonite men. They're holding towels. So, we just put our luggage down on the floor there, and they told us, 'Wet your hair.' I had long hair, like, I was an Aboriginal teenager, I grew long hair. So, they told us, 'Wash your hair.' Then they had this big bottle of chemical. I didn't know what it was. It looked like something you see in a science lab. So, they were pumping that thing into our hand, 'And put it all over your head,' they said. 'So, it will, this will kill all of the bugs on your head.' Just right away they assumed all of us had bugs, Aboriginal. I didn't like that. I was already a teenager. I was already taking care of myself. I knew I didn't have bugs. But right away they assumed I did because I'm Aboriginal. So after we washed our hair, everybody went through that, then we went to the next room. Then that's

---

[85] TRC, *Statement*, 2011-3203.

where I see a bunch of hair all over the floor. I see a guy standing over there with those clippers, the little buzz, was buzzing students. I kept on moving back. There was a line there. I kept going back. I didn't want to go. But it came down to the end, I had no choice, 'cause everybody was already going through it, couldn't go behind anybody no more. So, I made a big fuss about it, but couldn't stop them. It was a rule. So, they, they gave me a brush, and they gave us one comb, too, and told us this is your comb, you take care of it."[86]

As a child, **Bernice Jacks** had been proud of her long hair. "My mom used to braid it and French braid it and brush it. And my sister would look after my hair and do it." But, on her arrival at residential school in the Northwest Territories, a staff member sat her on a stool and cut her hair. "And I sat there, and I could hear, I could see my hair falling. And I couldn't do nothing. And I was so afraid my mom ... I wasn't thinking about myself. I was thinking about Mom. I say, 'Mom's gonna be really mad. And June is gonna be angry. And it's gonna be my fault.'"[87]

Victoria Boucher-Grant was shocked by the treatment she received upon enrolment at the Fort William, Ontario school. "And they, they took my braids, and they chopped my, they didn't even cut it, they just, I mean style it or anything, they just took the braid like that, and just cut it straight across. And I remember just crying and crying because it was almost like being violated, you know, like when you're, when I think about it now it was a violation,

---

[86] TRC, *Statement*, 2011-4200.
[87] TRC, *Statement*, 2011-3971.

like, your, your braids got cut, and it, I don't know how many years that you spent growing this long hair."[88]

Elaine Durocher found the first day at the Roman Catholic school in Kamsack, Saskatchewan to be overwhelming. "As soon we entered the residential school, the abuse started right away. We were stripped, taken up to a dormitory, stripped. Our hair was sprayed.... They put oxfords on our feet, 'cause I know my feet hurt. They put dresses on us. And were made, we were always praying, we were always on our knees. We were told we were little, stupid savages, and that they had to educate us."[89]

Brian Rae said he and the other boys at the Fort Frances, Ontario school were given a physical inspection by female staff. "You know, to get stripped like that by a female, you know, you don't even know, 'cause, you know, it was embarrassing, humiliating. And, and then she'd have this, you know, look or whatever it was in her eyes, eh, you know. And then she would comment about your private parts and stuff like that, eh, like, say, 'Oh, what a cute peanut,' and you know, just you know kind of rub you down there, and, and then, you know, just her eyes, the way she looked. So that kind of made me feel, feel all, you know, dirty and, you know, just, I don't know, just make me feel awful I guess because she was doing that. And then the others, you know, the other kids were there, you know, just laughing, eh, that was common. So, I think that was the first time I ever felt humiliated about my sexuality."[90]

---

[88] TRC, *Statement*, 01-ON-05FE11-004.
[89] TRC, *Statement*, 02-MB-16JU10-059.
[90] TRC, *Statement*, 2011-4198.

Julianna Alexander found the treatment she received upon arrival at the Kamloops, British Columbia school demeaning. "But they made us strip down naked, and I felt embarrassed, you know. They didn't, you know I just thought it was inappropriate, you know, people standing there, watching us, scrubbing us and everything, and then powdering us down with whatever it was that they powdered us with, and, and our hairs were covered, you know, really scrubbed out, and then they poured, I guess what they call now coal oil, or whatever that was, like, some kind of turpentine, I'm not sure what it was, but anyway, it really stunk."[91]

On their arrival at residential school, students often were required to exchange the clothes they were wearing for school-supplied clothing. This could mean the loss of homemade clothing that was of particular value and meaning to the students. **Murray Crowe** said his clothes from home were taken and burned at the school that he attended in northwestern Ontario.[92]

When **Wilbur Abrahams's** mother sent him to the Alert Bay school, she outfitted him in brand-new clothes. When he arrived at the school, he and all the other students were lined up. "They took us down the hall, and we were lined up again, and, and I couldn't figure out what we were lined up for, but I dare not say anything. And pretty soon it's my turn, they told me to take all of my clothes off, and, and they gave me clothes that looked like they were second-hand, but they were clean, and told me to put those on, and

---

[91] TRC, *Statement*, 2011-3286.
[92] TRC, *Statement*, 2011-0306.

that was the last time I saw my new clothes. Dare not ask questions."[93]

John B. Custer said that upon arrival at the Roman Catholic school near The Pas, Manitoba, all the students had their personal clothing taken away. "And we were dressed in, we were all dressed the same. Like, we had coveralls on. I remember when I went over there, I had these beaded moccasins. As soon as I got there, they took everything away."[94]

Elizabeth Tapiatic Chiskamish attended schools in Québec and northern Ontario. She recalled that when she arrived at school, her home clothing was taken from her. "The clothes we wore were taken away from us too. That was the last time we saw our clothes. I never saw the candy that my parents packed into my suitcase again. I don't know what they did with it. It was probably thrown away or given to someone else or simply kept. When I was given back the luggage, none of things that my parents packed were still in there. Only the clothes I wore were still sometimes in the suitcase."[95]

Phyllis Webstad recalled that her mother bought her a new shirt to wear on her first day at school at Williams Lake. "I remember it was an orange shiny colour. But when I got to the Mission it was taken and I never wore it again. I didn't understand why. Nothing was ever explained why things were happening."[96] Much later, her experience

---

[93] TRC, *Statement*, 2011-3301.
[94] TRC, *Statement*, 02-MB-19JU10-057.
[95] TRC, *Statement*, 2011-3363.
[96] TRC, Statement, SP111.

became the basis for what has come to be known as "Orange Shirt Day." Organized by the Cariboo Regional District, it was first observed on September 30, 2013. On that day, individuals were encouraged to wear an orange shirt as a memorial of the damage done to children by the residential school system.[97]

When **Larry Beardy** left Churchill, Manitoba for the Anglican school in Dauphin, he was wearing a "really nice, beautiful beaded" jacket his mother had made. "I think it was a caribou, a jacket, and she, she made that for me because she knew I was going to school." Shortly after he arrived at school, "all, all our clothes were taken away. My jacket I had mentioned was gone. And everybody was given the same, the same kind of clothing, with the old black army boots, we used to call them, and slacks."[98]

Ilene Nepoose recalled that the belongings she took to the Blue Quills residential school were taken away from her upon arrival. "I even brought my own utensils [laughing] and I never saw those things again, I often wonder what happen to them. But I remember at the end of the first school, the first year—they take our personal clothes away and they give us these dresses that are made out of our sacks." When she was to return home at Christmas time, the staff could not find the clothes she had worn to come to school. "I saw them on this other girl and I told the nuns that she was wearing my dress and they didn't believe me. So, that girl ended up keeping my dress and I don't remember what I wore, it was probably a school dress. But, that really

---

[97] Lamb-Yorski," Orange shirt day", *Williams Lake Tribune*.
[98] TRC, *Statement*, SP082.

bothered me because it was my own, like my mom made that dress for me and I was very proud of it and I couldn't—I wasn't allowed to wear that again."[99]

Nick Sibbeston attended the Fort Providence school for six years. He was enrolled in the school after his mother was sent to the Charles Camsell Hospital in Edmonton for tuberculosis treatment. The only language he spoke was Slavey (Dene); the only language the teachers spoke was French. "On arrival you're given a bath and you're de-liced and you're given a haircut and all your clothes are taken away. I know I arrived with a little bag that my mother had filled with winter things, you know, your mitts ... but all of that was taken away and put up high in a cupboard and we didn't see it again 'til next June."[100]

When **Carmen Petiquay** went to the Amos, Québec school, the staff "took away our things, our suitcases, my mother had put things that I loved in my suitcase. I had some toys. I had some clothing that my mother had made for me, and I never saw them again. I don't know what they did with those things."[101]

Martin Nicholas of Nelson House, Manitoba went to the Pine Creek, Manitoba school in the 1950s. "My mom had prepared me in a Native clothing. She had made me a buckskin jacket, beaded with fringes.... And my mom did beautiful work, and I was really proud of my clothes. And

---

[99] TRC, *Statement*, 2011-2380.
[100] TRC, *Statement*, NNE202.
[101] TRC, *Statement*, SP104.

Arriving at School

when I got to residential school, that first day I remember, they stripped us of our clothes."[102]

Frances Tait was sent to the Alberni, British Columbia school in 1951 when she was five years old. For her, as for so many students, the moment of arrival was a moment of tremendous loss. "And even right from day one, I remember they took everything I had. I went to that school with a silver teapot that my mother had left for me, and my family made sure that I had it. As soon as I walked into that school, they took all my clothes, and they took the teapot. And I never saw it again. And I got a haircut; I was issued school clothing."[103]

When **Dorothy Ross** went to school at Sioux Lookout, her clothes were taken from her and thrown away. "I was hanging on to my jacket really tight. I didn't want to let go. So once I set my jacket somewhere, I lost it. 'Cause what if my mom comes, I was looking for my mom, I need my jacket. They took that away from me."[104]

On her arrival at the Presbyterian school in Kenora, **Lorna Morgan** was wearing "these nice little beaded moccasins that my grandma had made me to wear for school, and I was very proud of them." She said they were taken from her and thrown in the garbage.[105]

The schools could not always provide students with a full range of shoe sizes. **Geraldine Bob** said that at the

---

[102] TRC, *Statement*, 07-MB-24FB10-001.
[103] TRC, *Statement*, 2011-3974.
[104] TRC, *Statement*, 01-ON-24NOV10-014.
[105] TRC, *Statement*, 02-MB-16JU10-041.

Kamloops school, "you got the closest fit whether it was too big or too small; so your feet hurt constantly." In the same way, she felt the clothing was never warm enough in winter. "I just remember the numbing cold. And being outside in the playground and a lot of us would dig holes in the bank and get in and pull tumbleweeds in after us, to try to stay warm."[106]

Stella August said that at the Christie, British Columbia, school, "we all had to wear the same shoes, whether they fit or not, and, and if they didn't fit, if we were caught without our shoes, we'd get whacked in the ear with our shoe."[107]

Other students recalled the school-issued clothing as being uncomfortable, ill- fitting, and insufficient in the winters. **William Herney** said that at the Shubenacadie school, the students would often huddle together in an effort to keep warm. "It was, it was just like a circle. The inner circle was the three-, the four-, five- year-olds and seven-year-olds in that circle, small ones, and the older you are, the outer circle you were, and the oldest ones wanted the outest, and the, the outer circle, the farthest out. We would huddle up in there, just huddle in close together to give that body heat. And the young ones were protected from the elements. And, well, we huddled up around there for maybe an hour, an hour and a half, and until suppertime, when, when the bell rang, you were all piled in there."[108]

---

[106] TRC, *Statement*, 2011-2685.
[107] TRC, *Statement*, 02-MB-16JU10-005.
[108] TRC, *Statement*, 2011-2923.

Margaret Plamondon said the children at the Fort Chipewyan, Alberta school were not dressed warmly enough for the winter recess periods. "And then it doesn't matter how cold it is, at recess, and you can't wear pants, you have to wear a little skinny dress, and it doesn't matter how cold it is, you were out there, and they wouldn't let you come in, even if you're crying and you're cold. You had to go play outside during recess, fifteen minutes, you can't get in, they lock the door on you, even if you try to go in, and same thing on weekends. There's no, it doesn't matter how cold it is in the wintertime, we have to ... sometimes we'd stand there by the door, freezing, freezing to death, a whole bunch of us, you know, just little kids, don't understand why we can't go in to warm up."[109]

The students' wardrobe at the schools was also limited in terms of quantity. **Joanne Morrison Methot** said that the students at the Shubenacadie school had a minimal supply of clothing. "And we didn't have a lot of clothes. We only had maybe two pair of pants, two socks, like two bras, two panties, and maybe two nightgowns, that's all we had. Sundays, it was a dress-up dress, like, for Sundays. We only wore that to go to church, and patent leather shoes, and little white socks. After church, we had to go back upstairs and change our clothes."[110]

Students spoke of the time they spent caring for their clothing. **Shirley Ida Moore** recalled that as a child at the Norway House, Manitoba, school, she used to get into trouble because she could not keep her clothes as neat and

---

[109] TRC, *Statement*, 2011-0387.
[110] TRC, *Statement*, 2011-2875.

clean as was expected. "We had these uniforms, they were, they were, we had a white blouse and then these tunics and I think they had like, three, three of those big pleat, pleaty things all around it. And every Sunday we had to iron those things razor sharp; like the pleats had to be sharp. And, and your shoes had to be polished and they had to be like glass. And, that's what I, that's what I got into trouble; that's why, because like, I was only little and she expected me to be able to iron those things like that well, and I couldn't and nobody could help me; so I would get punished. Just punished, and punished, and punished."[111]

Arthur Ron McKay arrived at the Sandy Bay, Manitoba school in the early 1940s with no knowledge of English. "I didn't know where to go, not even to the washroom sometimes. I just wet myself because I didn't know where to go and I couldn't speak to the teacher, and I know that the nuns was the teacher and I couldn't speak English. They told me not to speak my language and everything, so I always pretended to be asleep at my desk so they wouldn't ask me anything. The nun, first time she was nice but later on, as she began to know me, when I done that to lay my head on the desk pretending that I was sleeping not to be asked anything, she come and grab my hair, my ears and told me to listen and to sit up straight."[112]

When she first went to the Amos, Québec school, **Margo Wylde** could not speak any French. "I said to myself, 'How am I going to express myself? How will I make people understand what I'm saying?' And I wanted to find my sisters

---

[111] TRC, *Statement*, 2011-0089.
[112] TRC, *Statement*, 02-MB-18JU10-044.

to ask them to come and get me. You know it's sad to say, but I felt I was a captive."[113]

William Antoine grew up speaking Ojibway on the Sheshewaning Reserve in Ontario. When he was seven, he was taken to the Spanish, Ontario boys' school. "I was in Grade One, the work that was given to me I didn't know anything about and, and the teacher was speaking English to me and I didn't understand what he was saying. That's why it was so hard; I didn't understand English very much. I understand a little bit, at that time, but I did not understand what he told me. And he would get mad at me and angry at me because I couldn't do my work. I could not, I couldn't do it because I didn't understand what he was telling me what to do. So it was hard."[114]

When he first went to the Fort Albany, Ontario school, **Peter Nakogee** could speak no English. "That's where I had the most difficulty in school because I didn't understand English. My hand was hit because I wrote on my scribblers, the scribblers that were given on starting school, pencils, erasers, rulers and that, scribblers, and textbooks that were given. 'Write your names,' she said, so they don't get lost. But I wrote on my scribblers in Cree syllabics. And so I got the nun really mad that I was writing in Cree. And then I only knew my name was Ministik from the first time I heard my name, my name was Ministik. So I was whipped again because I didn't know my name was Peter Nakogee."[115]

---

[113] TRC, *Statement*, SP100.
[114] TRC, *Statement*, 2011-2002.
[115] TRC, *Statement*, 01-ON-4-6NOV10-023.

Arriving at School

For **Marcel Guiboche** at the Pine Creek school, the experience was frightening. "A sister, a nun started talking to me in English and French, and yelling at me. I did not speak English, and didn't understand what she, what she was asking. She got very upset, and started hitting me all over my body, hands, legs, and back. I began to cry, yell, and became very scared, and this infuriated her more. She got a black strap and hit me some more. My brother, Eddie, Edward, heard me screaming, and came to get me."[116]

Calvin Myerion recalled not being allowed to speak his language at the Brandon school. "And the time went on, and I was told not to speak my Native language, and I didn't know any other language other than my Native language. I didn't know a word of English, and my brother, who had been there before me, taught me in, said in my language not to talk the language. But the only way that I could communicate was through my language."[117]

The shock of her first night at the Alberni school left **Lily Bruce** in tears. Eventually, her auntie, who was a student at the school, was brought in to speak to her. "I was just getting dressed into pajamas, and I never, I never spoke English. [crying] My auntie was told to tell me that I wasn't allowed to speak Kwak'wala anymore. I told her, 'But Auntie, I don't know how to speak English.' And she says, 'Well you're gonna have to learn pretty quick.' [crying] She said, 'From now on, you have to speak English.' I don't know how long it took me. I kept my mouth shut most of the time. I'd rather keep quiet than get in trouble."[118]

---

[116] TRC, *Statement*, 02-MB-19JU10-034.
[117] TRC, *Statement*, 02-MB-16JU10-122.
[118] TRC, *Statement*, 2011-3285.

Andrew Bull Calf recalled that at the residential school in Cardston, Alberta, "I got strapped a lot of time because I didn't know English, you know, and the only language we spoke was Blackfoot in our community and so I got strapped a lot for that."[119]

Percy Thompson recalled being slapped in the face for speaking Cree shortly after his arrival at the Hobbema school in Alberta. "How was I to learn English within three or four days the first week I was there? Was I supposed to learn the English words, so the nun would be happy about it? It's impossible."[120]

When two sisters attended the Anglican school at Aklavik, they could not speak English. But, according to one sister, the staff would "spank us when we tried to talk our language. So, we just keep away from one another."[121]

Alfred Nolie attended the Alert Bay school, where, he said, "they strapped me right away, as soon as they heard me talking our language. I didn't know what they were saying to me."[122]

Martin Nicholas said that at the school he attended in Manitoba, the prohibition on speaking one's own language left him isolated. "I would be punished if I spoke my language, yet, that's the only language I knew. So, what am I

---

[119] TRC, *Statement*, 2011-0273.
[120] TRC, *Statement*, SP125.
[121] TRC, *Statement*, 07-NWT-02MR10-002.
[122] TRC, *Statement*, 2011-3293.

supposed to do? So, I kept quiet." Because he did not speak English, he became alarmed if anyone spoke to him.[123]

Meeka Alivaktuk came to the Pangnirtung school in what is now Nunavut with no knowledge of English. "For example, I knew how to knit. I learned before we came to school how to knit mittens but when we got to school and the teacher was speaking to us in English and he was saying 'knit, purl, knit, purl,' I had no idea what that meant so I put down my knitting and just sat there. The teacher came up to me and slapped my hands because they didn't know what to do and I couldn't understand what he was telling me. That's how my education began."[124]

After growing up speaking only Cree in northern Manitoba, **Emily Kematch** found that "learning how to speak English was a struggle." She said that "the only way I got by was my friend Sally taught me words, 'this is how you say, say words.' She taught me what to do so I wouldn't get into trouble and we weren't allowed to cry. If we cried, we got spanked."[125]

At the Qu'Appelle, Saskatchewan, school in the mid-1960s, **Greg Rainville** said, he was punished for speaking his own language and for failing to carry out instructions given him in a language he did not understand. "The nuns would get frustrated with you when they talked to you in French or English, and you're not knowing what they're talking about, and you're pulled around by the ear."[126]

---

[123] TRC, *Statement*, 07-MB-24FB10-001.
[124] TRC, *Statement*, SP045.
[125] TRC, *Statement*, 02-MB-18JU10-063.
[126] TRC, *Statement*, 2011-1752.

Arriving at School

When **Robert Malcolm** came to the Sandy Bay school, he did not speak a word of English. "I had to learn the hard way to communicate in school what the, the nuns or the teachers wanted. And if you didn't, if you didn't understand that, it was, you were being punished, sometimes physically, and then sometimes emotionally. Like you were made fun of sometimes by other people in your class, like if I said, or did something wrong everybody would laugh at you."[127]

The use of traditional Aboriginal languages were often banned, with the intention of forcing the students to learn English (or French). The anxiety caused by these rules remain one of the most commonly cited complaints of the residential school experience.

Jacqueline Barney said that one of her report cards from the Sault Ste. Marie, Ontario school complained that "Jackie still insists on speaking Cree."[128]

Dianne Bossum recalled being told not to speak her own language at the La Tuque, Québec, school she attended in the late 1960s and early 1970s.[129]

Geraldine Shingoose recalled being punished for not speaking English at the Lestock, Saskatchewan school. "I just remember, recalling the very first memories was just the beatings we'd get and the lickings, and just for speaking our

---

[127] TRC, *Statement*, 02-MB-16JU10-090.
[128] TRC, *Statement*, SP100.
[129] TRC, *Statement*, SP105.

language, and just for doing things that were against the rules."[130]

Dorothy Nolie recalled that at the Alert Bay school, she was caught speaking in her own language at the dinner table. "They put me in the middle of the floor, in front of everybody, and that was my punishment for speaking our language. I was hungry. I never ate nothing. Looked around, looked around, everybody eating. That's how mean they were to me, to all of us kids in there."[131]

At the Roman Catholic residence in Fort Smith in the 1960s, **Leon Wyallon** recalled, he was punished for speaking his own language. "We can't even talk in our own language. The minute you talked your own language then you would get sent to the corner. The minute those Grey Nuns found out that you're talking in your own language, whispering, you'd, if you don't tell us now then you get strapped on the hand until you say, what did you say. They let you stand in the corner 'til suppertime."[132]

David Nevin recalled seeing a young girl "savagely" beaten by staff at the Shubenacadie school for refusing to stop speaking Mi'kmaq. "This went on for—seemed like an eternity, and no matter what they did to her she spoke Mi'kmaq. You know, and to this day I, you know, that has been indelible in my mind and I think that's one of the reasons why when I went to school there I always spoke

---

[130] TRC, *Statement*, 02-MB-19JU10-033.
[131] TRC, *Statement*, 2011-3294.
[132] TRC, *Statement*, 2011-0244.

English, that fear of being hit with that strap, that leather strap."[133]

Alan Knockwood recalled being strapped for speaking his own language at Shubenacadie. "Just for saying thank you to someone who gave me something in the school. I was caught by a Brother or one of the workers, and I was strapped so severely that when we went to supper my cousin Ivan had to feed me because my hands were so swollen from the straps. And I remember sitting at the corner of the table and the guys got up and hid me, stood up and hid, so Ivan could feed me a few mouthfuls of food."[134]

Allen Kagak recalled being disciplined for speaking Inuktitut at the Coppermine tent hostel in the Northwest Territories (now Nunavut). "I couldn't speak English, they tell me to speak English, but I couldn't help it, I had to speak my Inuktitut language. When I speak my Inuktitut language, they, teachers, strapped, strapped, strapped me, pulled my ears, let me stand in a corner all morning."[135]

Richard Kaiyogan also attended the Coppermine tent hostel. "But over the years, if you talk in your own language you get strapped, and later on, I had to learn the hard way, but myself, I think over the years I earned that, we earn it, take this education. One time I got strapped and I didn't want to get strapped anymore so I said to myself, I said, 'What am I here for?' You know, education, I guess. Anyway, my culture is going to be—my language will be lost in the way. Okay, why not think like a white man? Talk like a white man? Eat

---

[133] TRC, *Statement*, SP029.
[134] TRC, *Statement*, SP029.
[135] TRC, *Statement*, SC090.

like a white man, that's what, so I don't have to get strapped anymore. You know, I followed their own rules."[136]

On his first day of school in Pangnirtung, the teacher overheard **Sam Kautainuk** speaking to a friend in Inuktitut. "He took a ruler and grabbed my head like this and then smacked me in the mouth with the ruler four times. That was very painful, it hurts! It hurt so much. That happened just for speaking to my friend in my own language."[137]

There are also reports of students being forced to eat soap if they were caught speaking an Aboriginal language. **Pierrette Benjamin** said this happened at the school at La Tuque. "They put a big chunk, and they put it in my mouth, and the principal, she put it in my mouth, and she said, 'Eat it, eat it,' and she just showed me what to do. She told me to swallow it. And she put her hand in front of my mouth, so I was chewing and chewing, and I had to swallow it, so I swallowed it, and then I had to open my mouth to show that I had swallowed it. And at the end, I understood, and she told me, 'That's a dirty language, that's the devil that speaks in your mouth, so we had to wash it because it's dirty.' So, every day I spent at the residential school, I was treated badly. I was almost slaughtered."[138]

Alphonsine McNeely attended the Roman Catholic school at Aklavik in the 1940s. On one occasion, she and a friend were overheard by a nun teaching each other their respective languages. "She took me, I don't know why they always target me. So anyway, she took me to the sink, and

---

[136] TRC, *Statement*, SC091.
[137] TRC, *Statement*, SP044.
[138] TRC, *Statement*, SP105.

she took this, they had this Sunlight soap, it's kind of a big bar, she took a brush, a floor brush, and she, she, I thought she was gonna tell me to scrub the floor or something. Instead of that she, she grabbed my hair, and she started rubbing my mouth with that."[139]

Ken A. Littledeer recalled seeing a fellow student at the Sioux Lookout school having his mouth washed out with soap for speaking an Aboriginal language. "I watched that incident, and, and I didn't like what I seen, bubbles coming out. It sounded like as if they were gonna kill him, or is he breathing, I would say, 'cause I see bubbles coming out of his nose and his mouth, and gagging."[140]

At the Shubenacadie school, a staff member once caught **William Herney** speaking Mi'kmaq with his brother. "And she says, 'What are you two boys doing?' 'Nothing, Sister.' 'Oh, yes, I heard you. You were talking that language, weren't you?' 'Yes, Sister.' 'Come here,' she said. I went over. She took a stick. She leaned me over to the bathtub, the bathtub, grabbed me by the neck, and I don't know how many whacks she gave me over my bum, and I was crying like I don't know what. Then, she took a piece of soap, and she washed my mouth in it. I can still even taste that lye soap. All my life I tasted that taste. And she said, 'You don't talk that language here. That's a no, no, no, you don't, you understand?' Looks at me straight in the eye. She said, 'Do you understand that?' And I said, 'Yes, Sister, I understand.'"[141]

---

[139] TRC, *Statement*, 01-NWT-JY10-002.
[140] TRC, *Statement*, 01-ON-24-NOV10-028.
[141] TRC, *Statement*, 2011-2923.

Arriving at School

In Roman Catholic schools in the West and North, it was most common for many of the staff members to have come originally from Québec or Europe. The fact that these staff members were allowed to speak to one another in French (their first language) bothered many students. **Mary Courchene** once asked one of the staff of the Fort Alexander, Manitoba, school, "'How come you get to talk your own language and we don't?' It was just, you know wanting to know why they could speak French and we couldn't speak Ojibway inside the, inside the school. We spoke it outside, but we couldn't speak it inside, inside the house; inside the school. And she looked at me and she was very angry but she didn't say anything." Later that evening, she was told to apologize to the nun in the dining room. At first she objected, only to be told that "'No one's going to eat until you say you're sorry.' Of course I had to say I was sorry; I didn't want all the rest of the students to have to go without supper, and just because I wouldn't say I was sorry. So I said I was sorry and but it was, I was made to feel humiliated. And there were, there was always humiliations like that, that made you feel small. And of course it was meant for the other, all the other students to laugh at this person that was made to feel ashamed. So it was always you know, that kind of, that kind of thing. So we weren't, we weren't encouraged to be ourselves. We weren't encouraged to, to do what was best for us. It was always what those … anyway."[142]

Students also objected to the fact that if they were taught an additional language, it was French. **Lydia Ross** attended the Cross Lake, Manitoba, school. "And in my Grade Eleven essay, I wrote out a French essay of 500 words, with

---

[142] TRC, *Statement*, 2011-2515.

all the verbs and adjectives, I had 90% in there. That's how, that's how much French that they taught me, and not my language. I couldn't speak our language."[143]

Despite the usual instruction to conduct school life in English (or in French in some of the Québec schools), many students continued to speak their own language when they could. **Monique Papatie** said that at the Amos, Québec, school, students "went to a corner to speak our language, even if we weren't allowed to do that. We kept our language, the Anishinabemowin language, and I speak it very well today, and this is what I want to teach the children, my mother's grandchildren and great-grandchildren."[144]

Arthur Ron McKay said he was able to hang on to his language at the Sandy Bay school. "Or else you'd get your ears pulled, your hair or get hit with a ruler. Well anyway, I just kept going and I couldn't speak my language but then I was speaking to boys in the, 'cause they came from the reserve and they speak my language. We use to speak lots, like behind, behind our supervisors or whatever you call it. That's why I didn't lose my language; we always sneak away when I was smaller."[145]

Ronalee Lavallee said that at the Grayson, Saskatchewan, school in the 1970s, there were a number of students from northern Saskatchewan who spoke fluent Cree. At night, they would teach the language to the other students. "We wanted to learn this language, and how we used to take turns watching for the nuns so that we wouldn't

---

[143] TRC, *Statement*, 02-MB-16JU10-029.
[144] TRC, *Statement*, SP101.
[145] TRC, *Statement*, 02-MB-18Ju10-044.

get into trouble. And I think, just think, that was 1970 or '71, that's not so long ago, and they were still doing that to us?"[146]

From the student perspective, the overall message was to speak English (or French). There were some exceptions. **Mary Stoney** said that at the school she attended in Alberta, at least one priest made an effort to preserve Aboriginal languages. "We were lucky to have Father Mullen, who helped preserve our Cree language by translating the Bible and hymns. If not, the language would be in worse shape. In school we often spoke Cree to each other, but some Sisters were strict with the rules and some were not."[147]

Both Catholic and Protestant missionaries had a long history of learning and encouraging the use of Aboriginal languages in religious settings. At the Beauval, Saskatchewan, school, **Albert Fiddler** recalled, Aboriginal languages were restricted to use in religious classes. "But that's the only thing they allow is learning how to pray in Cree. They won't allow us to talk to each other, and they make sure that we don't, we don't talk to each other in Cree either. We only, they only teach us how to pray in Cree in catechisms in the classroom, but not to talk to each other because it's un-polite for somebody that doesn't understand Cree."[148]

Alex Alikashuak said that at the school at Churchill, Manitoba, which operated in the 1960s, there were no restrictions on the use of Aboriginal languages. "We, we

---

[146] TRC, *Statement*, 2011-1776.
[147] TRC, *Statement*, SP124.
[148] TRC, *Statement*, 2011-1760.

almost never spoke English. The only time we spoke English was when we ran across, like, see the thing is in our school, some of our dormitory staff were Inuit people too, so we, we couldn't speak to them in English, anyway. The only time, real time we spoke English was when we were in the classroom, or we're talking to one of the administration staff, and or somebody from town that's not Inuit, but otherwise we, everybody spoke our language."[149]

The rule in the Aklavik residence, according to **Ellen Smith**, was "English please, English please." But, she said, "when we went on the playground in Aklavik we spoke our language; run around. There they even took us out on the land in the springtime. We went muskrat trapping."[150]

Despite the encouragement that was ordered in some schools, and the students' efforts to keep their language alive, the overall impact was language loss. **Russell Bone** felt he lost the ability to speak his language at the Pine Creek school. "I realized that nobody was, never used to talk their language. Some would, some would speak their language as long as the nuns weren't around, eh. And then, I started losing it. Forgetting how, what to say, about the words; what they meant; and when somebody, let's say, there'd be two people talking, eh, two young guys talking their language, and I wouldn't understand. I'd lost it."[151]

Of her experiences at the Baptist school in Whitehorse and the Anglican school in Carcross, **Rose Dorothy Charlie** said, "They took my language. They took it

---

[149] TRC, *Statement*, 02-MB-16JU10-137.
[150] TRC, *Statement*, 2011-0346.
[151] TRC, *Statement*, S-KFN-MB-01-001.

right out of my mouth. I never spoke it again. My mother asked me why, why you could hear me, she's, like, 'I could teach you.' I said, 'No.' And she said, 'Why?' I said, 'I'm tired of getting hit in the mouth, tired of it. I'm just tired of it, that's all.' Then I tried it, I went to Yukon College, I tried it, and then my own auntie laugh at me because I didn't say the, the words right, she laughed at me, so I quit. 'No more,' I said. Then people bothered me, and say, 'How come you don't speak your language?' And I said, 'You wouldn't want to know why.' So, I never speak, speak it again."[152]

Robert Joseph went to residential school at the age of six as a fluent speaker of Kwak'wala. "By the time I left that school, eleven years later, of course nobody in the school spoke that language. There are only 100 of us now in the entire Kwakiutl Nation who speak the language."[153]

Prior to the expansion of the residential school system in Québec in the 1960s, some Aboriginal students from that province were sent to schools in Ontario. **Paul Dixon** was one of these students. His younger brother, however, was educated at a residential school in Québec. "So, I couldn't talk to my brother in French 'cause I didn't know French, and he couldn't talk to me in English." His mother had insisted that they learn their Aboriginal language, which meant that they did have a language in common.[154]

When **John Kistabish** left the Amos school, he could no longer speak Algonquin, while his parents could not speak

---

[152] TRC, *Statement*, 2011-1134.
[153] TRC, *Statement*, SC093.
[154] TRC, *Statement*, SP101.

French, the language that he had been taught in the school. As a result, he found it almost impossible to communicate with them about the abuse he experienced at the school. "I had tried to talk with my parents, and, no, it didn't work. It's that we lived with them like if it was... We were well anyway because I knew that they were my parents, when I left the residential school, but the communication wasn't there."[155]

In some cases, the residential school experience led parents to decide not to teach their children anything but English. Both of Joline Huskey's parents attended residential school in the Northwest Territories. As a result of their experience in the schools, they raised their daughter to speak English. When **Bruce R. Dumont** was sent to residential school in Onion Lake, Saskatchewan, his mother warned him not to speak Cree. She told him that, "you got to learn the English language and, you know, so we, you know, we were instructed at home, and spoke freely, spoke Cree at home, but at school we, we weren't allowed to speak, speak our language."[156]

Andrew Bull Calf recalled that at the residential school in Cardston, students were not only punished for speaking their own languages, but they also were discouraged from participating in traditional cultural activities.[157]

Evelyn Kelman attended the Brocket, Alberta school. She recalled that the principal warned the students that if they attended a Sun Dance that was to be held during the

---

[155] TRC, *Statement*, 2011-6135
[156] TRC, *Statement*, 01-SK-18-25JY10-013.
[157] TRC, *Statement*, 2011-0273.

summer, they would be strapped on their return to school. "Today I still know one or two people who didn't go because they were afraid of that."[158]

Marilyn Buffalo recalled being told by Hobbema school staff that the Sun Dance was devil worship. "We were told by untrained, unprofessional teachers who took great joy in beating the heck out of the boys and the girls, that we were never going to amount to anything. And called savage."[159]

Sarah McLeod attended the Kamloops school. When she went home for the summer, her grandmother would teach her about traditional ways of healing. "My grandmother would saddle a horse for me, telling me, 'Go get this medicine for me up on the hill.' She'd name the medicine, and I was, like, eight years old, I'd get on a horse, and I'd go all by myself, and I'd get the medicines. I know which medicines she's talking about. I'd get on my horse, and I'd put some in the sack, and I'd have to go look around for a big rock, so I can get back on my horse again. One year, she returned to school with a miniature totem pole that a family member had given her for her birthday. When she proudly showed it to one of the nuns, it was taken from her and thrown out. I looked at her. I said, 'But that's my birthday present.' 'No, that's no good. That's all devil you see in that totem pole. It's all devil, can't you see all the devil in there? You throw it away right now.' And she made me throw it in the garbage, and it was, I didn't know, I said to myself, 'Oh,

---

[158] TRC, *Statement*, SP128.
[159] TRC, *Statement*, SP125.

my gosh. All this time I was, I was hugging this devil?' You know I didn't know that."[160]

At Akaitcho Hall, the residence in Yellowknife, Northwest Territories, **Mary Olibuk Tatty** roomed with students from a variety of backgrounds. "Three years of my life, I lost my Inuit values, even though I, I'm very strong. My mom was very strong at throat singing, and drum dancing, or whatever. But being a female Inuk, very proud Inuk I am, doesn't matter if my grandpa's a Newfe, what hit me was I couldn't say the Lord's Prayer in my room unless I whispered it, because I grew up so Anglican, because my roommate was Dogrib [Dene], or Kabluunak [a white person], 'cause they would ask me why are you, why are you saying this?" The common language of the residence and school was English. "The thing is I notice I spoke a lot of English to them, because back in my head, we had no choice but to speak English, 'cause our supervisors were all Kabluunak, nothing against Kabluunak, my grandpa's white, but I wish we had more support at residential schools with our Inuit values."[161]

One former student said that her time at the Catholic school in The Pas, Manitoba, left her feeling ashamed to be Aboriginal. "Even our own language was considered ugly; we weren't allowed to speak Cree language. I wasn't allowed to be myself as a Cree woman. Everything was filthy, even our monthlies and that's how I learned it at home and what I learned from the residential school, everything was ugly. And that's where I learned a lot of ugliness also, I became a compulsive liar, learned to live in the world of denial. When I

---

[160] TRC, *Statement*, 2011-5009.
[161] TRC, *Statement*, 2011-0156.

was younger, I learned how to hate, I hated my own mother, I blamed her for allowing us to be taken away even though at that time I didn't realize she didn't have a choice. It wasn't until 1990 that she told us that 'I didn't have a choice. It was either that, or me going to jail. I had to let you kids go to school,' 'cause that's when I disclosed to them both my mom and dad what I went through in residential school in 1990, August of 1990."[162]

Gordon James Pemmican recalled how at the Sioux Lookout school, the students used to watch western movies. "The ones they made us watch, Indians never won. I don't recall any show where Indians ever won. When we went out to play cowboys and Indians, none of us wanted to be the Indian."[163]

On occasion, some of the staff at the Blue Quills school had the students put on what one anonymous former student called "little powwows." "'Okay, everyone, want to see you guys dance like Indians,'" like, you know, like you pagans, or you people, you know, to go in the circle, and then she says, 'Here's your drum, and here is your stick,' and of course he sang though. I remember he's still a good singer, but they would laugh when he would bang that dust, that tin, steel dustpan, eh. But they had laughed at some of this, you know, make us do some of the things that was culturally done, eh, but to turn it around and make it look like it was more of a joke than anything else. It was pretty quiet when we would do those little dances. There was no pride. It's just

---

[162] TRC, *Statement*, 02-MB-18JU10-055.
[163] TRC, *Statement*, 02-MB-18JU10-069.

like we were all ashamed, and we were to dance like little puppets."[164]

It was during a confirmation class at the Sept-Îles, Québec, school that **Jeanette Basile Laloche** rebelled against the suppression of Aboriginal language and culture. "They gave us a lesson on the Pentecost, and then the principal Father came with the inspector. You had to be good in your person, and you had to have good posture. Then, they explained to us the Pentecost. Then he said: 'The Apostles had tongues of fire on the top of the head, then they started speaking all languages.' Then there I said: 'No, no, they didn't speak my language.' Then there, he insisted, he said: 'Yes, Jeanette, they spoke your language.' I said: 'No, it is impossible that they could have spoken my language.' Because, I began to be a rebel then: the God that my grandmother taught me about, my grandparents taught me, he was nothing like theirs. Then there, I said: 'No, they didn't speak my language.' I shouldn't have, we didn't have a word to say, and I remember what he said: 'Put your hand on the desk.' You couldn't contradict them, I placed my hand on the desk, and with the ruler, I had to repeat, repeat that the apostles spoke my language. Me, it took time before I said it, but you know that's it, I was marked: I was hit with the ruler, with ... there was a blade on the end of the ruler. I wrote a poem about it, my writing, and it was: 'I was a little flower that was uprooted and transplanted into another world.' My values were disrespected, my beliefs humiliated, I suffered infanticide. After all those horrors, my body, my mind had to adhere."[165]

---

[164] TRC, *Statement*, 2011-3279.
[165] TRC, *Statement*. 2011-6136.

Day to Day Life in a Residential School

As this book is being written in early 2022, Canada and most of the world is still dealing with Covid-19. Over the last couple of years the schooling system in Canada has been disrupted several times, leading to at home learning via computer or tablet. In my household, at least, this has had the effect of having my daughters reminiscing on the good old days when they could be in class with their cohorts, playing at recess, and learning new things with their friends. While it didn't always seem like it at the time, many of us remember our childhood school days fondly. A time in which we learned to communicate with other kids, often forged friendships that have lasted a lifetime, and interacted with teachers who had a lasting effect on our lives.

For nearly four generations school was a thing to be feared for Indigenous children in Canada, a place where loneliness, abuse and institutionalization were more likely to be the takeaway, rather than knowledge or friendship. Not only was the safety and security of the family and community taken away, but it was also to be demonized and condemned. The language children grew up on was to be forbidden and the culture and ceremonies fondly celebrated and remembered were to be condemned as evil, participated in at the price of your soul.

Life in the Shubenacadie school was strictly controlled in the early 1940s when **Noel Knockwood** attended the school. "We used to wake up in the morning, even before we had time to go to the bathroom, we would kneel down and we would say our prayers. 'Course it was orchestrated by the nuns and they told us what prayers to say. Then after prayers we were able to use the washroom and get dressed, then we would go downstairs in a single file. And then we would find our place in, in, in a, in a kitchen where, where we sat and we stood by our plates and waited for the nun to go give the command to sit down and she would clap her hands and by that sound we would all sit down. Then we would say grace, 'course they were Catholic prayers, Catholic grace that we said. We were forbidden to speak our own language."[166]

Lydia Ross said that the students at the Cross Lake, Manitoba, school were organized "just like an army.... And we used to go, oh, then the other one is you always file, file it by your number, always for everything. Go, go to cafeteria, you go by your number. Go to classroom, you go by number all in one row, up the stairs, up to the classroom. And everything was routinely done."[167]

Mel H. Buffalo spoke of how beds were to be made in precise, military style. "There's a main sheet from above and the second sheet goes partway and

---
[166] TRC, *Statement*, 2011-2922.
[167] TRC, *Statement*, 02-MB-16JU10-029.

you pull it under. And then the other sheet that covers—there's three—there's two sheets that cover and then the main blanket, that one, that covers as well. And then your pillowcase. There are two pillowcases, one that goes one way and the other goes the other way. And your dirty one comes to changing room, you have to take everything off and throw them in the center of the common room and that goes to the laundry room. There's a laundry crew that picks that up, in a little cage, and takes that down to the laundry room and brings it back the next day. So, after you've made your bed and the supervisor has inspected it to make sure there's no wrinkles or crinkles—if there is, he'll just rip off the whole thing again and you have to do it over 'til you get it right. First few times I was there, I couldn't get it right every morning. I used to have to do it at least twice and maybe if—if I'm—or if he's in a pretty bad mood, I could probably—he'd probably make me do it about three times."[168]

At the Sturgeon Landing school in Saskatchewan, one former student said, the students had to stand like soldiers: "We had to hold our head straight and not look anywhere else. We couldn't at all look at anybody. Especially not the boys where they were. No, we weren't allowed to look anywhere. We had to line up when we walked in school."[169]

---

[168] TRC, *Statement*, 2011-2535.
[169] TRC, *Statement*, 2011-3879.

Daniel Andre had a detailed memory of the routine at Grollier Hall, the Roman Catholic residence in Inuvik, Northwest Territories. "Our day consisted of just getting up the morning at, I don't know when, 6:30, 7:00, and we'd get up and say our prayers, and then go, and get dressed, and go for breakfast. And then after breakfast, we were all assigned a chore, so we did the chore, and then from there we just did whatever we did until school, and then we'd get dressed and go to school. And then come home at lunch, and have lunch, and then go back to school, and then come home, and, and or go to Grollier home. And then from 3:30 to 5:00, we would just, we'd play outside, or play in the gym, or whatever was, maybe something was assigned, like, go for a walk or whatever, and we'd do that until supper, and then have supper. And then in the evening after supper, about a half an hour later, we were assigned to gym time, which was in the evening from six to eight, something like that. It was 'til 8:00, anyway. And then after we were done in the gym we'd just go back upstairs, and then everybody had to have a shower. So, we showered and put on our pajamas, and then the boys would be, they'd be sent to bed by groups, like the first group, second group, third group, depending on your age. And so we went to bed, and then we'd just get up the next day, and it happened all over again. And then on Saturday and Sunday, we have a late breakfast. Sister Tremblay would bring our cereal and whatever, toast and whatnot, up to the, the boys' end, and, and we'd have breakfast, cereal and toast. And then, yeah, and sometimes we went down to the cafeteria, but depending how many students were upstairs, she would bring the stuff up, and then we'd eat, and then have lunch after that, after, and then we'd go for a walk in the afternoon. In the winter, or summer, spring, whenever it was, we always went to our walk to get out of the building, by a supervisor, a student supervisor from downstairs, the seniors, and sometimes they hired adults from the community or whatever. And, and yeah, so that was our life."[170]

Many students spoke of life that was regulated by the ringing of a bell. At the schools that **Percy Tuesday** attended in northwestern Ontario, everything was done with a whistle, a buzzer or a bell. "We were programmed, and we couldn't go or nothing. When the bell rang that's when you got up and when, you know, everything. When the whistle blew, you were playing outside, you had to come running in, and everything told you what to do. Every, you knew what everything meant to a buzzer or whistle; you know what you had to do. Even when we lined up to go and eat, we lined up at our benches, we'd stand there 'til the nun, I think, rang a bell or something for us to sit down, and then to start eating, you know."[171]

Stella Bone, who attended the Sandy Bay school in the 1960s, recalled, "Those bells that they used to use ring, ring, ring, okay, 'Time to get up.' Ring, ring, ring, like, you know, bells throughout the

---

[170] TRC, *Statement*, 2011-0202.
[171] TRC, *Statement*, 02-MB-18JU10-083.

day. Ring, ring, ring, recess bell, eh. Well, mind you, there was recess bells in other schools, too, but this drilling, conditioning was automatic, eh. And if you didn't do it, then of course, there was a consequence to that, really tough consequence."[172]

Bernadette Nadjiwan said that at the Spanish, Ontario girls' school, "I became acquainted with a regime of rules, which at first feel rigid and regimental." She too remembered the bells. "It rang in the morning when we'd wake up, to wake us up, to get ready for school, the bell rang again, and to get ready for bed, even to go to classes. We were so well trained, and everyone was likened to a soldier."[173]

David Charleson said that at the Christie, British Columbia school, "the bell would ring, and it would ring again to wash up, and it would ring again to line up at the dining room area, and I know we had to totally be quiet. We couldn't even talk to each other in the dining room while we're eating. Couldn't even ask for salt and pepper in language, English language."[174]

The schools afforded the children little in the way of privacy or dignity. **Louise Large** recalled "those little bathrooms" at the Blue Quills school. "There was maybe six in a row, and six sinks. And the

---

[172] TRC, *Statement*, S-KFN-MB-01-006.
[173] TRC, *Statement*, 2011-5029.
[174] TRC, *Statement*, 2011-5043.

nun stands there, and give us two little pieces of toilet paper, and they were almost see-through, and that's what we had to use to wipe ourselves after we used the bathroom. And later in the evening, we would get our panties checked and to see if there was, if they were soiled."[175]

Ilene Nepoose recalled that students were not allowed to close the bathroom doors in the Blue Quills dormitory. "It had to be opened and we were given three squares of toilet tissue, that's all we could use, that's all, three squares."[176]

Larry Roger Listener recalled how, when he attended residential school, female staff would supervise the boys when they were taking showers. "One had a ruler, would tell us, 'clean there, clean there, and wash there.'"[177]

Lydia Ross recalled that at the Cross Lake, Manitoba, school, "When you were small in a dormitory, we were in rows, two rows this way, two rows that way, and there was a, a little hole in there where the nun used to peek out of there with her white, she just wore white. You know those nuns, you only saw their face and their hands, that's it, you didn't see any, any of them dressed as an ordinary street person. They always wore, wore those, those black clothes."[178]

---

[175] TRC, *Statement*, 01-AB-06JA11-012.
[176] TRC, *Statement*, 2011-2380.
[177] TRC, *Statement*, SP125.
[178] TRC, *Statement*, 02-MB-16JU10-029.

Vitaline Elsie Jenner recalled her first sight of the junior dormitory at the Fort Chipewyan, Alberta, school. "And I looked up there, and, you know, and little rows of beds, you know, really not very close, 'cause they had a little space in between, so they can walk through. They walked through every night, you know, make sure that, make sure that your hands are not playing with yourself, 'cause that's all they ever thought of was gross things in their minds, you know. It was just awful."[179]

When checking students for health problems, the staff in some schools paid little attention to the children's dignity. **Shirley Waskewitch** felt humiliated by her experiences at the Catholic school in Onion Lake, Saskatchewan. "I had scabs, I had developed scabs all over my body, and they were all over my body, and they weren't looked after. This one time in the high dormitory with the, where the big girls slept, we're all standing in line, washing in our basins. The girls were standing in line with their basins just washing up, and, and this nun come and got me, and stood me up in front of all the girls, and kind of turned me around, and I was kind of bent over, and she must have took a ruler, I think it was a ruler, and she pulled my bloomers down, and lifted my nightgown to expose me in front of everybody, to expose the scabs I had on my bum."[180]

---

[179] TRC, *Statement*, 02-MB-16JU10-131.
[180] TRC, *Statement*, 2011-3521.

DAY TO DAY LIFE

To ease student identification for school administrators, the staff and Indian Affairs would use numbers. In many cases these numbers would become used in place of students names on a day to day basis, further degrading and dehumanizing the them.

At Cross Lake, **Lydia Ross** said, "My name was Lydia, but in the school I was, I didn't have a name, I had numbers. I had number 51, number 44, number 32, number 16, number 11, and then finally number one when I was just about coming to high school. So, I wasn't, I didn't have a name, I had numbers. You were called 32, that's me, and all our clothes were, had 32 on them. All our clothes and footwear, they all had number 32, number 16, whatever number they gave me."[181]

Marlene Kayseas never forgot the number she was given at the Lestock, Saskatchewan, school. "I remember when I first went, my number was 86. I was a little small girl and I was in a small girls' dorm. And you had to remember your number because if they called you, they wouldn't call you by your name, they'd call you by your number."[182]

Martha Minoose recalled how the students were numbered at the Roman Catholic school in Cardston, Alberta. "They didn't call us by our name, they just called numbers. So my number was 33 in

---
[181] TRC, *Statement*, 02-MB-16JU10-029.
[182] TRC, *Statement*, SP035.

the small girls. When I went to the senior girls, my number was 15. So our clothes were marked and they just call out numbers."[183]

At the Sandy Bay school, **Stella Bone** was number 66. "And everything that I had was marked with that number, eh. It may not affect others as much as it affected me, but being a number."[184]

Bernice Jacks felt that the practice at the Kamloops school denied her any personal identity. "I was called, 'Hey, 39. Where's 39? Yes, 39, come over here. Sit over here, 39.' at was the way it was. And that's ... I say it just the way they said it. I was 39."[185]

Wilbur Abrahams recalled how, on the first day of school at Alert Bay, British Columbia, the students were all given numbers. "They told us to remember our number, instead of calling my name, they'd call my number, and if you don't remember your number, you, you know you get yelled at. And I, I think we did extra chores, so you had to really keep memorizing your number. Mine was 989. And it was, so that's how they got my attention, you know, when they wanted you for something that, you know, could be for anything, could be for job placements or something, I don't know, you, 989, you had to pay attention, and just be there, I guess, or just be aware."[186]

---

[183] TRC, *Statement*, 2011-1748.
[184] TRC, *Statement*, S-KFN-MB-01-006.
[185] TRC, *Statement*, 2011-3971.
[186] TRC, *Statement*, 2011-3301.

Antonette White, who went to the Kuper Island school, said that "even though you have family, you still feel separated, you still, you don't have a name, you don't have an identity, you just have a number, and mine was 56."[187]

Kiatch Nahanni, who went to several residential schools and residences in the Northwest Territories, including those at Fort Providence and Fort Smith, recalled how strange and frightening she found the school at first. Not only was the language different, but she also lost her name and became simply a number. "Because I was given a number and whenever your number was called you, you, you had to be on the defensive because I think you were in trouble."[188]

At the Sioux Lookout school, students also were called by their numbers. According to **Ken A. Littledeer,** "They called me number 16, because that's the number that I was given when I walked in through those doors. So, 16, I was called. Whenever I heard that 16, I'm supposed to pay attention."[189]

Lorna Morgan recalled that at the Presbyterian school in Kenora, "They just gave me a number, which I'll never forget, you know. This is your number. When we call this number, you know,

---

[187] TRC, *Statement*, 2011-3984.
[188] TRC, *Statement*, 2011-2684.
[189] TRC, *Statement*, 01-ON-24-NOV10-028.

that's you, you know. And it was number 16, and I'll never forget that number."[190]

Again and again, former students spoke of how hungry they were at residential schools. Students who spoke of hunger also spoke of their efforts to improve their diet secretly. **Woodie Elias** recalled being hungry all the time at the Anglican school in Aklavik in the Northwest Territories. "You didn't get enough; hungry. So once in a while we go raid the cellar and you can't call that stealing; that was our food. I got somebody, go in the kitchen and get the bread."[191]

Dorothy Nolie said she was hungry all the time in the Alert Bay school. She thought it a lucky day when she was told to cut bread in the kitchen. "We'd eat it while we're cutting it, so that was good for a while. We were cutting bread for a long time, and kids would come to me and ask me for bread, and I'd sneak it to them, 'cause I know they were hungry, too."[192]

Of the food at the Fort Alexander school, **Faron Fontaine** said that all he could recall was kids starving. "Kids going in the kitchen to steal food. Lucky thing I knew some people that worked in there with my grandfather, they used to steal me, sneak me some food all the time, send me an apple or sandwich or something. It's pretty good to have

---

[190] TRC, *Statement*, 02-MB-16JU10-041.
[191] TRC, *Statement*, 2011-0343.
[192] TRC, *Statement*, 2011-3294.

Day to Day Life

connections in there I guess. As for those other kids, I don't know how they survived. Maybe their stomach shrunk enough that whatever they ate was filling them up, I don't know."[193]

Andrew Paul said that every night at the Roman Catholic school in Aklavik, "...we cried to have something good to eat before we sleep. A lot of the times the food we had was rancid, full of maggots, stink. Sometimes we would sneak away from school to go visit our aunts or uncles just to have a piece of bannock. They stayed in tents not far from the school. And when it's raining outside we could smell them frying doughnuts, homemade doughnuts, and those were the days when we ate good."[194]

Nellie Trapper recalled that whenever she would go through the kitchen to the laundry room at the Moose Factory, Ontario school," ... we used to steal food, peanut butter, whatever's cooking in a pot. There were big pots in there. I remember taking things from that pot. I just happened to walk by, you had to walk through the kitchen to the, to go to the laundromat, drop off the laundry there. You'd always take something from the kitchen when we're walking by there."[195]

While girls took food from the kitchens, boys might raid the school gardens. **Rick Gilbert** worked in the gardens at the Williams Lake, British Columbia,

---

[193] TRC, *Statement*, 01-MB-26JY10-009.
[194] TRC, *Statement*, SP067.
[195] TRC, *Statement*, 02-MB-16JU10-086.

school. "Kids would try and sneak to eat some of the carrots and potatoes and whatever else. If you get caught, if we call it stealing, if you get caught stealing any of the vegetables to eat the punishment for that was that they would paint your hands red. And so you had to suffer the humiliation for days and a week until the paint wore off your hands. To let everybody know that you were a thief I guess."[196]

Doris Young said that hunger was a constant presence at the Anglican schools she attended in Saskatchewan and Manitoba. "I was always hungry. And we stole food. I remember stealing bread. And they, the pies that, that I remember stealing were lined up on a counter, and, and they weren't for us to eat, they were for the, for the staff."[197]

At the Sioux Lookout school in the 1960s, the boys would slip into the kitchen at night to take extra food. **Ken A. Littledeer's** job in the raids was to stand by the doorway and listen to the steps, listen to the stairs, and echo, to hear if somebody was coming.[198]

Don Willie was one of the boys who used to make midnight raids on the kitchen at the Alert Bay school. "I guess, and steal pretty much, like, just chocolate, chocolate milk and stuff like that. They'd have it, they'd just, just have it with hot water in the bathrooms, and when they were caught there, they'd

---

[196] TRC, *Statement*, 2011-2389.
[197] TRC, *Statement*, 2011-3517.
[198] TRC, *Statement*, 01-ON-24-NOV10-028.

end up being strapped. But also we used to get strapped for being caught out of bed."[199]

Ray Silver recalled that a small grocery store used to dump spoiled fruits and vegetables by a creek near the Alberni, British Columbia, school. "And us kids, we used to sneak from the school, we must have had to walk about a mile, sneak away from the school, sneak over the bridge, and go to that dump, and pick up apples, they were half rotten or something, and they threw out, they were no more good to sell, but us kids that were starving, we'd go there and pick that stuff up, fill up our shirts, and run back across the bridge, and go back to the school."[200]

Many students spoke of the lack of variety in the school menu. At the Assumption, Alberta school, **Mary Beatrice Talley** recalled, there was "porridge every morning. Evening, eggs and potatoes. That's all we have. Milk and coffee, I think the bigger girls, they take coffee. They have milk and tea there too. But food is—every day, same, same, same."[201]

Many students recalled being served porridge every morning. At the boys' school in Spanish, Ontario, **William Antoine** remembered: "In the morning they would give you porridge; every morning, every morning. They call it "mush" back then. It was like lumpy, you know, very lumpy. It

---

[199] TRC, *Statement*, 2011-3284.
[200] TRC, *Statement*, 2011-3467.
[201] TRC, *Statement*, 2011-3197.

didn't taste very good ... but you had to eat it in order to, to have some food in you. You know you had to eat it so that's, and you had to get used to it. You had to get used to, you know. We got bread with no butter, just dry bread. Got a little milk, you know."[202]

Gerald McLeod said that at the Carcross school in Yukon Territory, "you would never see eggs, you know, for a couple of months. It was always mush. A lot of people didn't like eating liver. They had liver there that people couldn't eat, and they forced us to eat it."[203]

Louise Large said that at the Blue Quills school," ...the porridge would be burnt, black toast, and some lucky kids would get, no not, not burnt. But the food was horrible. I remember that I had to eat, because I was the youngest, every meal I had to eat everybody's leftover, and then I became real fat and chubby in school, 'cause we weren't allowed to throw away food, and because I was the smallest, I guess I was bullied into eating everybody's garbage."[204]

Shirley Ida Moore, who attended the Norway House, Manitoba, residential school in the 1960s, echoed the sentiments of other former students. "And, I hated, I hated, I hated breakfast. I didn't mind very much eating over there, but I hated

---

[202] TRC, *Statement*, 2011-2002.
[203] TRC, *Statement*, 2011-1130.
[204] TRC, *Statement*, 01-AB-06JA11-012.

breakfast because, I think what I didn't like was we always had to eat porridge; and this porridge was, like it, I was, I eat porridge at home before but it was good. You know when the porridge they gave us was, like when they put it into your bowl, it was this big lump; big ball, lump."[205]

Chris Frenchman recalled being forced to eat at the Hobbema, Alberta, school. "You either ate it or we, we would go hungry to bed. So we had no choice but to eat it."[206]

Mel H. Buffalo recalled being punished because he refused to eat his breakfast at the Edmonton, Alberta, school. "I was the last one to be let out of the cafeteria because I wouldn't eat my porridge. And they said, well you'll have this porridge again at lunch, and sure enough, again at lunch, and then again at supper, and the next day they got me a fresh bowl of porridge, but they said the same thing. And I still refused to eat that porridge, and I was taken to the principal's office, and I got five straps on each hand, and sent to my, to a room by myself, with no contact with the other students."[207]

Darlene Thomas said students "...were forced to eat that, whatever it was in our bowl, or our plate, we'd have to eat every bit of it. And if we got sick, we got strapped. And I start, put that food in my mouth and I wouldn't swallow it and keep putting

---

[205] TRC, *Statement*, 2011-0089.
[206] TRC, *Statement*, SP124.
[207] TRC, *Statement*, SP124.

food until I got a big piece and then I wrap it in the tissue and put it back in my sleeve and when I get caught I found another place, put it in my sock or pull up my, pull up my tunic and tie a knot in my bloomers, 'cause we had those big long bloomers we had to use. So I tie a knot with that tissue and all that ugly food so I wouldn't get sick."[208]

Connie McNab found it difficult to eat the food served at the Lapointe Hall residence in Fort Simpson, Northwest Territories. "And we sat down to eat, and the pork chops were just dry and I was so thirsty; my mouth was dry and I couldn't swallow. I couldn't eat them and they kept saying, 'You have to eat. They're going to check.' And I couldn't, I tried the wax beans, wax green beans; I ate some of those and it went on like that. And they wouldn't let them take food to me."[209]

The conflict over food turned to abuse when students could not keep their food down. **Bernard Catcheway** recalled that in the 1960s at the Pine Creek, Manitoba, school, "we had to eat all our food even though we didn't like it. There was a lot of times there I seen other students that threw up and they were forced to eat their own, their own vomit."[210]

Diane Bossum said that at the La Tuque, Québec, school, "We were obliged to eat everything

---

[208] TRC, *Statement*, 2011-3200.
[209] TRC, *Statement*, 2011-2715.
[210] TRC, *Statement*, 2011-2510.

we had on our plates. At a given time, I had, I got a soup, but in the soup there was an insect. Then I showed the soup to my educator. After that, she asked 'do you want another soup?' 'No.' But she brought another soup. I didn't want to eat, but my soup was there. I had to eat anyway."[211]

Bernard Sutherland recalled students at the Fort Albany, Ontario school being forced to eat food that they had vomited up. "I saw in person how the children eat their vomit. When they happened to be sick. And they threw up while eating. And that when he threw up his food. The food is not thrown away. The one whose vomit he eats it."[212]

Ethel Johnson had vivid memories of watching her younger sister struggling to eat food that she was not used to eating at the Shubenacadie school. "She didn't like it. And the nun was behind her saying, 'Eat it.' They used to call her Pussy when she was in school; blue eyes I guess. And she couldn't eat it, and she started crying. And then she tried to make her eat it; and she couldn't. And then she threw up, and then she put her face in there. And she couldn't; when you're crying you can't eat anyway."[213]

Mary Beatrice Talley recalled one conflict between a staff member and a student over food at the Assumption, Alberta school. "And then our

---

[211] TRC, *Statement*, 2011-5079.
[212] TRC, *Statement*, 2011-3180.
[213] TRC, *Statement*, 2011-2680.

supervisors, they were Sisters, and then she comes to this girl and then she told her that you have to eat the fat and everything. And this girl doesn't like it. So she just shoved it in her mouth like this. Just put everything in her mouth and asked her to swallow it. And we're watching that too, me and my friend, we're having supper. And then this girl was just crying and she told her to swallow it. And I—we're seeing—we're saying that she might choke on it. And we told Sister, we told Sister not to do that. And she told us, you two, you shut up. It's none of your business. I'm the one that's looking after you girls. And then that girl was just crying and she was just throwing up and she went to the washroom. I see that too."[214]

Victoria McIntosh said she was harshly disciplined for refusing to eat porridge with worms in it at the Fort Alexander school. "I really, really dislike porridge. And there was an incident where I wouldn't eat porridge, and, the first time, and I looked down, and there was a bowl in front of me, and I noticed there was worms in it, and I wouldn't eat it, and the nun come behind me, and she told me, 'Eat it,' and I wouldn't eat it, just nope, and she, she slammed my face in, in the bowl, and picked me up by my arm, and she, she threw me up against the wall, and she started strapping me. And I don't remember going up the stairs, but I remember her, she had my arm, had me up by one arm. And I don't remember that, that time gap in between, but after that I remember

---

[214] TRC, *Statement*, 2011-3197.

something broke inside of me that I wasn't stubborn, but I had to listen or else. And everybody was really terrified of this nun."[215]

At the Sandy Bay school, **Stella Bone** recalled, "we were made to eat our food regardless what type or shape or in what condition it was. And if we didn't eat, if we didn't eat it, or if it made us sick, you're guaranteed to eat your sick and your food at the same time. Even if you're gagging, you're just, used to be just, you had to eat it." She thought that nutrition was better in her home community. "At least, at home, I would have rabbit, fish, bannock, potatoes, you know. I thought about those things when I'd be starving in there."[216]

Many of the schools used to provide the students with a vitamin-enriched biscuit that had been developed by Indian Affairs in the 1940s.[217]

Alfred Nolie said that at the Alert Bay school, these biscuits were issued daily. "They gave us one biscuit in the afternoon, maybe two or three o'clock in the afternoon. We all line up. They gave us one biscuit for snack in the afternoon."[218]

Shirley M. Villeneuve, who attended the Fort Simpson, Northwest Territories, residence, recalled that the students used to refer to them as doggie

---

[215] TRC, *Statement*, 02-MB-16JU10-123.
[216] TRC, *Statement*, S-KFN-MB-01-006.
[217] Canada, *Annual Report*, 216.
[218] TRC, *Statement*, 2011-3293.

biscuits. "I wouldn't eat it, I would give it to somebody else. And the, the nun, the nun she saw me doing that and she didn't like that. She didn't like that I gave it away and she says, 'Why you gave it away?' I says, 'Because I don't, I'm not hungry; I don't want it.' And she says, 'Well, it's good for you it's good for you,' she kept telling me. And I said, 'No, I don't want it. I don't want it,' and so I was, I was scared."[219]

Stella Bone also reported her difficulty in eating the nutritional biscuit when she attended the Sandy Bay school. "They used to be really hard, eh, so you'd have to suck on it really long to make it soft, you know, just to appease your, your hunger, I guess." [220]

Mel H. Buffalo recalled with distaste the vitamin pills and biscuits that students were given. "They would ask you to swallow one of these every day. If you had bit into it—oh man, it was horrible, the taste was in your mouth for days. So you'd try not to bite it because—we would dare some of the new kids to bite the pills but they'd only do it once and that was it. And we used to—when we ran out of pucks, we'd use those cookies for pucks because they were hard. And we didn't have any of the regular pucks so, we saved up a bunch of those and used those."[221]

---

[219] TRC, *Statement*, 2011-2691.
[220] TRC, *Statement*, S-KFN-MB-01-006.
[221] TRC, *Statement*, 2011-2535.

Complaints about the limited, poorly prepared, monotonous diet were intensified by the fact that at many schools, the students knew the staff members were being served much better fare. When she helped in the kitchen to prepare staff meals at the Sechelt, British Columbia school, **Daisy Hill** could not help noticing "how well they ate compared to the food that was given to us, students."[222]

At the Kamloops school, **Julianna Alexander** was shocked by the difference between the student and staff dining room. "On their table they had beautiful food, and our table, we had slop. I call it slop because we were made to eat burnt whatever it was, you know, and compared to what they had in their dining room. You know they had all these silver plates, and beautiful glass stuff, and all these beautiful food and fruits and everything on there, and we didn't even have that. And so I, I became a thief, if you want. You know I figured a way to get that food to those hungry kids in intermediates, even the high school girls, the older ones were being punished as well."[223]

At the school she attended in Saskatchewan, **Inez Dieter** said, "the staff used to eat like kings, kings and queens." Like many students, she said she used the opportunity of working in the staff dining

---

[222] TRC, *Statement*, 2011-3967.
[223] TRC, *Statement*, 2011-3286.

room to help herself to leftovers. "I'd steal that and I'd eat, and I'd feel real good."[224]

When **Frances Tait** was given a position in the staff dining room, she said, she thought she had "died and gone to heaven 'cause even eating their leftovers were better than what we got. And anybody who got a job in there, their responsibility was to try and steal food and get it out to the other people."[225]

Hazel Bitternose, who attended schools in Lestock and Qu'Appelle, Saskatchewan, said she enjoyed working in the priests' dining room. "They had some good food there and I used to sneak some food and able to feed myself good there. So that's why I liked to work there." [226]

Gladys Prince recalled how at the Sandy Bay, Manitoba school, the "priests ate the apples, we ate the peelings. That is what they fed us. We never ate bread. They were stingy them, their own, their own baking."[227]

Doris Judy McKay said that at the Brandon, Manitoba, school, cleaning up the staff dining room was a prized chore. "There'd be about three or four of us working, we'd race for the supervisors' dining area because, why we raced was because they left a,

---

[224] TRC, *Statement*, SP035.
[225] TRC, *Statement*, 2011-3974.
[226] TRC, *Statement*, SP036.
[227] TRC, *Statement*, 2011-2498.

like platter of their meal there. Like say if they had steak, chicken or pork chops, and we'd race for that eh, 'cause what we got wasn't very much."[228]

Betty Smith-Titus said that her father paid extra to the Baptist-run school in Whitehorse, Yukon Territory, to ensure that she was given the same food as the staff. "I didn't get that. I ate like the rest of the kids. I ate the runny rolled oats in the morning, with a glass of milk. And my father paid for, I don't know how, how many years, and finally I told him I ate like the other kids, they didn't give me what the staff ate, so my dad didn't pay him anymore."[229]

Some students, however, spoke favourably of residential school food. One student, who attended the Gordon's, Saskatchewan school in the 1950s, said, "You know, I've heard a lot of people say that, you know, their experience in residential school, their meals were terrible. That wasn't so in Gordon's. Gordon's provided really good meals, a lot of times they were hot, good meals."[230]

Some students also reported improvements in the food, over time. **Mary Rose Julian** thought the food at the Shubenacadie school in the 1950s was not too bad. "I did like the porridge that we got every morning, 'cause I was, I was brought up on porridge. So, the porridge was pretty good, because they put sugar in it while they were, they mixed it with sugar,

---

[228] TRC, *Statement*, 2011-2514.
[229] TRC, *Statement*, 2011-1132.
[230] TRC, *Statement*, SP039.

and they never put sugar on the table, they mixed it, mixed the porridge with the sugar, and that was really good. Sometimes it was lumpy, you just bust the lumps in your mouth, you know, no big deal." But there were limits to her praise. She recalled that fish was served on Wednesday and Friday. "It wasn't, it wasn't like my, the way my father and mother prepared it. It was horrible. And then they put this sauce over it. It was white sauce, well, it was white, anyway, you know, and it was horrible. So, anyways, you had to eat that, and some kids didn't like it so much, you know, they got sick on it, but I didn't get sick on it. I managed to swallow it and everything. I forced myself to eat it. So, I start getting used to it after a while. So, the, the food and everything was fine."[231]

For many students, classroom life was foreign and traumatic. **David Charleson** said he found the regimentation at the Christie, British Columbia, school so disturbing that he never wanted to learn. "So I jumped into my shell. I took kindergarten twice because of what happened to me. I didn't want to learn. I never went home with any a's, or b's, or c's, and it was all under, under the bad, my baddest part of the book of knowledge. That's the way they graded me. That's what they put in my mind, I'm dumb, stupid, and they used to make an example of me all the time, 'cause I was one of the bigger kids in the school."[232]

---

[231] TRC, *Statement*, 2011-2880.
[232] TRC, *Statement*, 2011-5043.

At the Birtle, Manitoba, school, **Isabelle Whitford** said, she had a hard time adjusting to the new language and the classroom discipline. "I wasn't very good in math. I was poor. And, every time I couldn't get an answer, like, you know, she would pull my ears and shake my head. And I couldn't help it 'cause I couldn't understand, like, you know, the work."[233]

Betsy Olson described class work at the Prince Albert, Saskatchewan, school as a torment, in which her "spelling was always 30, 40, it was way down. And when we did spelling, sometimes I freeze, I couldn't move, I just scribbled because I couldn't move my hand. I can't remember to spell *b*, or *e*, or *c*. My mind was a blank. I could not bring any letters out. I just freeze."[234]

Noel Knockwood recalled that he was often frozen with fear in class: "We used to stand up with a reader in our hand and we will be given, each person will be given a paragraph to read. And when it came my turn I picked up the, the reader and turned to a page where I was supposed to. And other students took turns reading their paragraph. And then when it came my turn, I got up and I started to read the paragraph and I got down a little ways and I come across a word that I could not pronounce and I stopped, because I could not pronounce the word, I

---

[233] TRC, *Statement*, S-KFN-MB-01-004.
[234] TRC, Statement, 2011-4378.

didn't know what to say. [The teacher] had a long wooden pointer, they used to point to the blackboard and she had it in her hand. And she said, 'Read!' And I was very frightened and scared as a young, young boy. You know, then she took that pointer and pointed it at me and said, 'Read! Read! Read!' She was shouting at me and I, I couldn't 'cause I was afraid and she had that pointer, she came closer, then she took that pointer and I raised my hands and she broke the pointer over my arms. And in doing so, I dirtied my pants; I shit myself because of fear. And in doing so she seen what happened, and she said, 'You filthy little boy. Get upstairs and go to bed.'"[235]

Traumatized by her experiences at schools in Ontario and Québec, **Mary Lou Iahtail** had difficulty learning. Her inability to speak in class led a teacher to single her out for humiliation. "I was afraid I didn't know that word, and the teacher thought I was, I was just doing that, so she got mad at me, that I was just showing off. I really didn't know the word, and I was feeling so bad because so many people were staring at me. She, she brought a big, big yardstick ruler, yardstick, and she came after me, and I was afraid of her. I really was scared. She scared me so much, and I was afraid of the big stick. So, what I did is I run out of the classroom, and she ran after me, and I ran to next, next door, where our dorm is, our dorm was very close to the classroom."[236]

---

[235] TRC, *Statement*, 2011-2922.
[236] TRC, *Statement*, 01-ON-05FE11-005.

Day to Day Life

Leona Agawa never felt comfortable in the classroom at the Spanish school. For much of her time in school, she was frightened or intimidated. "I could hear [the teacher] say my name, but I couldn't hear her what, what she was asking me, and that happened all over. I, I just, I was just a person that couldn't hear anybody talking to me, or asking me questions. My mind would go blank. So, I never did have any, really any schooling. I would hide behind a girl, or who's ever behind, in front, I'd hide. And somebody would say, 'Leona.' I'd hear my name, but I never got to answer. I stood up, never got to answer what they were saying when they sat me down. And I'd get a good slap after, after you, you leave there for not being nice in school."[237]

Dorothy Ross recalled her time in the Sioux Lookout school classroom as being one of fear and punishment. "I remember the, the classroom. It was kind of dark, dingy–looking place. And I sat there, and holding a pencil, practice my name. She would write my name on a piece of paper, and the ABCs. It took me a while to understand those letters, the numbers. Like, I didn't, I guess some of them were hard for me. I couldn't pronounce them right, and I would, I would cry again if I do it again, make me do it all over again, over and over, and she would hit me. This is my first time that I experience. She had a, she had a, a stick, a ruler kind of, it was long, eh, a ruler stick. And if I didn't, if I, if she didn't like my, the

---

[237] TRC, *Statement*, 01-ON-4-6 NOV10-006.

way I was supposed to write with the pencil the first time, and this is where the first time ever being hit, right on my head. She would hit me three or four times across, over here, with that ruler, and my head would go down, and I would try to write at the same time, and she would hit me again."[238]

Mary Courchene described a similar education at the Fort Alexander school in the 1940s. "The first few years we were there I never had a teacher, a real teacher. The nuns that taught us weren't teachers; they weren't qualified. They had no qualifications whatsoever to, to, to be able to teach. Their only mandate was to Christianize and civilize; and it's written in black and white. And every single day we were reminded."[239]

At the Hobbema school in Alberta in the 1950s, **Flora Northwest** said, students were provided with a minimal education. The language training was compromised by the fact that neither teacher was a fluent English speaker. "And the English that I learned from there was ... it was really hard for me to speak the English language because of the teaching that was passed on to us through the teachers with their French accent, so I had difficult— difficulties with my English language."[240]

Some students said that the limits of the education they had received in residential school

---

[238] TRC, *Statement*, 01-ON-24NOV10-014.
[239] TRC, *Statement*, 2011-2515.
[240] TRC, *Statement*, SP124.

became apparent when they were integrated into the public school system. **Victoria McIntosh**, who had attended the Fort Alexander school, said that when she entered public school, she discovered that "I could hardly read and write. And I knew that I wasn't, you know, like, stupid, or, or dumb, or anything like that, it just, I didn't know how to read and write, and I didn't get a lot of these things. And I remember the teacher asking me where did you go to school? And I didn't know how to answer her."[241]

Many students said there was no expectation that they would succeed. **Walter Jones** never forgot the answer that a fellow student at the Alberni, British Columbia, school was given when he asked if he would be able to go to Grade Twelve. That supervisor said, "'You don't need to go that far,' he says. He says, 'Your people are never going to get education to be a professional worker, and it doesn't matter what lawyer, or doctor, or electrician, or anything, that a person has to go to school for.' He says, 'You're going to be working jobs that the white man don't want to do, that they figure it's too lowly only for them. And you will do the menial jobs, the jobs that doesn't require schooling.' I became a logger. I was a fisherman to start with, and I, most of our people do that. That had a lot of, I guess, a lot of things they did, like, teaching us our, like, to not speak our language, getting strapped for it, and telling us that we're never going to be able to take the good jobs and stuff like that, and the Commission

---

[241] TRC, *Statement*, 02-MB-16JU10-123.

happened. These things happened, and they, we lost so many of our people because of that residential school thing."²⁴²

For high school, **Roger Cromarty** lived in the Shingwauk Home in Sault Ste. Marie and attended local public schools. He recalled that he did not receive any guidance counselling. "We were all just shovelled into the technical program, technical school program, whether we wanted, we wanted to go in the technical stuff or not. Nobody asked us, or nobody showed us the vistas of going to the collegiate, and we were in a five-year program, or go into a technical program, which is a four-year. So, I end up being in a technical school, Sault Ste. Marie Technical and Commercial High School they called it."²⁴³

Lena Small recalled that when she turned sixteen, she was essentially forced to leave the Hobbema school. "We didn't have any future plans for us. The nuns didn't tell us there was a high school. They didn't tell us anything about life. They didn't tell us how to love one another, how to care for our families. We had no parenting, no nothing. All we had was religion."²⁴⁴

Nora Abou-Tibbett said that on one occasion, the girls at the Lower Post, British Columbia school were lined up and asked what they wanted to

---

²⁴² TRC, *Statement*, 2011-4008.
²⁴³ TRC, *Statement*, 02-MB-16JU10-132.
²⁴⁴ TRC, *Statement*, SP124.

be when they grew up. Many said they wanted to be nuns or missionaries. She said she did not know yet, but expected to know when she was older. "They put me up front, and said, 'Now, you see, there's this girl, now, how stupid she is, and I'm so happy that you kids aren't like her, because she is stupid to, to be saying, I mean she's the same age as you girls, and she doesn't know what she wants to be when she grows up.' And so I was labelled stupid and dumb, whatever. But I, I just said, 'Well, I know I just don't know, because until I grow a little older, I know by then what I want to be.'"[245]

When **Roddy Soosay** lived in residence, he attended a local public school. He credited his high school principal at the Ponoka, Alberta, public school for pushing him to succeed. "And one of the strangest things that happened in my life was our school principal was Halvar Jonson and Halvar Jonson called me into his office the next year and said, 'If you don't—if you don't behave yourself, you don't push yourself to do better this year, then that's it. I don't want you in my school ever again.' And I just said, 'Okay.' And he said, 'Condition is, you're going to take drama.' And I was like [laughs] 'Drama, what are you talking about? Why?' And he said, 'For— you'll probably benefit by looking at other people. And you'll probably benefit by pretending to be somebody else that you're not.' And he said, 'It'll do you some good for your own public speaking, it'll do you some good for your own confidence.' And I was

---

[245] TRC, *Statement*, 2011-0205.

just, whatever. Long story short, when I graduated, my highest grades were in law and in drama. And those two things got me through. And I was even more shocked when I graduated and they gave me a scholarship and awards and recognized me for those things. And I forever thanked him for that because, had he not done that, I'd probably would've never, ever, as the saying goes, to walk in somebody else's moccasins. I did that."[246]

Lawrence Wanakamik said that after he got over his initial fears, he did well academically at the McIntosh, Ontario school. "I used to be the, one of the top three students, you know, get 100s, get 95s, and no, no less than 90 in, in the marks, you know, 9 out of 10, or, you know, stuff like that." He had fond memories of one of his teachers. "Her name's Nancy, and she, she was nice, I liked her, everybody liked her, 'cause she was, she was friendly, and she was good to everybody. But the nun teachers, those were the ones that hit you with the ruler on your hands if you weren't listening, or you weren't behaving."[247]

Alice Quinney never forgot the positive impact that her Grade Four teacher at the Blue Quills school had on her life. "It was, it was so nice to have a teacher that really believed in, you know, in you, that you could, you know, that told you, you were smart, and that you were doing good, and, and not to hear anything negative from her, you know, like the

---

[246] TRC, *Statement*, 2011-2379.
[247] TRC, *Statement*, 01-ON-06JA11-002.

nuns always hounding you about this, 'Do this this way, do this that way,' you know. I, I was so thankful to have a, a teacher who really cared about me. And that teacher, she moved to California a few years later and we wrote to each other still when she was in California. Yeah, I didn't stop writing to her until I left school, when I was in Grade Nine. And I never forget her. Yeah, she was the first, first nice person in that school that made an impact in my life."[248]

Martha Loon said that at the Poplar Hill, Ontario school in the 1980s, there were staff people who befriended and helped her and her siblings. "We had staff members who took us under their wing. And one, over the years, started to recognize us as, like, younger siblings. So in a way, he was, like, protecting us, and other staff knew that, so other staff didn't really say or do anything against us because of that. So, sometimes I'll tell people, you know, when, they're talking about their experiences, I'll tell them, you know, this is what, this is what I went through, this is what my siblings and I went through. And I think that's what, how we didn't have those same experiences as some other students that went through a negative, bad experiences." There was one staff member to whom she could tell all her problems. "I could say anything to her, and we'd go for walks sometimes. So, I could tell her anything and she wouldn't, she wouldn't say anything to other staff members about it. So, in a way, that's, you

---

[248] TRC, *Statement*, 02-MB-18JU10-049.

know, gave me a chance to express my frustrations, and the things that I didn't like."[249]

Other students were able to concentrate on their studies. **Frederick Ernest Koe** said that at Stringer Hall in Inuvik, he devoted all his energies to studies and work. "You kind of develop a protective mechanism on the shell that you didn't rat on anybody, you kind of behave, you followed orders and things would go smooth. And what I did like is we had a study hall, and that study hall I was able to put a lot of time in there and get on with my studies and developed that discipline to work, and this is discipline that gave me to complete my studies to achieve my professional designation. I'm a professional accountant and have a degree in management. I helped a lot of the other kids because a lot of other kids had trouble in math and spelling and whatever, and I used to help the big boys, the bigger boys, because everybody was bigger than me then. But I used to help them."[250]

Helen Hanson thought the discipline in the classroom at the Sechelt, British Columbia, school was too strict in her early years there. She did, however, come to enjoy her schooling. "I like learning, and I liked the challenge of learning, spelling and stuff like that, getting that golden star. And so throughout my school years, seven years that I was there, I actually kind of enjoyed it because of

---

[249] TRC, *Statement*, 01-ON-24NOV10-021.
[250] TRC, *Statement*, SC091.

the schoolwork and the friends that I made there. I guess maybe in my grown-up years, like, in the last five years when things started coming up with the residential school issues, that, that I started thinking about what I had missed going to school there."[251]

Madeleine Dion Stout succeeded academically at the Blue Quills school. But she did not credit the school for her success. "It's not residential school that made me a good student. My, the fundamental values and good example I had before I went to residential school by my grandfather and my parents, and all the old people on the reserve where I grew up are the ones who made me a good student. Residential school had nothing to do with it, I swear by that. And the reason why I swear by that is because I would watch my grandfather work, and he made everything from scratch, and he didn't say do this, do that, it's, you know, memorize this or anything, he would just do what, what he had to do to survive, because in those days, there was no welfare. People were very self-reliant, and they worked very hard to be self-reliant. So that I was successful in school, and that I'm successful today academically, people might say, is not because I went to residential school; it's because I had, from a very early age, I was taught by example and through oral tradition how to live my life."[252]

---

[251] TRC, *Statement*, 2011-5045.
[252] TRC, *Statement*, 02-MB-18JU10-059.

Chores

The budgets for the schools were low, often 1/3 or less that of the average school in Canada at the time. To make up for the shortcomings in the funding of the schools, much of the workload would fall on the shoulders of the students. Whether it be cleaning, cooking, or manual labour, the students were expected to work for most of the hours that they weren't either in class or being indoctrinated into whichever religion the school operated under. It was not uncommon for studies to end at mid-day to make way for chores in the afternoon and evening workload so that the government and church could save money.

In many instances students would be injured or worse carrying out the workload operating machinery without proper supervision. While life was much harder for everybody at these times, students outside the residential school system were much more likely to spend their time in school learning. Chores were more likely to be done at home, helping to share the family's burden and help with harvests.

> Based on the chores that she and other students did at the Blue Quills school, **Ilene Nepoose** said, "We kind of run the school based on our own labour. We washed, we cleaned, they hired ladies to cook. There was no janitors, we were the janitors."[253]

---

[253] TRC, *Statement*, 2011-2380.

CHORES

Reflecting on the work he did at the Roman Catholic school in Kamsack, Saskatchewan, **Campbell Papequash** also noted that the students provided much of the labour needed to keep the school in operation. "I think there was a lot of slave labour in there because we had all the children, they all had to do, we all had our own jobs to do. You know all the residential school children maintained that whole building by cleaning it up and looking after the building. You know some guys worked in the boiler room and the furnace room, in the laundry room and with the dryers and the vegetables and working in the root cellar looking after the vegetables."[254]

Ula Hotonami recalled that at the school in Round Lake, Saskatchewan, she spent half the day in classes and half the day working. "We had to learn how to cook, how to do laundry, how to iron, how to do all those things, wash dishes, whatever, and clean out the, the both dormitories, and sweep the steps, and all those thing we had to do, we had to learn and that. And so it was, it was something that I never really expected, like, when I went to school."[255]

Andrew Speck said that at the Alert Bay school, "early in the morning you're up, like 5:30, 6:00 in the morning 'cause you had to do your chores before you had your breakfast. If you weren't up

---

[254] TRC, *Statement*, SP038.
[255] TRC, *Statement*, 2011-2654.

there, you were, you were literally ripped out of bed and thrown in a cold shower."[256]

Ellen Smith attended three different Anglican schools and residences in the Northwest Territories. In her memory, when students were not in class, they spent much of their time performing chores. "From the morning you get up seven o'clock in the morning, you were cleaning, cleaning, cleaning 'til you went to school. They kept us busy around the clock; right 'til we went to bed."[257]

One former student said that at the Shubenacadie school, chores took priority over classroom work. "I'm only in Grade Seven; I didn't even do Grade Seven! I spent most of the time working in a barn and duty. I got in there a little bit, you know, little bit of education or whatever they were commissioned to give to me, I didn't get."[258]

At the girls' school in Spanish, Ontario, **Josephine Eshkibok** said, she spent much of her time doing chores. "We used to work ... one week in the dairy and one week in the chicken coop. And the housework, sewing room, laundry; so we had to do all that work. There was one day there I was doing, a lot of stairs because the school is so high; I did the stairs and I guess I didn't do them right. I must have left some dust or something there in the corner. The

---

[256] TRC, *Statement*, 2011-3988.
[257] TRC, *Statement*, 2011-0346.
[258] TRC, *Statement*, 2011-2681.

teacher came there, said, 'You didn't do that right. Go back up there; start over again.' So I did."[259]

Darlene Wilson felt that the students at the Alberni school had little time to themselves. "Our time that we had was only time for us to do our job in the school. Some of us did the stairwells, some of us did the floors, stripping and waxing, laundry work, kitchen work, and some of us did dishes, pots and pans, helping with the cook, setting out the kitchen, the kitchen food. Our tables were set about four times a day for breakfast, lunch and supper, depending on the weekends. Each of us had our own jobs."[260]

There was a gendered division of labour, with the girls doing much of the cleaning and cooking. **Geraldine Bob** recalled that at the Kamloops school, the students did much of the cleaning. "We were just little kids, not even ten years old, eleven years old and we had to, if you can imagine the little kids in this school, cleaning the entire school and being forced to do things that are beyond them really. You know like cleaning the bathrooms, cleaning the tubs, shining the floors."[261]

Rose Marie Prosper's first chore at the Shubenacadie school was to sweep down the steps. "I had to sweep the steps down, make sure there was not a grain of sand or nothing in between those little

---

[259] TRC, *Statement*, 2011-2014.
[260] TRC, *Statement*, 2011-4065.
[261] TRC, *Statement*, 2011-2685.

runs. They checked everything we did. It had to be perfect. If not then we were made to do it over again, along with a strapping. I got strapped so many times down there because I had to learn about rules, regulations."[262]

Of the chores that she had to perform at the Sandy Bay school, **Isabelle Whitford** said, "We used to clean up in the, in the rectory. There was a long hallway. And then, they had hallways on the side for each rooms. We used to get on our hands and knees to wash the floors and wax them. We were like slaves."[263]

Emily Kematch said one of the things she learned at the Gordon's, Saskatchewan, school was how to clean. "As a result", she said, "I'm good at making a bed. We were taught how to make a bed perfectly. How to fold it, like each corner had to be folded just right and tucked in under the mattress, like the bottom sheet and then we put another sheet on top and our blanket. They were called fire blankets back then and our pillow and they had to be just right, or we'd get punished, if our beds weren't fixed just right."[264]

Shirley Ida Moore recalled that at the Norway House school in Manitoba, the students were supposed to make their beds in such a way that the sheets would be taut enough for an inspector to

---

[262] TRC, *Statement*, 2011-2868.
[263] TRC, *Statement*, S-KFN-MB-01-004.
[264] TRC, *Statement*, 02-MB-18JU10-063.

Chores

be able to bounce a nickel. She could never do this. "So my, my sister again would rescue me; she'd, she'd do her bed 'cause she could do it, 'cause she was bigger and then she'd come over and do mine so that, I didn't have to get punished so much all the time. And that's, that's what every morning was like, every morning waking up scared, afraid you are going to get punished."[265]

At the Fort Providence school in the Northwest Territories, **Florence Horassi** was assigned to clean toilets. "This one time, they give me a chore to do the lavatory, that bathroom area, the sink, the toilets. I cleaned the whole thing. And Sister came in the room, and I was standing a little bit aways, like from the middle, and I told her, 'I'm finished.' So she had to inspect, and she told me, 'You missed a spot there.' And, like, what spot? I couldn't see no spot. 'You missed a spot there. Look again.' And I know I'm not supposed to talk back, you speak only when you're spoken to, and when you're not spoken to, you don't speak, and you never talk back. And when I said, 'I didn't miss it, I washed it there.' 'I'll make you clean that,' she said, and she went out. When she came back, she came back with a toothbrush."[266]

The boys usually worked outdoors. **Thomas Keesick** said that at the McIntosh, Ontario school, "We cut firewood, four-foot-long logs because the school at that time was being heated by two furnaces

---

[265] TRC, *Statement*, 2011-0089.
[266] TRC, *Statement*, 2011-0394.

and we took turns. Half of the boys would go to morning classes, they call it, and they'd finish then go in the woods and cut wood or go in the barns to pick, clean the stables, pick up eggs. And there was an underground thing where they kept potatoes, carrots, cabbage, we worked there. We had gardens and stuff like that, that's what I remember."[267]

Rick Gilbert recalled that in the winter, the students at the Williams Lake school had to help put in the school's supply of firewood. "We had to cut big logs and have them chopped up and then packed in. We had to pack them into each building because we had wood furnaces. And I remember having to pack some of that wood and in the wintertime when now you're freezing, 'cause even though sometimes we did have gloves and it wasn't thick gloves. And sometimes we lost gloves 'cause kids are kids, you lose your gloves you put them somewhere and couldn't find them again. And then of course you'd get a strapping before they give you another set. And I remember that crying, packing this you know, a six-years-old packing blocks of wood inside."[268]

Roger Cromarty started at the Sioux Lookout school at the age of eight in 1945. He began by working in the barn. "First year and second year I was there, boys were expected to milk cows, and clean the school barn, and feed the farm animals, horses, cows and pig. Those assignments were designated

---

[267] TRC, *Statement*, 02-MB-16JU10-156.
[268] TRC, *Statement*, 2011-2389.

Chores

for the bigger boys." The school was heated by a coal-burning furnace. "And that coal came off the railroad track, which was a mile away, and then we started hauling coal, and that part I did too, shoveling all the coal for the school, and shovelling it into the bin." Cromarty also recalled being expected to help clean the school. "On Saturdays was, was the big day for cleaning. This, this is when we got on, on knee, hands and knees, and with just a scrub brush, we were expected to scrub the assigned chores we were given. And incidentally this, most of the floors were made of cement, so it was very difficult for, on our knees to, to do that." By 1952, his last year at the school, he was in charge of slaughtering animals for the kitchen. "I was a butcher for the whole school, cutting meat every day. That was my, my chore."[269]

Work at the schools could be dangerous. **Joanne Morrison Methot** said she was injured in the Shubenacadie laundry. "One time I was in there, and the thing was spinning, I don't know, to rinse the clothes, and I stuck my hand in there, and my hand twisted. It didn't break, though but it was just sore. But that wasn't her fault, that was my fault. I wanted to see what it was like. It was going so fast. And of course when you're young, you're curious, so I stuck my hand, and a good thing I didn't break my arm. Yeah, but I think there was one girl that did though, but I didn't, I just hurted it, but I didn't break it, thank God."[270]

---

[269] TRC, *Statement*, 02-MB-16JU10-132.
[270] TRC, *Statement*, 2011-2875.

CHORES

Lizette Olson said the students had to clean all the windows at the Prince Albert, Saskatchewan, school. "This was a big school and we had to clean it all, the windows, everything. Now, all the windows— one, two, three, four, five—the sanatorium windows, we used to lift the window like this. Some sat out the window to clean it. If there was an accident, one would have fell to his death."[271]

In some cases, students were paid small amounts of money for the work they did. For her work in the school kitchen at Fort Resolution, Northwest Territories, **Violet Beaulieu** could remember being paid a dollar by the priest. "This is my first dollar I ever earned. So, Sister said, 'All line up now, we're gonna go.' Wherever we went we always line up in two, and walking. We went to the store. She stood at the door there. She never told us anything before we went there. So, we all bought sweet stuff. When the children got back to the school, their supervisor asked to see their purchases. When she look at mine, she says, 'You bought only sweet stuff?' I said, 'Yeah.' 'You should have bought something more useful.' I didn't say nothing. I had nothing to say. I couldn't say nothing, you know. She just told me that. She said, 'I'll let it go for now, but next month it's not gonna be, you're not gonna do that,' she says. 'You're not gonna buy candy.'"[272]

---

[271] TRC, *Statement*, 2011-3878.
[272] TRC, *Statement*, 2011-0377.

CHORES

At the Roman Catholic school in Kamsack, Saskatchewan, **Campbell Papequash** had the opportunity to work with mechanized farm equipment. "I came from a family, you know, from a family that knew how to raise, how to look after horses and raise horses, and look after cattle and they put me out there. But there is a few good things that I learned in residential school because when I look back at the farming industry you know they had modern equipment there, modern machinery in the residential school, you know, they had these tractors and they had these combines and they had these swathers."[273]

Bernadette Fox was one of a number of students who spoke with pride of the skills she developed at a young age in residential school. While at the Roman Catholic school in Cardston, Alberta, she said, she "learned to be a good housekeeper. I learned how to clean myself personally and I was taught how to do housekeeping, make our beds, clean the floors and keep everything tidy. And so I continued that on in my life with my children, which is a positive thing for me."[274]

---

[273] TRC, *Statement*, SP038.
[274] TRC, *Statement*, SP127.

Religious Indoctrination

While there was a financial incentive in delegating the residential school program operations to the church it was also the fastest way to achieve the stated goals of assimilation. Breaking the family bond as well as the continuity of cultural upbringing would start the process, while replacing it with the dominant versions of Christianity. The entire school experience revolved around religion. Of course this was and remains to be fairly common in some communities in Canada today, the main difference being the mandatory nature of attendance coupled with the fact that these faiths were alien to the students.

During the process of being indoctrinated into these new beliefs, students would be discouraged from attending any traditional ceremonies while back at home with threats of an angry god. By this time all such events ceremonies had been outlawed by Canadian government. The view of the teachers was that community members that continued to participate in the traditional ceremonies were in some way evil, or devil worshipers.

>Religious observation and religious training were central to residential school life. **Noel Starblanket** recalled that prayer was a dominant aspect at the Qu'Appelle school. "And then we'd

finish, and we'd go to our, back to our playrooms, they called them, and we'd sit there until it was ready for class, then we'd go up for class, and when we sat down in class, they made us pray again. We have to pray. So, then we'd, we'd, we'd have our classes, and then, and then the noon bell rang, and we could hear the church bells. They have a big church there. Those bells would ring, and we'd have to pray again before we left the classroom. I think they called it the Angelus, or something like that. So, we'd pray again, and then we'd go to lunch, and, and before, when we sat down, they'd make us pray again. So, we prayed, and then we went back to our class, got ready for our playroom, went back, got ready for our class, class again in the afternoon. We went to class, they'd make us pray again, and then we'd go through our instructions, and then after school we'd come back, and they had, we had free time 'til about five or so, and then, then the nun would blow the whistle, and we'd have to come running in."[275]

Antonette White resented the amount of time that was given to religious observances at the Kuper Island residential school. "I think the worst thing, is the praying. It's, it's like you pray, pray, pray, and yet there's still no peace in that prayer of what they made you do."[276]

---

[275] TRC, *Statement*, 2011-3314.
[276] TRC, *Statement*, 2011-3984.

Geraldine Archie said that at the residential school she attended, "...they made us pray from morning until night, and we used to pray when we got up in the morning, and pray before we ate breakfast, and then pray again before we went and started class, and pray again when we went home, went downstairs for lunch, and prayed again to go to afternoon class, and then prayed again before supper, prayed again before bedtime. I was always kneeling down and I developed calluses on my knees. The schools were all the same there."[277]

Roger Cromarty had similar memories of the daily routine at the Sioux Lookout school. "Daily, we had the morning services in the chapel, grace at every meal, prayers at every class, evening services in the chapel, and the prayers at bedtime. On Sundays this was different. Again, we had morning, morning church services at the chapel, afternoon church services, Sunday school, and evening services."[278]

Louise Large joked that there was so much prayer at the Blue Quills school that she was left with *boarding school knees*. "It's always, you know, I'll make a comment, like, I don't need to pray anymore 'cause I prayed so much. I prayed first thing in the morning. When they opened the lights, you just shot out of bed, then we had to go on your knees, and close your eyes, and clamp your hands together, and,

---

[277] TRC, *Statement*, SC110.
[278] TRC, *Statement*, 02-MB-16JU10-132.

and pray, Our Father, Hail Mary. And then when we were done, we had to make our beds."[279]

Ronalee Lavallee was another former student who said that arthritis in her knees was the result of all the praying she had to do in residential school. [280]

According to **Geraldine Bob**, each day at the Kamloops school started with prayer. "Then we got dressed and we got, brushed our teeth, washed our face, combed our hair and we went to breakfast. And we prayed again and after breakfast we prayed to thank the Lord for what we had received. We went to school and we prayed before school; we had catechism. And before we went for lunch we prayed again; after lunch we prayed again, after school we went to more catechism lessons. And then prayed again before dinner, after dinner and then in the evening."[281]

Students also were introduced to the round of religious holy days. **Rita Carpenter** recalled how, when she lived at a hostel in Inuvik, "...we went, we'd, we'd, we'd practice every Saints Day, every like, St. Thomas, St. Michael, St. Francis of Assisi, St. Christopher, St. Mary, St. Bernadette, St. everything; everything. And we had on all our clothes for this special mass that we're going to have; our little tam, our little dress, our little fur coat, our little brown

---

[279] TRC, *Statement*, 01-AB-06JA11-012.
[280] TRC, *Statement*, 2011-1776.
[281] TRC, Statement, 2011-2685.

tights, our bloomers. And we'd all march two by two over to the Igloo Church; pray to a different Saint."[282]

Victoria Boucher-Grant recalled that at the Fort William, Ontario school, "I learned a lot about the Catholic church. I learned how to pray. I learned how to, this became a way of life, kneeling on my knees, and praying to, to some, some God that made me feel guilty because I was, I was not a very clean person." She also said that when they bathed, the students were told not to look at themselves. "So, we had this big guilt thing about our own bodies."[283]

Fred Brass recalled a copy of Father Lacombe's instructional ladder that hung at the end of the playroom of the Roman Catholic school in Kamsack, Saskatchewan. "There was a picture of stairs and at the bottom of those stairs was Indian people and there was fire. And above the stairs there was Jesus and the angels, and that's what we were told, if we didn't change our ways that's how we were going to end up. That's a picture that will always stay in my mind."[284]

Joseph Martin Larocque found religious education at the Qu'Appelle school frightening. "They scared us. From the time I was small 'til the time the, the priest, the nuns, the whole thing, they scared everybody with dead people, and, you know, talking about the devil. And, and they had this little

---

[282] TRC, *Statement*, 2011-0339.
[283] TRC, *Statement*, 01-ON-05FE11-004.
[284] TRC, *Statement*, SP039.

chart, catechism, where here's you're going up this road, and the, the roads are winding like this, and the, the devil's with a pitchfork. I was scared for a long time."[285]

Fred Kistabish attended the Amos, Québec, school. There, he encountered Father Lacombe's Ladder. "I don't understand the religious teachings of the priests and the nuns. There was a big blackboard that says if you're good boy you'll go to heaven. On the other side of the drawing, there's if you commit mortal sins, this is where you're gonna go, and then you have Lucifer and hell, and it said always, always forever, forever. That's traumatizing for a twelve-year-old, or a fifteen-year-old, or a fourteen year-old. Anyways, when I left the residential school, I knew that if I died, for sure I was going straight to hell because I was disobedient, because there are things lacking in my childhood."[286]

Martha Minoose encountered the poster at the Roman Catholic school in Cardston. "At the front they had a poster. It was really long and there was a black ugly road going down and there were people in the fire at the bottom and their hands were raised and they were suffering and they were stuck there and the priest ... oh priest, he taught religion. He said if you want to go down this road, you are going to be in there. You are going to go to hell and then the other road was so beautiful, they had a picture, it

---

[285] TRC, *Statement*, 2011-4386.
[286] TRC, *Statement*, SP101.

was going to heaven. There was angels and the lord and talk and it was so beautiful and you didn't want to go with that other one, I was so terrified of hell."[287]

In religious studies, student discipline might be linked to the lessons that were being taught. Once, in the religious studies class at the Fort Chipewyan, Alberta school, **Vitaline Elsie Jenner** was caught speaking to a friend during a lesson. She was called to the front of the class. "I thought, oh boy, I'm in trouble now. So, I walked up to the front of the class, and he, and he made me turn around to face my peers, and how embarrassing that was. I was kind of, I was a shy, a shy gal, a shy girl, and I turn around, and I knew I was in trouble, and he said, 'I was teaching you. What did I tell you, anyway?' he said. And I said, 'Something about forty days, forty nights Jesus fasted, right.' He said, 'Oh, see, you weren't listening,' he said. 'So, for your punishment,' he said, 'this is what you're gonna do. You're gonna,' he took headpins out of his, on his desk, there was a little container full of headpins, he took it out of his desk, and he said, 'Spread your hand out.' So, I spread my hand out like this, both hands, and he started jabbing me in front of the students, jabbing me in the hand, and he said, 'You're, you're gonna feel what Jesus felt on the cross. You're, you're gonna feel the same pain.' So, he was just jabbing me and jabbing me and jabbing me, and my tears were just streaming down my eyes, and looking at all the, the students that

---

[287] TRC, *Statement*, 2011-1748.

were all looking at me, right. They were shocked, like. And then after that, he stopped, finally he stopped, anyway, and so he stuck me underneath his, underneath, they used to have a great big desk, he stuck me underneath his desk. He said, 'This is where you're gonna stay now 'til the lesson is over. You're gonna hear it from where you are now.' So, oh, my goodness, so I sat there, and I was just crying, but I cried quietly."[288]

Students were confused by the requirement that they regularly confess their sins. At the Grouard, Alberta school, **Frank Tomkins** said, he never really learned anything except to pray and catechism and confessions. "And I used to lie like hell and go to confession. The priest would ask you all kinds of questions that had nothing to do with religion. They just wanna know all about you—what your thoughts and everything else. And I'd lie like hell because they used to say that God knew everything anyway! You know, God knew everything."[289]

Fred Brass said that at the Roman Catholic school in Kamsack, Saskatchewan, he was taught to lie. "I had to lie to keep from being beat and it is not a very nice feeling. When we went to confession, what they called confession, we had to lie, make up lies just to get through our confession."[290]

---

[288] TRC, *Statement*, 02-MB-16JU10-131.
[289] TRC, *Statement*, 01-SK-18-25JY10-009.
[290] TRC, *Statement*, SP039.

Although much of the initial religious training was done by rote, students internalized the lessons they were taught. In his later years at the Sandy Bay school, **Arthur Ron McKay** decided, in his words, "to try their way." He said he took to reading the Bible and became an altar boy. "That's how I lost all my …beliefs, traditional things that I knew from my grandfather, the songs that he tried to show me because I knew some songs before I left for school and I forgot all about those songs, traditional songs, Sun Dance songs, even when I was younger, that young I knew and I knew how to do all the little things that the medicines, he used to pick. By this time then I was going back on the last years, I forgot all about those."[291]

Not all teachers attempted to frighten students out of their traditional beliefs. **Ula Hotonami** recalled telling a sympathetic teacher at the United Church school that she attended in Round Lake that her family did not attend church. "I said, 'We, I like to go to Sun Dances.' I said, 'It's getting summer time now, I want to go to Sun Dance, 'cause I always go to Sun Dance with my grandma and them, and we always take part in there. We fast, and we don't, she doesn't make us fast all day,' I said, 'because we're still young and, and that,' I told her. 'Then, but as we got older, our, our, every summer,' I said, 'was a little bit more hours we had to fast,' I said, but she made sure that we, she got us up before sunrise. We had to, we could eat before sunrise. And

---

[291] TRC, *Statement*, 02-MB-18JU10-044.

then she'd talk to the Elders after. She'd tell them how long we were gonna fast, and we would fast that long. We wouldn't eat nor drink, but she made us sit in a lodge, and listen to them talking and that." According to Hotonami, the teacher told her, "'Keep faith, 'cause you won't be here very long, then you could go back to that again,' she'd tell, tell me that. And I told her, 'But that's not right.' I said, 'Like, we have to go to church every Sunday, and I don't like going to church,' I told her, and she said, 'Well, we can't, we can't stop it,' she said. 'So just try hard, and just go to church, and just sit there.'"[292]

Many students were confused by the contradictory combination of religious teaching and harsh discipline. **Julianna Alexander**, a former Kamloops school student, said, "You know they were trying to tell me that's this church, or this place we're in, you know, I had to do, I had to be this perfect, perfect person or whatever. And yet at the same time, that's not what I saw. Because I thought to myself, well, if you're a priest and nun, how come you're doing this to this child, or you're doing this to me, and I would say it out loud, and I'd get more lickings."[293]

For other students, a religious education was one of the key benefits of residential schooling. **Mary Stoney** was proud of both the religious training she received at residential school and the skills she

---

[292] TRC, *Statement*, 2011-2654.
[293] TRC, *Statement*, 2011-3286.

took away from her education. "I learned a lot of good things at the residential school over the years, my church beliefs and culture has brought happiness and healing to my family."[294]

Elizabeth Papatie said she learned important skills at the Amos, Québec, school. "I learned to look after myself, to dress properly, and to, to brush my hair, and to be nice and tidy, because the woman I had stayed with, she had told me how to look after myself and be nice and tidy, and to my, my manners and to speak well." She also valued her religious education. "I learned religion at a very early age. I learned about Christianity and I loved it. I love beautiful things, I love beauty."[295]

---

[294] TRC, *Statement*, SP124.
[295] TRC, *Statement*, SP101.

Breaking up Siblings

Further to the disruptions already faced within the families of the children destined for Residential Schools, those lucky enough to face the new reality with a sibling would soon find out that would not be the case. Even when siblings were housed at the same school often times they would only see each other in situations in which they couldn't communicate, or on rare occasions. If the sibling was one of the opposite sex the chances of communication became almost non-existent.

In recollecting these times more than one of the students said it seemed as though the Residential School system was actively discouraging family relationships form forming or continuing. This makes a little more sense when considered through the assimilation lens that was active at the time, the less connections someone has, the more likely they are to assimilate.

> **Inez Dieter** said the only time she got to spend with her brother was when she was in class. "I used to turn around and smile at him and if I got caught, of course I'd go to the front again to be punished." Sometimes, she said, they would communicate with each other in sign language.[296]

---

[296] TRC, *Statement*, SP035.

Daniel Nanooch recalled how he and his sister were separated at the Wabasca, Alberta school. "So even though I was there with my sister and I only seen her about four times in that year and we're in the same building in the same mission. They had a fence in the playground. Nobody was allowed near the fence. The boys played on this side, the girls played on the other side. Nobody was allowed to go to that fence there and talk to the girls through the fence or whatever, you can't. When I look at these old army movies, I see these jails, these prisoners standing there with rifles and there was a fence. It felt the same way, 'Don't approach that fence' when I think back."[297]

Madeleine Dion Stout, who attended the Blue Quills school, thought the school deliberately discouraged the development of family connections. "There was a sense of separation and the sense of, of not connecting to your own, you know, the people who would mean the most to you, your family members, and your community members, a complete separation. And if it wasn't that we were taught by my mother to always love one another no matter how big the transgressions we committed against each other, that we would always, always love one another, and I think that's, that's what we carry today, not what residential school taught us, but there's still a deep conflict there, you know, that separation, but be together, separate but be

---

[297] TRC, *Statement*, 2011-1868.

together. So, there's this, there's this, these conflicting messages I think that I still carry."[298]

Wilbur Abrahams had a strong memory of being separated from his sisters on their arrival at the Alert Bay school. "My sisters were kind of in front of me. My two sisters, and we got up the stairs, got up. Somebody guided us through the door, and going down the hallway, and I didn't realize it, but they were separating us, girls on this side, and boys on this side, and I was following my sisters. And all of a sudden this, I felt this little pain in my, my left ear, and this, I looked up, and I saw this guy with a collar, and he pulling me back with, by my ear, and telling me I was going the wrong way. 'You're going this way.' Pull, still pulling my ear. I have always believed that, I think at that particular moment, my spirit left."[299]

The only reason **Bernice Jacks** had wanted to go to residential school in the Northwest Territories was to be with her older sister. But once she was there, she discovered they were to sleep in separate dormitories. "They wouldn't allow us to be with our sisters. The juniors had to be with the juniors. Intermediates have to be with the intermediates." On the occasions when she slipped into the older girls' dormitory and crawled into her sister's bed, her sister scolded her and sent her away. "My sister never talked to me like that before."[300]

---

[298] TRC, *Statement*, 02-MB-18JU10-059.
[299] TRC, *Statement*, 2011-3301.
[300] TRC, *Statement*, 2011-3971.

Sheila Gunderson was in residential schools in the Northwest Territories from 1958 to 1971, living in both the Fort Providence school and Lapointe Hall (Fort Simpson). She was enrolled when her mother was institutionalized; she never met her mother again until she was sixteen years old. "And, I didn't know I had an older sister until I was I think probably thirteen years old and somebody came and introduced us and said that we were sisters. And anyway, then my older brother was also raised by my grandmother and so I got to know him and over the years he had left Simpson and I never really got to know him until the last few years and it's like, we're strangers 'cause we, we were, I was raised in residential school and he was raised by my grandmother. But anyway, living in residential school, I don't know, it just seemed, you were alone. There was always so many people there and you were always [audible crying] you were always alone and you didn't know who to talk to because you weren't allowed to become friends or, or mingle with your brothers or sisters."[301]

When **Peter Ross** was enrolled at the Immaculate Conception school in Aklavik, Northwest Territories, it was the first time he had ever been parted from his sisters. "In all that time I was there I never had a chance to talk to my sisters. You know, we're segregated even in church. The girls had one side, the boys one side. You went to school, same

---

[301] TRC, *Statement*, 2011-2687.

thing. You never had a chance to, only at Christmas and Easter feasts I think is the only time that, we sat in the same dining room to eat together. And that's the only time, you know, my sisters and I had a chance to talk together."[302]

Older brothers and sisters were both a source of comfort and protection. It was not always an easy role to play. **Margaret Simpson** had to look out for her younger sister at the Fort Chipewyan, Alberta, school. "I needed to protect my sister and boy, that was hard. Especially when she's going to get a strapping or something, maybe she wet the bed or something and is going to get a, be put in the water there, in the tub and I couldn't just go in there, and I tried once and I got a good licking for that. I was happy that she didn't just pee every night in bed. Some of the girls did every night and every morning they got up and they had to be in that tub. Never mind how cold it was, getting washed in there, there was no privacy, no nothing like that."[303]

At Lapointe Hall in Fort Simpson, **Connie McNab** found herself separated from her older sister. "I remember telling her like, 'Don't leave me.' She would come and sit with me and at night one of her dorm mates would come and get me and bring me there so I could just see her at night; after everything was dark, 'cause I had nobody and I was seven, six."[304]

---

[302] TRC, *Statement*, 2011-0340.
[303] TRC, *Statement*, 02-MB-18JU10-051.
[304] TRC, *Statement*, 2011-2715.

Bernard Catcheway said that even though he and his sister were both attending the Pine Creek, Manitoba, school, they could not communicate with each other. "I couldn't talk to her, I couldn't wave at her. If you did you'd get, you know a push in the head by a nun; you know because you were not loved."[305]

The rules regarding the separation of siblings could be violently enforced. **Dorene Bernard** said that one day at the Shubenacadie school, she saw her brother walking down a hallway to go to church. "We met right at the same, we met right across from each other turning the corner to go down to the chapel. And when I waved to him, 'cause we weren't allowed to speak, so I kind of waved to him, and he kind of waved back, and one of the boys, the men, that were watching the boys, they weren't a priest, they weren't a brother, they were just civilians, men. [A staff member] grabbed Robert out of the line and threw him against the radiator right outside the priest's office, and he smashed his head on a radiator and he was rolling around on the floor holding his head, and then Morris was kicking him, telling him to 'Get up! Get up!' And I turned around and seen that and I ran out, ran back to help him. And I ran back and I jumped on his back and I started pulling his hair, telling him to 'Leave him alone, he didn't do anything.' And I was ten years old at that time and I bit him, I scratched him. I knew I was going to get it

---

[305] TRC, *Statement*, 2011-2510.

and I knew Robert was going to get it; he was going to get beaten bad. So we were fighting, and of course, yeah, I did, I got, you know, I got locked in the dormitory and I wasn't allowed out. And I was, I don't remember if they brought me food or not, but it didn't really matter, my punishment was that I would never be able to speak to him, my brother."[306]

On her second day at the Kamloops school, **Julianna Alexander** went to speak to her brother. "Did I ever get a good pounding and licking, get over there, you can't go over there, you can't talk to him, you know. I said, 'Yeah, but he's my brother.' You know it's not any, anybody different, you know, you can't talk to him, you can't go over there, can't sit with him, you know, so this was the beginning of our, our daily routine, I guess, you know, can't talk, can't see them, can't anything. I knew he was there, I just, you know, and he knew I was there, too."[307]

In strange surroundings, contact with siblings was especially important. Of her time at the Alberni school, **Elizabeth Good** recalled that "the only thing that was familiar to, to me were my siblings, and my home was a world away. And so whenever I did get to see them, it was, that was all that existed within the world was my siblings, I could see them, and I ached for them."[308]

---

[306] TRC, *Statement*, SP029.
[307] TRC, *Statement*, 2011-3286.
[308] TRC, *Statement*, 2011-3469.

In some cases, family members were not told if their siblings were sick, even when they were all enrolled in the same school. **Joanne Morrison Methot** recalled: "I remember one time my brother, he had an abscess or something here, and it busted. They took him to the hospital. They didn't even tell us that my brother almost died. They didn't tell us nothing. Then we find out after, we just found out he was gone. I think it was to a hospital they brought him, and they didn't tell us my brother almost died. They didn't tell us anything, you know, like, if something happened."[309]

Beverley Anne Machelle said the separation from her siblings increased her sense of loneliness at the Lytton, British Columbia, school. "I wasn't even allowed to talk to my brothers, and I had three brothers there. Two of those brothers committed suicide. Yeah, it really hurt not to be able to, and I couldn't even talk to my sister, and she was on the same side as me, but she was a, she was a junior girl. And maybe if she was, you know, in intermediate, I would have had more access to her. But it was, it was really lonely not having my mom, and not having my brothers or my sister."[310]

---

[309] TRC, *Statement*, 2011-2875.
[310] TRC, *Statement*, 2011-1133.

Student Gender Relations

The policy of separating brothers and sisters was part of a larger policy segregating students by sex, although students often circumvented these restrictions, as children will do. However, the complete lack of family guidance and supervision could lead to more than acceptable levels of exploration and experimentation, and often turn to abuse. In addition to students' interest in each other, the schools themselves would also arrange marriages. It should be noted that at this time no school system in Canada offered much in the way of sex education and usually fell to parents to ensure that children were educated on puberty and sex.

Among First Nations people, this points in an adolescent's life were often marked by ceremony, during which women spoke to young girls and older men counselled young boys. Residential school students were unable to turn to their parents or families for such knowledge and tribal ceremonies were banned. When the students did return home for the summer it may be too late and traditional relationships would prove to be strained by newly implemented language and growing cultural differences.

Lena McKay stayed at Breynat Hall, one of the two Roman Catholic–run residences in Fort Smith, Northwest Territories. She recalled the expectations for girls and boys there: "And we're not

Gender Relations

allowed to talk to the boys. We, you know, we go for meals and that, 'cause they used to meet us in the stairway, like, you know, we'd turn our heads, she'd tell us we're pants crazy. Can't even leave our shirt, like this open, you know, button shirts. Boy, she, one time she came to me, she just about choked me, 'cause, you know, my shirt was, one button was open. Here she was just fiddling around, trying to, you know, she just about choked me buttoning my shirt, because she said, 'You want to show yourself to, to the men?' you know. 'You're boy crazy. You're pants crazy,' things like that." [311]

Andy Norwegian said he found the separation of the sexes to be unnatural at Lapointe Hall, the Roman Catholic hostel in Fort Simpson. "When I was still living at home we had the freedom to move around the community and interact with our female cousins. In just the first two months that I arrived here there were three boys that went to talk to some girls on the girls' side and what happened as a result of that was that evening we were called into the gymnasium like this, and the three boys were sent to the mechanical room and they were stripped down to their undershorts. They were forced to come out, one at a time, and lay down, face down on a table in the middle of the gymnasium. The boys that came out laid down on a table like this, face down, and the supervisor pulled down their undershorts and strapped them with a leather strap, about three inches wide and a half inch thick. It had a

---

[311] TRC, *Statement*, 2011-0382.

Gender Relations

wooden handle and he put both hands on it and strapped them across the buttocks and you could hear the impact throughout the whole gymnasium and also the boys that were on the table, every time they were hit, they would cringe and put their arms around the table very hard, and you could hear that too."[312]

At the Blue Quills school, **Ilene Nepoose** said, boys and girls would meet in the boiler room. "I would be her lookout. I had to look out for anybody in authority. I don't know what the heck she did in there but she was in there with boys. She would say they would be necking. She made it sound like such a romantic moment."[313]

When she was fourteen years old, **Isabelle Whitford**, a student at a Manitoba school, became pregnant. "I just wanted to get out of school. And sure enough, they kicked me out of school."[314]

John Edwards met his future wife when they were both living in Grollier Hall in Inuvik, Northwest Territories. "I told all the buddies there, you know, 'Don't touch her, she's my girlfriend; going to be my girlfriend,' and then I told her that. Got into a lot of trouble over her and, went into the girls' end and went upstairs to see her and told her that, you know, 'I'm not going to do anything, nothing bad, just come to hold you and tell you that, you know I love you, I

---

[312] TRC, *Statement*, SP033.
[313] TRC, *Statement*, 2011-2380.
[314] TRC, *Statement*, S-KFN-MB-01-004.

want you to be my girlfriend.' And I was going to jump out the second story window in the middle of the winter so I don't get caught. But the supervisor making her rounds and caught me and I just walked down the girls' end. Walked right down to the boys' end and I got, I had to wait in the hall. And they had their discussion and they came out and I had to go see the boys' supervisors. And, they told me, told me, what I did was very serious and shouldn't be done and it's not tolerable. So I'll probably get a suspension or grounded for sure. So they told me, 'You want anything done? 'Cause we're going to have to call your parents.' And I said, 'Sure, call them,' and they told them basically that I had been caught in the girls' end, in a girl's room and, 'You have anything to say?' Said, 'No; just got to deal with it' and, so I'm trying to phone and I just told them, 'Mom, I met this girl and I think she's the one; I'm going to love her.'"[315]

Such romances were not uncommon. **Donald Copenace's** parents met at the Presbyterian school in northwestern Ontario.[316]

Violet Beaulieu was enrolled in the Fort Resolution school when she was four years old in 1936. An orphan, she was still in the school at age twenty-one in 1953. By then, she had rejected a number of men the school officials had tried to get her to marry. "They had to get rid of me, I guess.

---

[315] TRC, *Statement*, 2011-0328.
[316] TRC, *Statement*, 02-MB-17JU10-062.

GENDER RELATIONS

Where are they gonna send me? They, 'cause they had to set up a marriage for me, somebody I didn't know. So, she sent me to bring a book to a priest. I brought a book to a priest, and he said, 'Sit down, I want to talk to you.' So, I sat down, and he says, 'You're getting old.' So, I thought I was old. And he says that you should be getting married, and so many guys came to see you, and you refused. So next time somebody comes, you go out there, and you're gonna marry that guy..." She said that on January 6, 1953, she was told there was someone at the school to see her. "And then the parlour bell rang, and Sister said, 'Somebody came to see you.' So, I went to the door there, and he says, 'I came to see Father to ask to marry you.' It's, like, yeah, I said, 'Okay,' and I walk away. Then that was January 6, and I guess I didn't know the wedding was set for January 12th, six days later." She was upset by the prospect of having the wedding announced in advance. "I was gonna get married that Monday morning. And the custom then was Sunday church, they used to announce wedding, like, Monday morning. In those days, the church used to be just full of people. Every Sunday people would just, all the time. And that Sunday morning I got up, I was so sick. I was just throwing up. I was just sick just thinking that they're gonna announce my wedding, like, I'm gonna get married. I was so sick I couldn't go to church. They, you know, usually if you're sick they don't let you, I was sick. When the church was over, the girls came back, oh, they're just teasing, 'Oh, Violet, you're getting married.' And oh, I, I didn't like that, but I just, I had to do it." She could recall little of the marriage ceremony itself. "Next morning, 6:00

Gender Relations

o'clock in the morning, my sister-in-law come, a wedding gown, veil, everything, and she was, oh, the whole set of clothes, helped me dress up now. And she must have knew by my expression that, I didn't say nothing to her, but she must have known I didn't want to. She kept saying, 'Don't say no, don't say no,' she kept saying to me. I didn't say nothing. And you know 'til to this day, I don't remember going in church. I blocked everything. I don't remember going in there. I know the church was full. I don't remember nothing. Only one time I came to when the priest asked me, 'Will you take Jonas for your husband?' I woke up, and just like I woke up, not a sound, and they're waiting for my answer, and then, like, in the back of my head I could hear my sister-in-law saying, 'Don't say no, don't say no.' I said, 'Yes.' And from there, I don't know, just the day went. Like, that's how I got married, without, I didn't want to, and I still got married."[317]

Muriel Morrisseau said that she and the other girls at the Fort Alexander school did not know about the physical changes they would undergo at puberty. "I didn't know what was going on because they never told us. All they did was mark the calendar and give you a piece of rag that was already stained, dirty looking, ugh. We had to use that but I didn't even know what was happening with me. Even a brassiere, they gave us something to make us more flat, skin-tight homemade bras and you grow up very sad and I'm still, still lost. I figured out everything on

---

[317] TRC, *Statement*, 2011-0377.

Gender Relations

my own, it's very hard, nobody to ask. I didn't want to ask the other girls when you start having puberty, I didn't even know the words. After I grew up I became pregnant because I didn't know the facts of life."[318]

Vitaline Elsie Jenner said students were left with a feeling of shame. "And you know they never explain anything, like you're developing into a woman, and all that good stuff, you know, which is not nothing shameful about it, it's, it's natural, you know. But to me I, I came out of it, out of there, just being shamed about everything. Everything was a shame, shame-based. And finally I got used to, you know, the every month and that, so I took care of myself that way."[319]

Her first menstrual period caught **Alphonsine McNeely** by complete surprise. At the time, she was attending the Roman Catholic school in Aklavik. "I told one of the older girls, 'Sister is gonna really spank me now.' I said, 'I don't know, I must have cut myself down there because I'm bleeding now.' My pajamas is full of blood, and my, and my sheets, and I was so scared. I thought this time they're gonna kill me. And then she laugh at me, and she told me, 'Go tell Sister. She's not gonna tell you nothing.' I was scared. Told her, 'Come with me.' She came with me. And then I told her what happened. I showed her my pajamas. She started laughing, and I start crying

---

[318] TRC, *Statement*, 02-MB-18JU10-057.
[319] TRC, *Statement*, 02-MB-16JU10-131.

more, because why, why are they laughing? And I was already fourteen years old. And, and she said, that nun told me, 'Even I go like that,' she said. I used to think they never go pee, they never go poop, or nothing, eh, so I was thinking how come they go like that then?"[320]

One student, who attended school in northern Ontario, in the 1960s, was fifteen when she got married. "I didn't know anything. I was sixteen when I had my first child. No one ever told me what to expect. I didn't feel connected to my parents or anybody. I wasn't told anything, I wasn't told anything about how to raise, raise my children."[321]

---

[320] TRC, *Statement*, 01-NWT-JY10-002.
[321] TRC, *Statement*, 02-MB-18JU10-062.

Contact with Parents

Contact with parents and other family varied greatly depending on the distance between the reserve and the schools. While some were quite close, others would be thousands of kilometers away. Some students could see their parents on a weekly basis while others could wait months or more. Students were encouraged to write to family; however, all incoming and outgoing correspondence was to be read by staff, making it hard to complain about treatment. There were many reports of parcels being intercepted and stolen. At some schools, the visits were also closely monitored.

Given these restrictions, parents would lose contact with their children. The problem was exacerbated further when parents were not informed that their children would be transferred to another school. Holidays could provide some families with an opportunity to reconnect, but in many cases the distance was to vast for the short amount of time over the holidays. In most cases these travel costs would need to be covered by the family. The results would be some students remaining in the school for up to ten months straight before seeing family again for two. The strain on interfamily relations in these cases was extreme.

Students keenly anticipated visits from their parents. **Gerald McLeod** recalled that when his parents visited him at the Carcross, Yukon Territory,

Contact with Parents

school, they brought him candy and treats. When they left, the staff made him share it with other children. "They'd put it away, and they said, 'No, you can't have it. You got to share it,' and stuff like that. And it was just, you know, they had so much control over us." [322]

Because **Nellie Ningewance's** parents lived close to the school, they were able to visit her regularly. "They'd come in by cab; stay over for the weekend Friday night and Saturday night and away they go again. They give me fruit, they buy me candy, bring me new clothes I couldn't even wear." They would also bring baked bannock. "We'd smuggle that under our pillows and have bannock, after the lights go out."[323]

Even though her parents lived only a five-minute walk from the Fort Alexander school, **Mary Courchene** saw them for only one hour a week. "The parents were allowed to come into, to visit their children using the back door where the, where the boys' playroom was and the basement and that's where they would, they would wait. And then our names would be called in the, in our playroom across the way, in across the long corridor. And my, when my name would be called I'd be so happy. We'd line up and then we'd, we'd go walk, we had to walk, couldn't run. Walk to the, to the playroom and there was my mom and dad. They always sat on that side

---

[322] TRC, *Statement*, 2011-1130.
[323] TRC, *Statement*, 2011-0305.

Contact with Parents

of that, on the left. And I would go rushing to, to my, to my mom. I would jump on her knee and I would hug her and I would kiss her."[324]

Ben Sylliboy recalled that a nun was always present when his parents came to visit him and his siblings at the Shubenacadie school. "The nun told us to speak English so 'I can understand you.' So we couldn't tell them what was really going on in our world in that residential school."[325]

Loretta Mainville went to school at Fort Frances, Ontario, which was located near the reserve on which her parents lived. From the school, she could see her parents' house. On occasion, she caught sight of her parents. "And I remember one time we were, we were always in lineups all the time, and, and one time we were going by a hall, and I saw him. He had work boots and his work clothes, and he was talking to a nun, and apparently later on I found out that the nuns refused him a visit, but he tried to visit us all the time, but they wouldn't allow him."[326]

Madeleine Dion Stout had a vivid memory of her parents visiting her at the Blue Quills school. "I remember looking out the window, look, thinking they were going to appear anytime, and so they did drive up, and I remember my father tying the horses to the posts at the school, and my mother getting out of the wagon. And I really, I looked harder at my

---

[324] TRC, *Statement*, 2011-2515.
[325] TRC, *Statement*, SP030.
[326] TRC, *Statement*, 02-MB-16JU10-089.

mother for some reason. I saw her getting out of the wagon. She had, I can't remember what she had on, but I remember her red tam, and I remember how she wore it. Today, I'd probably describe it as very coquettishly, you know, sort of slanted. And, and [audible crying] I started crying then because I was missing them already. I knew they couldn't stay."[327]

Students were often encouraged to write home, but incoming and outgoing letters were read. One of **Tina Duguay's** letters to her parents was blocked because she had mentioned another student in the letter, and a second letter was blocked because she described school activities. "So, I used to wonder, 'what in the heck am I supposed to talk about?' You know I want to write letters to Mom and Dad, 'what am I supposed to say?' So, letter writing started to dwindle, and they didn't hear from me that often."[328]

Leon Wyallon felt terribly isolated from his parents when he lived in residence in Fort Smith. He also thought he could not describe what he felt in letters home. "Every time you write a letter they read it, and then they, I don't know what they do with it."[329]

Doris Young said that when she attended Anglican schools in Manitoba and Saskatchewan, she never received letters and parcels that her parents

---

[327] TRC, *Statement*, 02-MB-18JU10-059.
[328] TRC, *Statement*, 2011-5002.
[329] TRC, *Statement*, 2011-0244.

Contact with Parents

had sent her. "My mother would, would write us letters, and my dad, and we never received them, or they'd send parcels, and they were opened, and we, we just don't know what happened to them, but I know that my mother when I, when I would, we'd come home, and said she would write to us. Her English was limited, but she still wrote, and my dad send, would send us money, but we never received it either."[330]

Because the staff read all outgoing letters, **Josephine Eshkibok** attempted to have a school employee smuggle a letter out for her. "And one day I wrote a letter to my mother and it was that lady, an Indian lady that worked in laundry. I went to the laundry and I gave her that letter. I said, 'Can you post this for me?' you know. I didn't want to tell anybody, just her. So she took that letter; I was so happy she's gonna post it. 'Cause I was writing to my mom, told her to come and get me; they're too mean over here, at the school; strap all the time." The next day, she was called into the office. "There and on the table there was my letter. Then she opened it up you know, 'Is this your letter?' and I, I had my head down. And she read it, eh." The principal tore up the letter. According to Eshkibok, "I got a strap, as usual. I got the strap for sending that letter out."[331]

Given these restrictions, parents and children lost contact with each other. The problem was

---

[330] TRC, *Statement*, 2011-3517.
[331] TRC, *Statement*, 2011-2014.

exacerbated if parents were not informed that their children were going to be transferred from one school to another. This happened to **Doris Judy McKay** in Manitoba in the 1950s. "I found out that I was transferred to Birtle without them letting my parents know or anything they just transferred us. Then my mother didn't find out 'til later on that we were in Birtle, when we wrote her a letter from there. She was pretty upset about it." [332]

Geraldine Shingoose's home in northern Saskatchewan was too distant from the Lestock school for her to return at Christmas and Easter. She stayed in the school for ten months out of the year. "We didn't go home for Christmas, spring break, like all the other kids did, 'cause we lived so far. We lived up north in Saskatchewan. And, and then when I'd see my parents, it was such a, a beautiful feeling, just going back home to them for those two months. And, and then when September would come, I would, I would dread it."[333]

At the end of every summer, **Ula Hotonami** would try to talk her mother out of sending her back to school. "And every summer when they'd go home for holidays for a couple of months, then I didn't really want to go back, you know, I'd want to stay out, but then, then my mother asked me why, and I told her,' Cause I don't like getting lickings all the time,' I told her. And I was getting lickings for no

---

[332] TRC, *Statement*, 2011-2514.
[333] TRC, *Statement*, 02-MB-19JU10-033.

Contact with Parents

reason. Well, well I still, I used to get lickings for nothing. I don't know."[334]

Some children stayed at the schools year-round. **Frances Tait** recalled that every June, the school supervisor at the Alberni school would come with the list of students who were going home for the summer. "And I remember hoping, crossing my fingers, crossing my toes that my name would be on that list, but it never was. And finally, one, one summer, I guess when I was about ten years old, I guess, in a way, I bet that I was thinking that maybe if I had a suitcase I would go home. So I went into the cloakroom, and I stole a suitcase and didn't put my name in it but put my brother's name in it and waited. And still, my name was not on that list. But because I stole the suitcase and because I had gone into the cloakroom without permission, I got punished. And it was to scrub the stairs from top to bottom with a toothbrush."[335]

Don Willie recalled how hard it was on students at the Alert Bay school as they waited at the end of the school year to see if their parents would come to take them home. "Kids would take turns sitting by the window, waiting for somebody to pick them up, pressing their faces against the window, and they were all happy if somebody came to pick them up, but pretty sad when nobody came."[336]

---

[334] TRC, *Statement*, 2011-2654.
[335] TRC, *Statement*, 2011-3974.
[336] TRC, *Statement*, 2011-3284.

Contact with Parents

For students whose families had fallen apart, life at the school was particularly lonely. One **former student** recalled that at the Chapleau, Ontario, school, he never got letters from home. "Other kids on holidays, going home, everybody's supposed to be good. I knew I wasn't going home; and my mom was drunk. 'Cause one brother said, 'Your, your mother's drunk right now drinking.' They phoned the store that's in Mobert, 'She's incapable of accepting,' taking his call or something. There was no phone to the house, but I mean there was phone that goes down to the store. And, he said, I guess the brother said, 'No, your mother's not in the condition right now.' I knew right away what was happening, I'm not going home man."[337]

Wilbur Abrahams and his sisters were not sent home from the Alert Bay school for the summer holiday. "I remember the first year that, summertime, just before the summer holidays they had, they had a list of names, and the students that were going home for the summer. My name never came up. Must have been hard on my sisters, too, because they, they had the same list up on that side. I don't know, maybe there was about a handful of us that never went home. And it, it was a little, a little more freedom."[338]

Victoria Boucher-Grant attended the Fort William, Ontario, school. She was one of the children

---

[337] TRC, *Statement*, 2011-2012.
[338] TRC, *Statement*, 2011-3301.

Contact with Parents

who did not get to go home in the summer. "But in those times that I, when my uncle wasn't there, there was three of us that our, our families never came to get us in the, in the summer. One, the other was a boy, and two girls. And everybody used to think we were orphans, but we weren't orphans. It's just that our big family never came to get us."[339]

Ben Sylliboy, a student at the Shubenacadie school, was not able to go home for the summer holidays. "Some people were lucky, they went home in June; June 30th was known as Freedom Day for all the boys that were fortunate enough to go home a couple of months of the summer. But there was quite a few of us that didn't go home. We stayed at the residential school all summer. It was hard."[340]

Julianna Alexander recalled that at the Kamloops school, the "Girls that were allowed to go home, or the boys that were allowed to go home were only allowed because their parents could afford to take them home, and the majority got left there for the holidays. And that was kind of like hell, because the load of having to do all the dirty work there." [341]

William Francis Paul said he enjoyed staying at the Shubenacadie school in the summer. "There was no school. We were outside all day. It seemed like that was the only time we had a lot of fresh air.

---

[339] TRC, *Statement*, 01-ON-05FE11-004.
[340] TRC, *Statement*, SP030.
[341] TRC, *Statement*, 2011-3286.

We got to be outside most of the day, and we got to mingle with other kids, instead of your teacher, where I was outside."[342]

Darryl Siah said that some of the summer activities that were organized at the Mission, British Columbia school were the best part of his residential school years. "But the best part was, we weren't, we couldn't go to our homes for the summer, we got to stay here for a while and go on camping trips, and we were canoe pulling and stuff, hiking up the cross up here in the mountain was good."[343]

Mary Teya said the summers with her parents were the best memories of her life. "For two months our parents would take us right out, back out to our fish camp and that would be one of the best memories in my life. Where we would be able to speak our language and live our way of life. For two months we stayed out there. We never came into town. And that's how come I think today I still have my language and I still have my way of, my way, my culture and my tradition and all the wonderful values of being a Gwich'in person, I still hold that. And I thank God for that."[344]

For some students, visits home had their own unique stresses. When **Kiatch Nahanni** and her sisters returned home from residential school in the Northwest Territories, they found that they were

---

[342] TRC, *Statement*, 2011-2873.
[343] TRC, *Statement*, 2011-3473.
[344] TRC, *Statement*, SP019.

estranged from their father. "He would talk to us in Slavey, and we would answer him back in English; because we understand what he said. And so when I was in Grade Three I, I came home and he, he talked to me in Slavey and I opened my mouth, nothing came out. I was, and I answered back in English and so that summer my cousin talked to me and slowly I got the language back. But it was like that every summer for the longest time."[345]

Residential schooling left **Rosie Kagak** completely unprepared for a return to her home community, and forgetful of traditional ways and foods. "Finally, we're on our way home and I'm looking at everybody in the plane wondering where we're going. We land in Kugluktuk, originally Coppermine, and my parents travelled to Coppermine from their outpost camp to pick us up. One of my older brothers came with a dog team to where the plane had landed on the ice. He took me and my brothers to the tent and this lady looks at me and tells me to sit beside her. I'm looking at her, and beside her was a man. She said something to me I could not understand. So I looked at my older sister, and I asked her, 'What is she saying?' And she picked up a piece of frozen char and had her hand out with the char for me to have. I looked at her, I looked at her, I looked at my older sister, and I asked her, 'Why does she want me to eat raw fish?'"[346]

---

[345] TRC, *Statement*, 2011-2684.
[346] TRC, *Statement*, SC090.

After years of separation, many family connections were broken. When **Dorothy Hart** returned to her home in northern Manitoba after six years in residential school, she discovered that her mother had remarried. "We were so happy to knock on their door; but this man appeared. And I called my mom, and she saw us, but she couldn't do anything. That guy said, 'They're not staying here.' He shut the door. So I took my sisters to my granny's, that's in Hart's Point. And we just got home after all these years. [audible crying]"[347]

Going away to residential school in the Northwest Territories brought **Frederick Ernest Koe's** home life to an end. "I said that year had a monumental effect on my life and my relationship with my family because I came, spent a year here, went back, everything that I thought I owned was gone and a month or so later my family moved over here because my dad moved with the armed forces, and you know, we lived here. And from that day on, the day we moved here, I never, ever went hunting with my dad again."[348]

Mollie Roy said that her years at the Spanish, Ontario girls' school left her struggling with a sense of abandonment. "I think the thing about the school more than anything else is the feeling of abandonment. Why was, why was I there, and why didn't you come to see me? Because all of us, with

---

[347] TRC, *Statement*, 2011-2586.
[348] TRC, *Statement* SC091.

Contact with Parents

the exception of few, were just, parents were, like, ten miles down the road, ten miles, and the people wouldn't even come. You know it's not that my parents didn't have a car. My dad worked at Denison, and made good money, and, like, there was no, you know, you'd wait and wait, and nobody showed up, and I think that's the thing more than anything else that bothered me. It's not the school, it's the fact that I wasn't wanted."[349]

Florence Horassi said that at the residential school she attended in the Northwest Territories, she was made to feel ashamed of being Aboriginal. "When I was in residential school, then they told me I'm a dirty Indian, I'm a lousy Indian, I'm a starving Indian, and my mom and dad were drunkards, that I'm to pray for them, so when they died, they can go to heaven. They don't even know my mom had died while I was in there, or do they know that she died when I was in there? I never saw my mom drink. I never saw my mom drunk. But they tell me that, to pray for them, so they don't go to hell."[350]

Agnes Moses said that her time in residential schools in northern Canada left her wanting "to be white so bad."
"The worst thing I ever did was I was ashamed of my mother, that honourable woman, because she couldn't speak English, she never went to school, and we used to go home to her on Saturdays, and they

---

[349] TRC, *Statement*, 2011-1129.
[350] TRC, *Statement*, 2011-0394.

told us that we couldn't talk Gwich'in to her and, and she couldn't, like couldn't communicate. And my sister was the one that had the nerve to tell her. 'We can't talk Loucheux [Gwich'in] to you, they told us not to.'"[351]

By belittling Aboriginal culture, the schools drove a wedge between children and their parents. **Mary Courchene** recalled that in the 1940s at the Fort Alexander school in Manitoba, she was taught that her people were no good. "This is what we were told every day: 'You savage. Your ancestors are no good. What did they do when they, your, your, your people, your ancestors you know what they used to do? They used to go and they, they would worship trees and they would, they would worship the animals." She became so ashamed of being Aboriginal. "I looked at my dad, I looked at my mom, I looked at my dad again. You know what? I hated them. I just absolutely hated my own parents. Not because I thought they abandon me; I hated their brown faces. I hated them because they were Indians; they were Indian. And here I was, you know coming from. So I, I looked at my dad and I challenged him and he, and I said, 'From now on we speak only English in this house,' I said to my dad. And you know when we, when, in a traditional home where I was raised, the first thing that we all were always taught was to respect your elders and never to, you know, to challenge them. And here I was eleven years old, and I challenged." Her father's eyes

---

[351] TRC, *Statement*, SC090.

Contact with Parents

filled with tears. Then he looked at her mother and said, in Ojibway, "I guess we'll never speak to this little girl again. Don't know her."[352]

Feelings of shame complicated many parental visits. At the Amos, Québec school, **Carmen Petiquay** felt ashamed of her parents also. "And I was ashamed of my parents because I was told Indians smell bad and they don't talk, and I said to myself, 'As long as they don't come,' cause I was ashamed I hoped they wouldn't come because I, I hoped that they would come sometime. At, at one point my parents came and I was happy. I was pleased to see them, and I hoped that they would leave soon. Because it hurt so much to be taken away from one's parents like that, and it hurts to say things about one's parents and to be ashamed of them. I had believed because I was told that Indians smell bad and that they don't wash. And my mother brought me an orange, and I kept the orange for the long time, I never even ate it, I kept it because it came from my mother. This is something that I now regret having thought that of my parents, that they smelled bad."[353]

After six years at the Mohawk Institute in Brantford, Ontario, **Jennie Blackbird** came to see the English language as being superior to her family's language. "When I returned home, I heard my grandparents and my family around me, only

---

[352] TRC, *Statement*, 2011-2515.
[353] TRC, *Statement*, SP104.

speaking our language. I was a very angry person when I heard them speak the Anishinaabe, our language. I remember telling my grandparents, don't you dare talk to me in that language, and feeling superior to them, as they did not know how to make the English sounds. This, I now regret having said that to my loved ones."[354]

When **Vitaline Elsie Jenner** went home for the summer holidays from the Fort Chipewyan school in Alberta, she was ashamed of her ancestry. "In the summers, when I went home from the residential school, I did not want to know my parents anymore. I was so programmed that at one time I looked down at my mom and dad, my family life, my culture, I looked down on it, ashamed, and that's how I felt." She tried to deny who she was. "I didn't want to be an Aboriginal person. No way did I want to be an Aboriginal person. I did everything. Dyed my hair and whatever else, you know, just so I wouldn't look like an Aboriginal person, denied my heritage, my culture, I denied it. I drank. I worked as well. I worked and partied hard. When I had that opportunity on my days off, I would party."[355]

When he returned home after spending three years at the Anglican school in Aklavik, **Albert Elias** no longer fit in with his family. "I was a different person, you know. I had, I kind of knew everything after being in residential school. I couldn't, I couldn't,

---

[354] TRC, *Statement*, 2011-4188.
[355] TRC, *Statement*, 02-MB-16JU10-131.

you know, get along and cope with life in Tuktoyaktuk 'cause I was rebelling against my parents and didn't listen to them and I was changed. I, and I had lost my language, but, you know, I'm very lucky, in those days everybody in Tuktoyaktuk still spoke Inuvialuktun, so it didn't take me long to learn my language back, so, and I know lots of people that are, don't have that experience."[356]

When **Betsy Olson** went home after three years at the Prince Albert school, she had difficulty adjusting to reserve life. "And, the food we had the first day was a rabbit, a rabbit, and I couldn't eat it. I told my sister, 'I can't eat this. This is Peter Rabbit. I can't eat Peter Rabbit,' I told her, 'cause Peter Rabbit was our favourite story in our books there, and I couldn't eat Peter Rabbit. All the wildlife we had for about a month, Mom had to buy white man's food to feed me 'cause I couldn't eat our, our way of eating back home. I couldn't eat soup. I couldn't eat fish. I couldn't eat bannock. Couldn't eat nothing. I had to, so Mom had to get extra money to try and buy extra food just for me."[357]

Ellen Smith, who was born in Fort McPherson, Northwest Territories, found that residential schooling made it impossible for her to fit back into her home community. "I can't sew; I can't cut up caribou meat; I can't cut up moose meat; work with fish and speak my language. So I was

---

[356] TRC, *Statement*, SC092.
[357] TRC, *Statement*, 2011-4378.

starting to become alienated from my parents and my grandparents; everything."[358]

Raphael Victor Paul spent ten years at the Beauval, Saskatchewan, school. I thought for a long time that I was better than my parents. "That's the thought that they gave you, because my parents didn't talk English, but I did. My parents were very Catholic, and I was very Catholic, but I knew both languages, the catechism and all that. So, you get, I got the feeling that maybe I know more than my parents." His father believed that the residential school education had prevented his son and his friends from learning the skills they need to survive. He said, "You know you guys that went to residential school are useless, because you don't know how to survive like they did." "'Cause they never taught us that, you know, how to. At that time, there was no welfare, there was, there was no running waters or lights, so we had to do all those things by ourselves, but we didn't know how. So, the people that went back had to relearn how to survive. And at that time, survival washing, hunting, and trapping. To this day, I don't know how to hunt. I can trap, I can fish, but I don't know how to hunt, 'cause I, I was never taught that."[359]

Some people never adjusted. Although she had not enjoyed her time at the Alberni, British Columbia, school, **Frances Tait** discovered she could

---

[358] TRC, *Statement*, 2011-0346.
[359] TRC, *Statement*, 02-MB-19JU10-051.

Contact with Parents

not find a place for herself in her home community when she returned. "I couldn't survive in the village. I was different. I was an outcast. And my brothers weren't there." As a result, she asked to be sent back to Alberni, where she boarded with a Euro-Canadian family.[360]

---

[360] TRC, *Statement*, 2011-3974.

Trauma, Emotional Neglect, and Despair

Many of the former students who spoke to the Commission emphasized a general atmosphere of fear that permeated their school lives. Despite being surrounded by dozens of children; they were lonely and deprived of affection and approval. Childhood loneliness often drove students to take desperate and destructive measures resulting in self harm. To this day suicide and substance abuse remain prevalent in many First Nations communities, with Inuit 15–24-year old's being the hardest hit at over 35 times that of their non-indigenous counterparts while the average among the rest of the First Nations is closer to 8 times the non-indigenous rate. Add to this that poverty and substance abuse remain ongoing symptoms of generational trauma that continues to this day and unfortunately, probably far into the future. The effects of the residential school system will continue to be felt for generations to come and even today, while accounting for only 7% of the adolescent population of Canada, Indigenous children make up 48% of all children in foster care.

Raymond Cutknife recalled that when he attended the Hobbema school, he "lived with fear." As he grew older, this turned into anger and bitterness. "The abuse that I went through and then I grew with anger, as I grow a little older, and that stayed with me for a long, long time. Anger into bitterness as I grew a little older again and you know at the, and it's about the mid-grades or going into Grade Nine, and then the last part of my experience with my life, that reflected on hatred, with such intense hatred that I never thought what it meant but when I think about that, you know it, as I grow older even today when I think about it you know, I didn't realize how close I came to destroying my own life spiritually speaking, that is."[361]

Of his years in two different Manitoba schools, **Timothy Henderson** said: "Every day was, you were in constant fear that, your hope was that it wasn't you today that were going to, that was going to be the target, the victim. You know, you weren't going to have to suffer any form of humiliation, 'cause they were good at that. You know and they always had nasty, nasty remarks all day long. There was never, you never heard a kind word; I never heard a kind word."[362]

William Herney, who attended the Shubenacadie school, recalled the first few days in the school as frightening and bewildering. "And you had to understand, you had to learn. Within those few days, you had to learn, because otherwise you're gonna get your head knocked off. Anyway, you learned everything. You learned to obey. And one of the rules that you didn't break, you obey, and you were scared, you were very scared. You, you don't

---

[361] TRC, *Statement*, SP125.
[362] TRC, *Statement*, 2011-0291.

know what to come up with next. I was scared. I was, like, always afraid, always looking over my shoulder."[363]

Shirley Waskewitch said that in Kindergarten at the Catholic school in Onion Lake, Saskatchewan, "I learned the fear, how to be so fearful at six years old. It was instilled in me. I was scared and fearful all the time, and that stayed with me throughout my life."[364]

At the Fort Alexander, Manitoba school, **Patrick Bruyere** used to cry himself to sleep. "There was, you know, a few nights I remember that I just, you know, cried myself to sleep, I guess, because of, you know, wanting to see my mom and dad. I could never figure out why we had to be in there, you know."[365]

Ernest Barkman, who attended the Pine Creek school, recalled, "I was really lonely and I cried a lot, my brother who was with me said I cried a lot."[366]

Paul Dixon, who attended schools in Québec and Ontario, described life at residential school as one of unbearable loneliness. "You hear children crying at bedtime, you know. But all that time, you know, you know we had to weep silently. You were

---

[363] TRC, *Statement*, 2011-2923.
[364] TRC, *Statement*, 2011-3521.
[365] TRC, *Statement*, 02-MB-16JU10-157.
[366] TRC, *Statement*, 2011-0123.

not allowed to cry, and we were in fear that we, as nobody to hear us, you know. If one child was caught crying, eh, oh, everybody was in trouble. You'd get up, and you'd get up at the real fastest way. Now, they hit you between your legs, or pull you out of bed by the hair, even if it was a top bunk, you know. Homesickness was your constant companion besides hunger, loneliness, and fear."[367]

Rick Gilbert said that in the junior dormitory at the Williams Lake school, children cried themselves to sleep at the beginning of each school year. "That one kid would be lonesome and starting to cry and then pretty soon the next bed another kid heard that and started crying and that's how it really spread next bed and next bed. And pretty soon almost the whole dorm was filled with kids crying because they are, you know and then, just knowing that they're not going to be, their mom and dad's not going to be coming to tell you goodnight and that things are okay. Nobody who has, that was one thing about this school was that when you got hurt or got beat up or something, and you started crying, nobody comforted you. You just sat in the corner and cried and cried till you got tired of crying then you got up and carried on with life."[368]

Bob Baxter said it was hard to come up with good memories of his time at the Sioux Lookout school. One of his strongest recollections was "the

---

[367] TRC, *Statement*, SP101.
[368] TRC, *Statement*, 2011-2389.

loneliness of being alone and being away from your parents." At night, he said, the dormitories were full of lonely children. "I remember when the lights used to go out everybody used to cry when I first got there, I guess being lonesome, I guess. All the kids are, he's crying, and I guess I was crying, too."[369]

Betsy Annahatak grew up in Kangirsuk, in northern Québec, which was then known as Payne Bay. When her parents were on the land, she lived in a small hostel in the community. Like many students, she has strong memories of the loneliness she experienced at the school. "I remember the, the time the first few nights we were in the residential school, when one person would start crying, all the, all the little girls would start crying; all of us. We were different ages. And we would cry like little puppies or dogs, right into the night, until we go to sleep; longing for our families. That's the memory I have."[370]

Noel Knockwood recalled boys crying themselves to sleep at the Shubenacadie school in the 1940s. "At nighttime I could hear some boys trying to smother their, their crying by putting a pillow over their mouth. And they would, not be heard too much, but we could hear them because they were in the same room with us. And, and we slept in a large dormitory which had perhaps about twenty-five or thirty beds and we were side by side.

---

[369] TRC, *Statement*, 01-ON-24NOV10-012.
[370] TRC, *Statement*, 2011-2896.

So we could hear some kids crying at night and they would say, you know, 'I'm lonesome, I want my mother, I want my father.'"[371]

For the first three days that **Nellie Ningewance** was at the Sioux Lookout school, all she did was cry. "There was lots of us; other girls didn't seem to, seem to be doing the same thing, the younger ones. So my, my hiding place was in the washroom. I'd sneak to the washroom and sit in the washroom and they would look for me; I wouldn't answer. I hid in the washroom. I sat on the toilet tank with my feet on the toilet seat; and nobody didn't see me where I was. I wouldn't open the door. Somebody had to crawl under to get me out."[372]

On her first night at the Spanish, Ontario girls' school, **Shirley Williams** recalled, "no sooner did we have the, the lights off, and in our, our beds, I could hear people sniffling, and I knew they were crying. I think the loneliness swept in and for me, too, and but I slept at least, you know, but I think I woke up every hour and that, but I did, but I did go to sleep finally."[373]

Daniel Andre was frightened and lonely when he went to Grollier Hall, the Roman Catholic residence in Inuvik, Northwest Territories. "And the hardest part that I had to deal with was when I would go to sleep at night, and I'd cry myself to sleep every

---

[371] TRC, *Statement*, 2011-2922.
[372] TRC, *Statement*, 2011-0305.
[373] TRC, *Statement*, 2011-5040.

night, wondering what I did wrong to, to be away from my mom and dad, and not to have them with me, or beside me, or protecting me."[374]

Students commented on how they felt lonely even in a crowded school. **Alan Knockwood** said about his time at Shubenacadie, "Biggest thing I remember from the school was that I was lonely. I was surrounded by people all the time, but I was alone. And it took a long time for me to finally acknowledge that I do live in a loving community."[375]

Despite the fact that there were over 100 students at the Mission, British Columbia, school, **Jeanne Paul** felt alone and isolated. "But again it was the loneliness of, of crying under my sheets at night, you know, just covering my head, underneath my blankets and sniffling, you know, very quietly, so nobody could hear me. And I imagine there were a lot of other ones in the room, I didn't know, might be having the same problem as well."[376]

Josiah Fiddler went to school at McIntosh, Ontario. "My first few weeks in school, I cried every day. Either it was on the beating of the seniors, the beatings, the pulling of the ears by the nuns, and my first introduction to the principal was a slap across the head and told me to get downstairs and join the other 100 boys there. After those first few weeks I finally said, I'm not going to give them that

---

[374] TRC, *Statement*, 2011-0202.
[375] TRC, *Statement*, SP029.
[376] TRC, *Statement*, 2011-3464.

satisfaction any more, I stopped crying. And to this day, I haven't cried. I really can't. And I feel so good for people that have the ability to be able to cry because as I said, I don't know how to cry."[377]

Nick Sibbeston, who was placed in the Fort Providence school in the Northwest Territories at the age of five, recalled it as a place where children hid their emotions. "In residential school you quickly learn that you should not cry. If you cry you're teased, you're shamed out, you're even punished. So you brace yourself and learn not to cry, you have to be a big boy, you have to toughen up." There was one nun at the school who would give students an empty sardine can in which to collect their tears. "And I've always thought, you know, what's so hard about just putting your hand on a child and saying, 'Don't cry, don't be sad,' you know, but there was never anything of that."[378]

Jack Anawak recalled of his time at Chesterfield Inlet in the 1950s that "there was no love, there was no feelings, it was just supervisory. For the nuns that were in there it was just, they supervised us, they told us what to do, they told us when to do it, they told us how to do it, and we didn't even have to think, we didn't even have to feel."[379]

---

[377] TRC, *Statement*, SC111.
[378] TRC, *Statement*, NNE202.
[379] TRC, *Statement*, NNE202.

Murray Crowe was very homesick at the school he attended in northwestern Ontario. At nights I was crying. "And, I was crying and there was other students that were crying. We had double bunks; we were all crying in the dorm. And then the workers Jeanne Paul there, they kept taking other kids out because they were disturbing the other kids from sleeping and.... When I couldn't stop crying they came and got me. And they came and got me; they took me out, out to the dark room we called it. And they pulled my trousers down and they spanked me. But I didn't stop crying; I was screaming and crying. They checked me up. They checked me, they locked me there, in the dark room. And they checked me and I wouldn't stop crying and I was hurting, because they, they, they hit me too hard; and I was so, I was hurt so much."[380]

Of her years at Shubenacadie, **Joanne Morrison Methot** said, "We never, nobody ever told us they loved us. We couldn't hug each other, you know, like, you know, [the Sister] said, 'You can't do that.' You know you can't say you love somebody, or hug somebody, you can't kiss boys, and stuff, and of course I was too young for that, but she said we couldn't do that."[381]

Even though **Lydia Ross's** parents lived in the same community in which the school was located, she rarely saw them when she was enrolled at the

---

[380] TRC, *Statement*, 2011-0306.
[381] TRC, *Statement*, 2011-2875.

Cross Lake, Manitoba, school. "If you cried, if you got hurt and cried, there was no, nobody to, nobody to comfort, comfort you, nobody to put their arms. I missed my mom and dad, and my brothers and sisters." On one occasion, she looked out the school window and saw her father. "I knocked on the window, and he looked and I said, I waved at him. I wanted to go outside, but you're not supposed to. If you see your parents out on a Sunday, you're not supposed to go to them. You can't go and hug your little brother and sister, and go and talk to your mom and dad. You can only see them from a distance."[382]

Robert Malcolm said that when he was placed in the Sandy Bay school in Manitoba, he was "taken from a loving environment and put into a, a place where there was no love, and that we had to fend for ourselves pretty much. It was very traumatizing that we, we had to go through something like that."[383]

Clara Quisess was six when she was sent to the Fort William, Ontario, school. She found the experience traumatic. She became fearful of the nun who had responsibility for her at the school. "I had to learn the language that she was teaching me to speak. I was not allowed to talk in my language that whenever she asked me something, whenever she tried to tell me to pronounce this, I have to talk in English, no Native language. And she would yell at

---

[382] TRC, *Statement*, 02-MB-16JU10-029.
[383] TRC, *Statement*, 02-MB-16JU10-090.

me if I was saying, I'm trying to tell her I don't understand and I'm confused and I don't know what to say and how to say it, I was very scared of her. She, Murray Crowe, was always raising her voice at me and she always had this angry look on her face and it felt really intimidating. And I was homesick. I was, like, crying and she yelled at me and told me to stop crying and she called me a crybaby in front of the students and it made me not want to cry anymore. I didn't like her. Deep inside I hated her for being so mean to me and when she told me not to cry and she told me not to speak my language, I felt like I had to keep everything inside me and it made me lonely, that there's nothing out here that could make me happy and feel like it was home."[384]

For **Florence Horassi**, loneliness was a constant feature of life at the schools she attended in the Northwest Territories. "Like, the nuns in there, they're cold. There was nobody there to give any hugs. There was nobody there to say goodnight. There was nobody there to even wipe your tears, or we will hide our tears. We're not to cry, so we have to hide and cry. But at night, you could hear a lot of muffling crying, muffling, sometime all night. Late at night you can hear somebody crying. I don't know what time it is. There's no time or nothing that I know, but I know it's very late at night. There's nobody to tell us. Everything we do in there is wrong,

---

[384] TRC, *Statement*, 02-MB-17JU10-032.

wrong, wrong, wrong, is what I hear. Couldn't do anything right."[385]

This lack of compassion affected the way students treated one another. **Stephen Kakfwi** attended Grandin College in Fort Smith, Northwest Territories when he was twelve years old. "And one day, a week after I got to Fort Smith, I had a meltdown 'cause I realized I wasn't going to go home for ten months and I was homesick, and my older brother didn't know what to do with me." When another student came into the room and asked what was wrong, Kakfwi's brother said, "He's homesick." "'He'll get over it,' [the other student] said, turned around and walked back out. And I think that's how we were, you know, every kid that came after that, that's what we all said, 'He'll get over it.' No hugs, nothing, no comfort. Everything that, I think, happened in the residential schools, we picked it up: we didn't get any hugs; you ain't going to get one out of me I'll tell you that."[386]

Victoria McIntosh said that life at the Fort Alexander, Manitoba, school taught her not to trust anyone. "You learn not to cry anymore. You just get harder. And yeah, you learn to shut down. And you know those feelings are there, and but they're, they're so deep down inside, you know, and they come out as some pretty, some pretty wicked

---

[385] TRC, *Statement*, 2011-0394.
[386] TRC, *Statement*, NNE202.

nightmares at times, and then some days are good."[387]

Megan Molaluk lived at both the Anglican and Catholic hostels in Inuvik. As was the case with many students, her loneliness led her to engage in behaviour intended to get her kicked out of school. "I missed camping, I missed having country food. There are so many things I wanted to say, all right, but I really wanted to go home. It was bugging home, and bugging, bugging, bugging. I guess they got tired of me bugging them, so they moved me to Grollier Hall. I didn't know nobody over there. So I start behaving, I asked Mr. Holman if I could move back. I'm tired of being with strangers everywhere. So I started doing bad things in Inuvik, drinking, sneaking out. I hated doing those things, but I really wanted to go home."[388]

Elizabeth Joyce Brass attempted to take her own life at the Dauphin, Manitoba, school in the 1960s. "And I remember one time going downtown with, and this was probably when I was, like they had junior dorm, intermediate dorm, senior dorm, I was in the senior dorm at that time. I must have been about eleven, twelve years old, and I remember, and I don't even know where this thought came from, but I remember I wanted to go downtown, and I had a plan, I was gonna go steal some Aspirins, which I did. I can't remember what store it was, and, you know,

---

[387] TRC, *Statement*, 02-MB-16JU10-123.
[388] TRC, *Statement*, SC090.

later on that night I, I took a whole bunch of them, and I remember, you know, going to sleep, and then I remember the next morning, you know, someone waking me up, but I couldn't hear them, because there was that really loud buzzing in my ears, so I guess that, you know that was, that must have been the way the Aspirin had affected me. And I couldn't get up, and I could remember the supervisor, you know, telling me, you know, 'You're just not wanting to go to school today,' you know, 'You're just pretending to be sick.' And she sent me off to see the nurse. And on my way I, you know, threw up, and it was all brown, and so I went and seen the nurse on the top floor, and same thing, too, she says, 'You need to get to school. There's nothing wrong with you.' So that was, you know, the first time in my life that I attempted suicide, and, you know, just at a young age."[389]

Antonette White has her own disturbing memories related to suicide. The students at her Kuper Island school were forced to look at a suicide victim. "I remember the one young fellow that hung himself in the gym, and they brought us in there, and showed, showed us, as kids, and they just left him hanging there, and, like, what was that supposed to teach us? You know I'm fifty-five years old, and I still remember that, and that's one thing out of that school that I remember."[390]

---

[389] TRC, *Statement*, 02-MB-19JU10-005.
[390] TRC, *Statement*, 2011-3984.

Truancy, Learning to Lie, or Worse

Many students would run away to escape the often times harsh discipline of the schools. Emotional, physical, and even sexual abuse were prevalent, leaving many to feel the only way out was to leave. In some cases, students ran away even though they had no expectation of making home. They just could not bear the life in the institution any longer. This unfortunately resulted in countless children missing or worse. The true number of children dead or missing will never be known.

Some lessons the schools taught too well: many students mentioned that one of the major things they learned in the schools was the ability to hide, if not completely suppress their feelings. Learning to give the responses needed to 'just get by.' Having little or no support structures in place left them feeling alone and afraid, often expressing bad behavior. While all children find themselves in this situation at some point in their lives, having no family and little friends, along with the authoritarian nature of the school system, little outlet was allowed for these feelings.

Chanie Wenjack was 12 years old in 1963, and unfortunate to fall into the latter category. His story, made famous by now-deceased Gord Downie Jr., stands out to me as Chanie attended the Kenora Residential School less than 3 hours from where I grew up, and the

Truancy

school I could have attended, had I been born a couple of decades earlier. Chanie's body was found beside the railway tracks on October 22, 1966, a week after he fled. He had succumbed to starvation and exposure. In his pocket was nothing but a little glass jar with seven wooden matches.

> **Margaret Simpson**, who attended the Fort Chipewyan, Alberta school, described it as a survival technique. "I learned how to lie, to lie so that I will get away with whatever Sister wanted me to do and that whatever she wanted to hear, that's what I told her even if it was a lie. So it got easier and I got pretty good at lying and I had a real time to get out of that lying as I got older in life to be able to tell the truth and to know the difference of what was happening because of that lie that it became such a habit for me. I had a real hard time even after I left the residential school."[391]
>
> **Noel Knockwood** said that at the Shubenacadie school, he learned to fake submission. "We learned how to play the game and acknowledged and bowed our heads in agreement and whatever they said we agreed with them, because they were too powerful to fight and they were too strong to, to, for us to change their, their habits and their ways of living."[392]

---

[391] TRC, *Statement*, 02-MB-18JU10-051.
[392] TRC, *Statement*, 2011-2922.

TRUANCY

John B. Custer learned to rebel at residential school. The only things he took away from his years at the Roman Catholic school near The Pas, Manitoba, were a guilty conscience and a bad attitude. "So instead of learning anything in that residential school, we, we learned just the opposite from good. We learned how to steal, we learned how to fight, we learned how to cheat, we learned how to lie. And to tell the truth, I thought I was gonna go to hell, so I didn't give a shit. I was sort of a rebel in the residential school. I didn't listen, so I was always being punished."[393]

Elaine Durocher felt that she received no meaningful education at the Roman Catholic school at Kamsack, Saskatchewan. Rather, she learned the tools for a life on the fringes of society in the sex trade. "They were there to discipline you, teach you, beat you, rape you, molest you, but I never got an education. I knew how to run. I knew how to manipulate. Once I knew that I could get money for touching, and this may sound bad, but once I knew that I could touch a man's penis for candy, that set the pace for when I was a teenager, and I could pull tricks as a prostitute. That, that's what the residential school taught me. It taught me how to lie, how to manipulate, how to exchange sexual favours for cash, meals, whatever, whatever the case may be."[394]

---

[393] TRC, *Statement*, 02-MB-19JU10-057.
[394] TRC, *Statement*, 02-MB-16JU10-059.

Truancy

Ken Lacquette attended residential schools in Brandon and Portage la Prairie, Manitoba. He found the discipline so harsh that he and his friends regularly ran away. "They used to give us straps all the time with our pants down, they'd give us straps right in the public. Then ... this started happening, after a while when I was getting old enough I started taking off from there, running away."

After being subjected to ongoing sexual abuse, **Anthony Wilson** ran away from the Alberni school. "I barely even remember how I made it home, but ... I got bits of pieces of how I made it home, I took off from residential school in Port Alberni, and I hitchhiked from Port Alberni to Nanaimo, and I made it as far as where the BC ferries were. And when I was a young child, and I was so messed up after the abuse, I didn't know what to do, and so I was hiding."

When she returned to the Qu'Appelle school after being sexually abused by a fellow student the year before, **Shirley Brass** decided to run away. She did not even bother to unpack her suitcase on the first day at the school. "I took it down to the laundry room and everybody was taking their suitcases down to wherever they kept them. I took my suitcase down. I told the nun, I said, 'I have to do my laundry,' I said so I took it to the laundry room. I hid it there and that night this other girl was supposed to run away with me but everybody was going up to the dorm and I went and I asked her, 'Are you coming with me?' And she said, 'No, I'm staying.' So I said,

'Well, I'm going.' So I left, went and got my suitcase and I sneaked out. I went by the lake. I stayed there for I don't know how long. I walked by the lake and I sneaked through the little village of Lebret, stayed in a ditch. I saw the school truck passing twice and I just stayed there. I never went back. I hiked to—I had an aunt in Gordon's Reserve so I went there. I had a brother who was living—a half-brother who was living with his grandparents in Gordon's and he found me and somehow he got word to my mom and dad where I was and they came and got me. My dad wouldn't send me back to Lebret so I went to school in Norquay, put myself back in Grade Ten. I didn't think much of myself. I quit when I was [in] Grade Eleven in Norquay."

In the 1940s, **Arthur Ron McKay** regularly ran away from the Sandy Bay school. "I didn't even know where my home was, the first time right away. But these guys are the ones; my friends were living in nearby reserve, what they call Ebb and Flow, that's where they were going so I followed." He said he was physically abused for running away. "... and that my supervisors, they'd hit me, like a man hitting somebody else, like a fist and all that. So this went on and on and on, I don't exactly know how to say. And then one time the principal threatened us, 'If you run away one more time, we're going to send you to a reform school in Portage, boys' reform school.' The boys' home, they call it a reform school, 'If you run away one more time that's where I'm going to send you and take you down there.' I was thinking about

Truancy

that and I said, oh it's better to go away, maybe it's better down at the reform school."

Ivan George and a group of his friends ran away from the Mission, British Columbia, school when he was eleven years old. "Got as far as Abbotsford, and they recognized our clothes, or whatever, and haircut, I guess, and said, 'Where are you guys going?' I says, 'Chilliwack.' He said, 'Okay.' He picked us up, drove us right around, right back to here. He gave us a warning. 'Next time you get the strap.' So, I stayed for another month or so, and I took off by myself. Got as far as the freeway, and the police picked me up, took me back. This time they made me take my pants down, and strapped me. So about two months later, me and this other guy decided to run again." This time, he got as far as his home in Chilliwack. Indian Affairs officials sent them back. "That guy was getting the strap first, my best friend, and he said, 'You again.' I says, 'Yeah.' He was just gonna strap me, and I took the strap, and I threw it down in the dormitory. He said, 'Go pick it up.' And I says, 'You go pick it up.' He gave me extra strappings for that, what I did to him. So, I stayed the whole year."

Muriel Morrisseau ran away from the Fort Alexander school almost every year she was at the school. "I ran away for, I don't know, just to make the nuns angry, the priests angry I guess. I didn't get anything out of running away, more punishment. I remember one time when the priest come and got us, me and this girl that I was close to, we went home for a night and he'd come and get us the next day. Nothing good became out of it anyway. I remember running away again trying to cross the river and it started freezing up, we all got scared, we had to come back again with a tail under our legs."

Walter Jones attended the Alberni school in British Columbia. He ran away several times and was harshly punished in front of other students on his return. "We were all thinking we're not gonna cry when that happens. Come to my turn, too, all three of us, one after the other, I cried, they cried, and all the other ones cried." Despite this humiliation, he continued to run away. "We knew it was, we might not be able to get where we come from, but we didn't think of that, you know, we're just running away because we were, wanted to run away, you know, 'cause we were, didn't, we couldn't stay there."

Even when it was not fatal, running away was frightening. **Isaac Daniels** ran away from the Prince Albert, Saskatchewan, school with two older boys. Their escape route involved crossing a railway bridge. Partway across, Daniels became too frightened to continue and turned back. "And it was already late, it must have been about 11:00, 12:00. So, I said to myself, well, I'll go back, I'll go back, follow this track all the way, I'll go back to residential school. So, so that, that was already the sun was coming up by the time I got back to the residential school. And I was just a young fella, you know. So, anyway, I couldn't get in. Dormitory locked, doors were locked, so I went around the corner, and I slept on the, by my window there. I just have a window, and I used to sneak in and out from the, through the window there. So, I must have sat down there, and I must have fell asleep."

Dora Necan ran away from the Fort Frances school with a friend. "Then we ran away to, me and a girl, we, by Fort Frances, it's, you know, the States is on the other side of the tracks, so we were crawling there just to run away, that was in the springtime. There was a lot of ice, and there was river flowing down, down there. There was a train coming behind us, so we were crawling to go past this bridge. And it's a good thing my friend had long hair, that's where I grabbed her, was so she wouldn't slip into the river, yeah." They made it to the United States and stayed there for three days before returning to the school.

When **Lawrence Waquan** ran away from the Fort Chipewyan school in 1965, there was no one along the way to support him. "I walked from Fort Chipewyan to Fort Smith, 130 miles. It took me about five days. I was only about sixteen. And I just ate berries and drank water to survive. But at that time I knew my brother was living in Fort Smith. Simon Waquan, he was living there that time. That's when he took me under his wing, in 1966."

There were many students who considered running away but, in the end, decided against it because they had no place to go. **Roy Denny**, for example, carefully prepared his escape from the Shubenacadie school. "It's been like, I tried running away once; and I saved all my lunch, I hid it away. And one night I went down and tried to make a run for it. I went downstairs, I was at the door, big door, I opened it, it was around midnight, after midnight I think. And I stood there; I'm thinking where in the hell am I going to go? Didn't have family; the only I have is my grandmother. So I went back in, I went back to my bed. I felt so helpless or I couldn't, I don't know the feeling I had and I didn't want to leave my sisters there; that's another thing too. I couldn't take them with me 'cause they're, they're on the other side. So I said I might as well tough it out."

When **Beverley Anne Machelle** and her friends ran away from the Lytton, British Columbia, school, they had to contend with the school's isolated and mountainous location. "It's a plateau region, and the residence was here, and then we walked up onto the road, and then the road goes along, and then it goes a little bit up, and then, and then there's a great big hill going down, and it was halfway down this big hill, and then from there you could see town. And we got halfway down there, and we were all feeling, like, woo-hoo, you know, and we got out of there, and, and we're gonna go do something fun, and, and then we got halfway down, and then we realized, well, we have no money, and we have no place to go. There was no place to go. There was no safe place to go. And that was really weird to me because, because where the residential school was and where I lived just before I went into the residential school, I lived on the reserve just, like, it was, like, less than a mile away, and yet I had no place to go. Yeah, so we were very sad, and we all agreed that we had to go back because we had no place to go, so we went back."

One student even flew away from school. **Doug Beardy** left the Stirland Lake, Ontario, school for good, shortly before his two years at the school were completed. "There was a plane that, that used to come there with, I think, with fish, tubs of fish that they, they would drop them off there, and they were thrown onto a truck, a semi-truck. And so this plane landed, and I went down to the plane and stood around until the pilot was ready to go, and, you know, he was right about ready to close the door, and when he was ready to close door, I jumped into the plane. This, this pilot was in Round Lake for many years, and he has since passed away. He didn't ask me anything. He didn't ask me why I jumped into the plane. He just looked at me when I jumped into, into the plane, he just looked at me and didn't say anything, and he just took off. And, and that's how I left the school."

Harsh Discipline

Many students were caught by surprise by the violent nature of the discipline at the schools. Flogging, strapping and other forms of physical violence were to be expected. The line between punishment and abuse was blurry at best and frequently crossed. Many of the school administrators believed that the students had to have their spirit broken. This resulted in students who would not adhere to school schedules and regulations receiving strappings and were often humiliated in front of their peers. Trying to run away from the schools and being caught would result in their hair being cut very short regardless of sex and solitary confinement and withholding of food were also common practice. The relationship between staff and student at times getting so bad as to result in death.

> **Isabelle Whitford** said that prior to coming to the Sandy Bay school, she had not been physically disciplined. "All my dad have to do was raise his voice, and we knew what he meant. So, when I first got hit by the nuns, it was really devastating 'cause how can they hit me when my parents didn't hit me, you know? Never did I ever get a licking from my parents. It was just ... my dad raising his voice. And, and, we knew what he meant. We had our chores to do; we would do them."[395]

---

[395] TRC, *Statement*, S-KFN-MB-01-004.

Harsh Discipline

Rachel Chakasim said that at the Fort Albany, Ontario school, "...I saw violence for the first time. I would see kids getting hit. Sometimes in the classrooms, a yardstick was being used to hit. A nun would hit us. Even though our hair was short as it is, the nuns would grab us by the hair, and throw us on the floor of the classroom.... We never knew such fear before. It was very scary. I witness as other children were being mistreated."[396]

Ricky Kakekagumick said that students at the Poplar Hill, Ontario school were often disciplined at night. "You try and sleep, you just hear that noise of somebody crying. I don't know how long, maybe a month later, that's when I finally found out what was going on. Whoever was bad, didn't listen, well, the, the ones they wanted to punish, they'd come and get them in the middle of the night, when everybody's asleep, that's what they did, that's why I kept hearing this whimpering and crying at night. They came and got them at the night, took them down, wherever they wanted to strap them, and they brought them back."[397]

Stella Marie Tookate never forgot being called to the principal's office at the Fort Albany, Ontario school. "There was a priest there, standing, and the Sister standing, a nun. And then, they were two in the office. And at that time, I remember, they were strapping me five times— five times on my

---

[396] TRC, *Statement*, 01-ON-4-6NOV10-019.
[397] TRC, *Statement*, 2011-4200.

hands and five times the other hand. And that's where, that's where I stopped going to school because I was ... I showed my dad my hands at that time, and then he took me away from school. It was hard for me to continue my school at that time. It was hard to feel that stripes on my hands.... My hands were red at that time— painful. Sometimes, I could, I could tell, sometimes how I was feeling. I feel that pain sometimes. And I stopped going to school after that."[398]

Fred Brass said that his years at the Roman Catholic school at Kamsack, Saskatchewan, were "the hellish years of my life. You know to be degraded by our so-called educators, to be beat by these people that were supposed to have been there to look after us, to teach us right from wrong. It makes me wonder now today a lot of times I ask that question, who was right and who was wrong?" Brass described a school dominated by a violent regime of punishment. "I saw my brother with his face held to a hot steaming pipe and then getting burned on the arm by the supervisor. And I took my brother, tried to get him out of there. And I saw my cousin get beat up to the point where he was getting kicked where he couldn't even walk and then it was my turn. I got beat so bad that I wet my pants. Fears I lived with day and night to the point where at nighttime when you want to go to the bathroom you can't because there is someone sitting there with a stick or a strap ready to beat on you if you try to go to that

---

[398] TRC, *Statement*, 01-ON-8-10NOV10-003.

bathroom. And the only choice we had was to pee in our beds. That's not a nice feeling to have to sleep in that kind of a bed."[399]

Joanne Morrison Methot told the Commission that noisy behaviour was punished severely at the Shubenacadie school. "I used to count. One girl got strapped forty-five times, I was counting, yeah, and then it came to my turn, I got a beating, and I wouldn't cry. I just let her beat me and beat me, and I wouldn't cry. I just let her do that because, well, sometimes I would pretend I'm crying just so she'll stop, but then other times I just didn't cry, 'cause I knew I was talking, maybe it was my fault, so I just let her beat me, and then next one, then after we'd go to bed."[400]

Alfred Nolie said that corporal punishment at the Alert Bay school was strict and painful. "There was one big staff there. He used to lay me over a desk, big square thing there. I think because I used to work up at the farm up here, there were horses up here, they had those big leather straps, big leather, heavy ones, about that thick, I guess, I'd lean over a desk, take my pants down, and hit me in the bum with that strap, and that hurts really bad. Every time I get caught talking our language that's when it's usually big staff, was 300 pounds, really big guy."[401]

---

[399] TRC, *Statement*, SP039.
[400] TRC, *Statement*, 2011-2875.
[401] TRC, *Statement*, 2011-3293.

Ron Windsor had strong memories of being punished for laughing at the dining-room table at the Alert Bay school. "I didn't know what he was gonna do. He grabbed my hair, put his knee in my back, and held me right on the floor, and I tried to tell him my neck is sore, and I was crying. And he caught me off guard, I didn't expect that. Now, why would you do [that] to a little boy like me at that time?"[402]

For crossing into the girls' playground at the Sioux Lookout school, **Ken A. Littledeer** was grabbed by two staff members. One of them then beat him on the hands with branches from a thorny bush. "I was crying. Never cried hard before. I never felt this sharp pain before, and anger build up, and resentment build up, that if I grow bigger I would get this person back. I knew that I was small, and I can't hit him back."[403]

Doug Beardy said that at the Stirland Lake, Ontario school, the principal punished him with blows administered with "a hockey stick, a goalie stick ... that was cut off like ... a paddle."[404]

For going to the washroom in the middle of the night at the Sault Ste. Marie residence, **Diana Lariviere** said, she was sent "down to the basement, and I was in the basement practically all night, scrubbing the cement floor, on my hands and knees, and that was my punishment for that night. Now it, it

---

[402] TRC, *Statement*, 2011-3307.
[403] TRC, *Statement*, 01-ON-24-NOV10-028.
[404] TRC, *Statement*, 2011-4197.

was a, a scary, a very frightening situation because of all the creaks and the noises that were going on in the basement."[405]

Lynda Pahpasay McDonald said that on one occasion, she was placed in a closet as punishment at the Roman Catholic school in Kenora. "There's just a little bit of light coming through that door, and, and I sat there I don't know how many hours. It felt like a long time. And that's where they put any child that acted up, into the closet. I remember my sister going there a couple of times, too, my younger one. She would go in there also."[406]

Extended periods of kneeling were another form of discipline. **Wesley Keewatin** said that at the Qu'Appelle school, students might have to kneel in front of a statue of the Virgin Mary for half an hour to an hour. Keewatin also recalled that at the Qu'Appelle school, a teacher he had thought had always treated him well slapped him so hard that he "went flying." He attributed his deafness in one ear to this incident.[407]

Inez Dieter felt that her hearing was damaged by the punishment she received at a Saskatchewan school. "I was speaking out of turn and there was a male supervisor, I was about fourteen, maybe thirteen. He was a male supervisor, he was big, he came up to me and instead of talking to me in

---

[405] TRC, *Statement*, 2011-2011.
[406] TRC, *Statement*, 02-MB-16JU10-130.
[407] TRC, *Statement*, 2011-3276.

a nice way, he just ploughed into my ear like this. Today I wear hearing aids. Today I can't hear, I can't hear well enough. And that really hurt because there was nobody there to say, 'I'm sorry,' because everybody was scared. Nobody wanted to say anything but I felt it. I felt the blow and again I cried."[408]

Delores Adolph also said that the punishment she received at the Mission school impaired her hearing. "The nun slapped me across the face, and, and I had too much soap in my hair, and my ears, and I was trying to get the soap out of my ears and my face, and she gave me one good slap, and, like, and all I saw was stars. And so I didn't know that my eardrum was broken at that, at that point. So, after a while, you know, they were getting mad because I, I couldn't hear what they were saying."[409]

Edmund Metatawabin spoke of how he and other students at the Fort Albany school had been punished by being placed in what students referred to as the "electric chair." According to Metatawabin, this was a metal-framed chair with a wooden seat and back. After being buckled into the chair an electric current from a hand-cranked generator was run into their bodies. The chair had been constructed by Brother Goulet, the school's electrician, and had apparently been initially used as an entertainment. It

---

[408] TRC, *Statement*, SP035.
[409] TRC, *Statement*, 2011-3458.

came, however, to be used as an instrument of punishment. Metatawabin said he had "sat on the electric chair three times."[410]

Simeon Nakoochee was another student who was put in the chair. "To them it's, like, entertainment, like it was just, like, 'Who wants to get in?' There wasn't, it was like a selection. I never wanted to get in that chair, you know. I saw that chair. I could even describe it, that thing too, you know. That thing just right out of my mind, I could, I could describe it, you know, what the, what the chair looked like, you know, what, what they use. Then they, well, I never volunteer, or raised my hand, you know, and I just, and then she called my name, the nun, you know, 'Just sit on that chair.' It was almost like a crack, you know. She wouldn't let me get off there until, and then I, I probably cried after that, you know, and she wouldn't let me get out after this. People thought it was, kids were laughing asking why I cry, you know. He said he thought the chair was later destroyed."[411]

Jonas Grandjambe recalled how the nun in charge of the boys' dormitory at the Roman Catholic school in Aklavik gave the students what he called a "rough time". "A strapping, grabbing us by the ear, and pushing us against the corner to kneel down. Sometimes we had to kneel down all day. And if we spilt something, she would do the same thing, grab

---

[410] TRC, *Statement*, SP098.
[411] TRC, *Statement*, 2011-4316.

our ear and twist it until we, make us get down on the floor, and whatever we dropped there we have to eat it or lick it. I don't know."[412]

Margaret Plamondon, who attended the Holy Angels Residential School in Fort Chipewyan, Alberta, said she once saw a nun push a student down a flight of stairs. "It was one of my, one of my friends, and we were lining up to go to the bathrooms before school was, was to start, and I don't know what happened, and one of the nuns, one of the nuns that were looking after us, not the teacher, and then she, as, as I turn around, I see the nun push that girl down a flight of stairs, and she never got up, we were chased away, down to go away from there. I don't know what happened, but she never came back for months. And when she came back, she was kind of crippled. She was never the same after that. She even likely, she had a broken back after. She came back, and she was almost gone a year before I see her again. They didn't tell us what went wrong."[413]

Noel Starblanket recalled being constantly "slapped on the side of the head" at the Qu'Appelle school. One teacher struck him in the face and broke his nose. "My nose started bleeding, I ran out, I went to the bathroom, was wiping my face with cold water, and it took a long time to stop it, and I plugged it with toilet paper, and toilet, paper towel,

---

[412] TRC, *Statement*, 01-NWT-JY10-024.
[413] TRC, *Statement*, 2011-0387.

whatever I could find. I went back in class, and everybody was teasing me, bugging me, and ha-ha-ha, look at, look at him, you know, all that, humiliating me. And, and so, anyway, it started swelling up, getting blue under here, and I wondered, gee, you know, is there something wrong? I was sore here. So, a couple of days after it started going down, and I remember waking up in the middle of the night, and my nose would be bleeding, and I'd have to run to the bathroom, and wash it and plug it again."[414]

Adam Highway recalled a beating that he witnessed the principal of the Sturgeon Landing, Saskatchewan, school administer in the 1920s. "The priest grabbed him, grabbed him by the hair, threw him down. Now, that was a cement floor where we played. And here he kicked him repeatedly. There was no stick. He had brand new boots, leather. I was sitting not too far away. I wasn't very big. I still can't forget to this day. It's like I'm still watching him. It must have been ten minutes. These were brand new boots. On the thighs and the buttocks. He bounced his boots off him as he kicked him. And the Brother that looked at him. Now the principal said to him. 'George,' he said, 'you will kneel there until six o'clock,' he told him."[415]

There are also reports of group punishment. **Earl Clarke** recalled how at the Prince Albert, Saskatchewan school, many of the boys would start

---

[414] TRC, *Statement*, 2011-3314.
[415] TRC, *Statement*, 2011-1781.

fooling around when the lights went out in the dormitory. Eventually, he said, the supervisor would come out and line up the boys he suspected to have been making noise. He would then "take them down to the end of the hall, and would get out a, a leather strap, just like a conveyor belt type of material. And the kids would come hopping out, crying, bawling, you know, little, little ones 'cause the little ones would get forced to go first."[416]

Ernest Barkman, who went to the Fort Albany school, said that, on one occasion, all the boys were punished for the actions of one student. "We all stood in rows (three or four rows, all the boys, and we had to stand there for an hour) one hour and we were told not to move, and if we moved we got hit, that's one thing I remember."[417]

At the Norway House school, **Shirley Ida Moore** recalled: "When, when something would happen, like one of the girls would get into trouble or somebody would, or somebody, or somebody would get into trouble, they'd haul us all down to the playroom and we'd stand in these lines, we had to stand at attention. And you would walk around, we would, we would be forced to stand there until somebody, whoever did what confessed. And, and I guess the, the memory that I have is like, we stood there for so long, I saw girls falling; that's, that's how

---

[416] TRC, *Statement*, 01-SK-JU10-002.
[417] TRC, *Statement*, 2011-0123.

long we had stood there. So I guess it was really a battle of wills."[418]

Gerald McLeod recalled being subjected to group punishments at the Carcross, Yukon school. "And another place where, where we used to play downstairs, they call it the play area ... where they make us stand up in line, and if one guy got in trouble, all of us would have to stand there 'til we confessed who did, like, stole candy from the candy place, or whatever went wrong, or something, we always all got punished for it."[419]

Students might also be punished if it was felt they were withholding information about the activities of other students. **Eli Carpenter** recalled that the principal of the Presbyterian school in Kenora in the early 1940s was very strict. On one occasion, Carpenter was strapped because the principal believed he was not revealing information about the destination of a boy who had run away. Carpenter said the boy had not shared his plans with him.[420]

Mary Vivier saw her brother publicly flogged at the Fort Frances school. "I don't know what my, what my brother ... what he did. All I know is that it was, we were all in the dining area when they brought him in, when they brought them in. They had, I don't know, I was just pretty small, but it

---

[418] TRC, *Statement*, 2011-0089.
[419] TRC, *Statement*, 2011-1130.
[420] TRC, *Statement*, 02-MB-17JU10-018.

looked like a big, long rod to me, maybe it was smaller. That's when they were hit in front of all the students. Maybe it was a lesson for us, or scare tactic, I'm not sure, but I was, I cried. I had one of the nuns holding me down, so I don't go running to my brother. They had another one by my sister. I remember that day. I cried, I cried and I cried."[421]

Daniel Andre was disciplined in front of other students at Grollier Hall, the Roman Catholic residence in Inuvik. "All I remember is being singled out, and the center of attention, and being abused physically. And when he couldn't make me cry, or, or weaken me that way, he would get all the students to call me all different kinds of names, and, and laugh at me, forcibly make them laugh at me so that I cried, and I cried every single time when it happened. I couldn't help it."[422]

Not only were runaway students often punished as a group, but they were also often disciplined in front of the entire student body and subjected to punishments that were clearly intended to humiliate them and intimidate the rest of the students. When a group of runaway girls were brought back to the Sioux Lookout school, they were punished in front of the assembled students. According to **Nellie Ningewance**, "We were all lined up. Boys on one side, girls on one side, to watch them being punished. Their pants were pulled down

---

[421] TRC, *Statement*, 02-MB-18JU10-082.
[422] TRC, *Statement*, 2011-0202.

right to bare butt, they were strapped with a belt; bent over. And all the boys and girls were watching that."[423]

Boys who ran away from the Spanish school also were punished in front of their fellow students. **William Antoine** said, "What they did to them, they cut all their hair off. And ... they got all the boys to look at what is happening to this boy, what they were doing to him because he ran away. They cut all his hair off and they pulled, pulled his pants down and he was kneeling on the floor, and holding onto the chair. And they were, whipping him, with this big belt. I mean hard too. They were hitting him, for I don't know how long. He, he started to cry after; it was hurting so bad eh. But I don't know how many times they hit him, but they hit him lots of times. And those boys that got whipped that time, was, there was two of them, they, they couldn't sit down for two months; that's how bad it was. That's how bad they got beat because they ran away. And that's what the priest said, 'If any of you boys run away, that's what you're going to get.'"

According to **Lawrence Wanakamik**, students who ran away from the McIntosh, Ontario school were subjected to a similar punishment. "When they got caught a couple of days after, they'd, they'd haul them into the, into the playroom, and they told us, you know, gather around. There used to be benches along the walls in the playroom, and

---

[423] TRC, *Statement*, 2011-0305.

everybody would sit down, and we'd sit down there, and we knew, we knew it was those kids got caught, and we didn't know where they were though. We didn't know what happened. But then after everybody was gathered, you know, they'd bring them in, wherever how much they were, two, three, sometimes four. And they, one of the nuns brought in a big strap, real big strap, about two feet long. It was one of those hard rubber conveyor belt type of rubber. They'd bring that out. They'd tell the kids to put their hands out, and they did pow! pow! I don't know how many times."[424]

J.G. Michel Sutherland recalled the public punishment of boys who ran away from the Fort Albany, Ontario school in the 1960s. "So, all the boys were lined up, and at the west side of the building where the sun side was, they were lining up these four boys that had been caught, that ran away. I'm six years old, and there was about twenty-five of us, you know, you know starting, and then the Grade Ones. There was another twenty-five of them, so there was quite a few of us, six, seven years old. And the brothers in black robes were standing there. There was about five of them. And there was some nuns. So, we were there to learn a lesson. They stripped the four boys naked. They tied them up on this big, big thing, and it looked like a wheel, it was, well, they, they, they got 'em by the hands, and they started whipping them one by one."[425]

---

[424] TRC, *Statement*, 2011-2002.
[425] TRC, *Statement*, 01-ON-06JA11-002.

Doris Young recalled that runaways from the Anglican schools she attended in Manitoba and Saskatchewan were punished in front of the assembled students. "They both were brought back into the dining room, where we witnessed them getting their head shaved. And, and then they had to remove their clothes, they'd remove their clothes, and they strapped them in front of all of us. And we all had to go into the dining room, where, where the, where usually the, the boys' and the girls' dining rooms were separated, and but we, we were all taken into the dining room, and we were, we had to witness this beating, and I thought, oh, I hope it's not one of my brothers, but, but it wasn't, and still they, they were boys and girls that, the boys and girls, and everybody, the, the supervisors were all standing there witnessing this, these horrible beatings that these boys were getting because they ran away from school."[426]

Even when the students were not disciplined in public, they were subjected to invasive and humiliating punishment. Once, **Violet Beaulieu** and her friends slipped out of the Fort Resolution school in the middle of winter. "I don't know why I did that. So, we planned it all out. And it was a really, really cold winter night, blizzard." They were quickly caught and accused of attempting to get into the boys' dormitory. "They got the Father there to, took us each our turn in the room, and really gave it to us.

---

[426] TRC, *Statement*, 2011-3517.

'Better tell the truth. Lay down there, pull your pants down.' Whack, whack. 'What did you do?' 'Nothing.' Again, whack. Holy smokes I was just bruised. And they tried to make us say that we saw somebody. Who did we see? All that stuff, just for a dare, you know. And they put us in penance for, like we were, we were forbidden to do anything, go anywhere. Like, they'd have Sunday movies, stuff like that, and we were, shut us out, and they tried to get us to say we did something."[427]

Dorothy Ross and a friend ran away from the Sioux Lookout school. "We ran as fast as we could. Down the lake, along the shore, we followed that girl, through the bush. I remember the tracks. I just followed, you know, and that, there's the tracks, a train. We didn't get too far. We ran on the tracks, the side of the tracks, and I could see lights coming, lights coming, eh, and people running, chasing after us. They were caught, returned to the school, and sent to the principal's office." There, she was told to pull her pants down so she could be strapped on her bare bottom. "'Pull your pants down,' he would yell at me, but I won't, I won't let him. So, he grabbed me by my collar, took me to the, the desk. It's a long desk. Put me against that desk. 'Pull your pants down,' I remember him saying that all the time, 'pull your pants down' and I wasn't gonna give in. He had to force me. He forced me to pull my pants down. He had to do it; I didn't do it. So, he put me against that desk, and he whacked me with that, I remember the

---

[427] TRC, *Statement*, 2011-0377.

strap, it was a big thick strap, brown, that, and he hit me on my bum. I started crying, that's how much it hurted. 'You're a bad girl. You don't run away again, or you will, you're gonna get it again.'"[428]

When she was at the Lestock, Saskatchewan, school, **Clara Munroe** joined a group of girls who were running away. "One evening they said, 'Come with us,' and I said, 'Okay.' I thought, okay, I'll go with them. Here I didn't know they were planning to run away. There was twelve of us. So that's what I did, I followed them. Next thing I knew there was a wagon, team of horses, picked us up like a bunch of cattle, throw us in the wagon, brought us back. Didn't say nothing, they just, and we used to line up, we used to get in line and we were on our way to the dormitories, bedtime, who do they call? They called me. They called on another girl there. The two of us and I was blamed for that and I didn't even know a thing about it, so they wouldn't listen to me. So what did they do? They took us to the principal's office. The principal was there, there was three nuns there, and not a word, they just pulled my pants down [pause] and the priest, the Father principal, gave me a strap. And yet it was I know I was so ashamed I start laughing and that nun said, 'She's laughing,' and he strapped, strapped me harder and longer. I was so embarrassed."[429]

---

[428] TRC, *Statement*, 01-ON-24NOV10-014.
[429] TRC, *Statement*, SP039.

Some students said they tried not to show any signs of pain when they were being punished. Once, when **Tina Duguay** and her friend Sandra were about to be punished at their school in British Columbia, Tina told herself, "This time they're not breaking me. I don't care what, they're not gonna break me." She recalled receiving 100 strokes on each hand without crying. "So after she sent us out of her office, walking down the stairs, and Sandra says, 'Man, you're tough,' and I said, 'No, I just stopped it,' and I says, 'Now I'm gonna cry.' So, I ended up crying. We went in the bathroom, and let, just let it out, and I said, 'There,' and I said, 'That's it. She didn't see me do it though.'"[430]

To their frustration, some students were not able to convince their parents of the severity of the punishment at the schools. **Noel Knockwood** found it difficult to get his parents to believe that he and his fellow students were being harshly punished at Shubenacadie in the 1940s. "And when we would tell our mothers and fathers and when, when Mother and Father will come and visit us on, on, on the Sunday, they usually have visiting days on Sunday, we would all go into the, the, to the room where we would meet and I would tell my mother and father that we seen some boys and some girls getting beaten. Some of them were whipped; some of them were beaten with a leather strap. And Mom and Dad, they always said, 'Oh no, the priests and nuns wouldn't do that because they are the people of

---

[430] TRC, *Statement*, 2011-5002.

Harsh Discipline

God.' My mother and father were very strong Catholics."[431]

Students recalled that some staff members were clearly uncomfortable with the harsh disciplinary regimes that prevailed at so many schools. **Eugene Tetreault** was an Aboriginal man who worked as a boys' supervisor at the Fort Frances school. It was his job to discipline students who had been referred to him by one of the nuns at the school. He said, "It's not my thing to do that kind of work." He said he would tell boys, "'I'll take the slap, I'll, I'll slap on the, on, on my desk, and you scream.' And I'll say the boy was really happy about that, so I, I slap on the table, and the boy screamed 'Ow, ow, ouch!,' and that was the end of it."[432]

Once, at the Anglican school in Onion Lake, **Ula Hotonami** was strapped by the laundry superintendent for joking with a student in the hallway. The principal encountered her shortly afterwards and asked her why she was crying. When she explained what happened, the principal told her to go into his office. "And he put me in his office, and he had told me, 'You wait there,' and so I, I waited in his office. We were never allowed in his office, like, not, and he, he went down to the laundry room, and must have went and talked to her. Within two weeks she was gone, anyway. So, I don't know. His name was Mr. Card and that. And so he told me, 'You can

---

[431] TRC, *Statement*, 2011-2922.
[432] TRC, *Statement*, 01-BC-20DE10-001.

miss school 'til the swelling goes down.' So, I was thinking what's going on here, like, you know, why, why do I have to miss school now? I can't go to work. I can't go to school. And so I asked him, 'Well, what am I gonna do? Like, I have to go to school and that.' And he told me, 'Well just, you, you can't do anything, anyway. You can't hold anything in your hand,' he said, 'they're all swollen.' Like, my hand was just puffed up, like, from the strapping that I got."[433]

Roger Cromarty said that at the Sioux Lookout school, different staff members were allowed to discipline students in different ways. "While teachers might use a yardstick, dormitory supervisors used a strap. This would be a strap about one and half inches wide, quarter-inch thick and about twelve inches long, that they, those, they would use that on, on us boys either open hand, or in some cases if the principal is there, they would strap them in the bum, bare bum with, with the principal as a witness. Now when you got punished by, if the punishment was being done by the principal, he had a, a longer strap. That's about fifteen inches long, and it's an inch and a half wide, and a quarter-inch thick, and he was the one, he didn't have to have a witness I never saw him, when he hit me with it, he never, there was no witness, and you're supposed to have a witness."[434]

---

[433] TRC, *Statement*, 2011-2654.
[434] TRC, *Statement*, 02-MB-16JU10-132.

Harsh Discipline

Strict discipline bred animosity. **Roy Johnson** said that at the Carcross school, students came to hate their supervisors. "But I remember hating. It's, it's, it's really something to behold to hate a person. You look them right in the eye, and say over and over, you know, you're going down last day, which means you can go to hell last day, over and over. Then when you're getting strapping, you keep, you try to keep that frame of mind burning, that hatred burning in, in you, until finally you can't take it anymore." On one occasion, Johnson said, the older boys went on a "rampage" in response to the school discipline. "They were upstairs and downstairs, locked themselves in the dormitory, or whatever, but the supervisor was chasing them, and the principal. And I was looking up from the playroom, and from the fire door, a tin garbage can came flying down, and got me here. I think a boy was taking off running. He was, he was hollering back, 'Sorry, Roy.' You know I was holding my head. I had Kleenex. I had to be taken to dispensary. I guess those, they were dealt with when they were all caught. And there's another boy from here, fire hose was used on him. But his older brother would get in a fight with his, with the supervisor. They would fight up in the, up in the dormitory, they fight there, and then again in the kitchen. I think then again in the playroom. The kitchen one was sort of a ... whose who, who is tougher, I guess, I don't know. But that boy grab a pot of mashed potatoes, and just lift it up and put it over the supervisor's head, and they were fighting, wrestling around for a while. That's funny, it wasn't funny to me, but it was, you know it was, that's how life was there."[435]

Mollie Roy recalled fighting when a teacher at the girls' school in Spanish tried to punish her. "[The teacher] was tall, and she was mean, and she'd grab us by the cheeks, and just twist, just turn, and she'd do this every time. Well, I guess one day I was her victim, and that was the last time. She turned, she put her finger, and I bit on it, and bit it just about to the bone. There was blood pouring down. She was just freaking out. 'Let go.' And I kept shaking my head ... and that was the last time she ever touched anybody's cheeks. But we'd have big marks on our cheeks all the time."[436]

Larry Beardy recalled how, at the Dauphin school, the students eventually rebelled. "But one of the saddest things that I, I want to share is in the, in the dormitories we were in, young boys, we started to notice a lot of my colleagues running away, and, and every time somebody ran away, the whole dorm would get physically strapped by the principal of that school, and also the supervisors. And this kept continuing, and it escalated so bad, a eight-year-old, a nine-year-old, ten-year-old, we ransacked the whole dorm. We went violent."[437]

---

[435] TRC, *Statement*, 2011-0203.
[436] TRC, *Statement*, 2011-1129.
[437] TRC, *Statement*, SP082.

Outright Abuse

Due to the power relation and age differentials in a residential school, no sexual relationship between a staff member and student could be considered consensual, and many former students recalled having been raped at school. Some sexual abusers purportedly carefully recruited their victims, providing them treats and small favours, while others made use of simple threats and physical force.

At the Fort Albany school, one of the lay Brothers cornered **Josephine Sutherland** in the school garage. "I couldn't call for help, I couldn't. And he did awful things to me, and I was just a little girl, not even thirteen years old yet, and he did something to me that the experience as having a horrible pain. You know he got me from the back, and he was holding me down with his, covering my mouth, and, you know, and, and I couldn't yell out. I was so stunned, I couldn't move, I couldn't."[438]

As a student at the Fort Frances school in the 1960s, **Richard Morrison** said, he was called into a change room by a staff member. Once he was in the room, a bag was put over his head and his clothes were removed. "I remember that he had struggled with me really, really hard and I fought back and fought back and I don't know how long it was, I just fought and pretty soon he just, I don't know what he

---

[438] TRC, *Statement*, 01-ON4-6NOV10-013.

did, he had restrained me somehow. And when that happened, he had sexually abused me, he penetrated me and I was just, all I remember was just a pain. A pain was just strong. It was really hurtful and I remember that day after that I was a very, very angry kid."[439]

At the Qu'Appelle school, **Raynie Tuckanow** said, he witnessed staff committing sadistic acts of abuse. "But I know what they did. I know what they did to me and I know what they did to others, too. Looking up here, just like that up here, I watched the young man. They tied him. And I know him today, I see him today. They tied him by his ankles and they tied him to the [heat] register and they put him out the window with a broomstick handle shoved up his ass. And I witnessed that."[440]

Leonard Peter Alexcee was abused at the Alberni school. The abuse began one night when a staff member tapped him on the shoulder and told him it was time for him to take a shower. Middle of the night. "So, I thought that was one of the things going on there. I'll go back a bit. First morning, he woke us up about 6:30. Take us down to the playroom and this big, big guy. I was a small, very small, but you know and he start pushing me around, pushing me around, slapping me. 'Come on! Let's fight,' he said. 'I'm the boss here.' There was no kids in the playroom. They're all looking through the little

---

[439] TRC, *Statement*, 02-MB-17JU10-080.
[440] TRC, *Statement*, SP036.

Outright Abuse

window outside, so I just fell down and cried, and cried, and cried. Finally, he left me alone. And then we went into the dining room." Later, Leonard was told to take his clothes off. "The next thing I know he had all his clothes off too. He said, 'I'm gonna wash you.' He washed me down. He started fooling around with my part—private parts and then he took his—he took my hand and put it on his private parts. And then I started crying."[441]

In some cases, students said that discipline was mixed with sexual abuse. **Mary Vivier** told the Commission about her experience at the Fort Frances school. "And there was a priest, I'm not sure what he, what he was, I don't know, but he was the head priest at the time, the principal, I don't what they call it. He had a chair. Whenever, whenever we were brought up to his office to get our strapping, he, there was chairs outside his office, and then there was, like, a leaning chair, I guess. It was low enough for us to, from here on down. He'd remove our, our unders, our pants, our underpants. He would strap us, and he would rub us, saying. 'You shouldn't have done that, you shouldn't have done this.' Another strap, another fondling. Where, where I was, we were exposed. I think I was, when I was younger, I only got five, but as I grew older I got more and more."[442]

---

[441] TRC, *Statement*, 2011-3228.
[442] TRC, *Statement*, 02-MB-18JU10-082.

Donna Antoine was exposed to ongoing harassment from a staff member at one of the Roman Catholic schools she attended in the interior of British Columbia. "He was [the] maintenance person, he would come over, and he, he would stand in my way. He did that for a while, and then he just, and other times he would tap me on the backside, and that felt very uncomfortable. And then when I was go-, when I'd go by, 'cause he'd stand right by the table and we had to squeeze by him in a little, little area, he made sure that he stood in the way, and he grabbed me by the backside. And so I told my sister about it. I was afraid to tell the Sister because she might think I was an evil person; I didn't want to displease her. So and the next time, he, he found me carrying up a load of laundry in my hands, going up the stairs, and then he took that opportunity to put his hands between my legs. And I thought why, why is that happening? What did I do to deserve to be treated like this?"[443]

Vitaline Elsie Jenner said that a bishop used to seat children on his lap when he visited the Fort Chipewyan school. "I just went and sat on his lap, but when I sat on his lap, he, he was holding me, you know, holding me around like that, and pressing me against his, his penis, and, you know, like, kind of like moving me up and down, and I could feel, like, a hardness of his penis underneath my bottom, and I didn't know what to do. I became scared."[444]

---

[443] TRC, *Statement*, 2011-3287.
[444] TRC, *Statement*, 02-MB-16JU10-131.

Louisa Papatie said that at the Amos school, the head of the school once summoned her upstairs. "'Come.' That's what she said, 'Come with me.' She gave me a, a kiss on the mouth. And at one point she started caressing my back, and I fought back, and I tried to get away, but I didn't have the strength, because I was just a child, and she was bigger than me."[445]

Ricky Kakekagumick said that one of the supervisors at the Poplar Hills, Ontario, school used to invite him into his room every weekend. "When he would start changing, taking his church clothes off, he kept his underwear on though. He would just stand there only in his underwear, every Sunday that was me in there. I didn't like being in there. I was so uncomfortable. It's a smaller room, just enough for his bed to fit and a drawer and a chair. So every Sunday I had to go in there. I felt violated, I was so uncomfortable. I didn't, like he liked me being in there, him standing there, 'cause he didn't put his pants back on right away, he just stands there, talks to me, in his underwear. He made me feel uncomfortable, 'cause usually you can see the bulginess of, of that underwear. I think he was getting his thrills like that. I don't know if he wanted, I don't know if he wanted to violate me, physically. I just kept on ignoring him, try and look away. That still bugs me this day."[446]

---

[445] TRC, *Statement*, SP101.
[446] TRC, *Statement*, 2011-4200.

Doris Judy McKay said that at the Birtle, Manitoba school, the principal would come into the girls' shower area. "And then we'd have our, we'd go and have our showers, and when we were in the shower, he'd come there, walk around, check us out, and as we try and hide ourselves we'd crouch into a corner of the shower and try and hide, and he'd be walking around there, check, just back and forth, checking us out."[447]

At the Beauval school in Saskatchewan, **Mervin Mirasty** was told to take a lunch pail to a priest's room. He had not been warned that boys who were sent on such errands were likely to be abused, as Mirasty was in this instance. When he returned, he felt that boys who knew what had happened to him were mocking him. "The boys looked at me, and some of the older ones, they were all smiling." He warned his own brother to never take the lunch pail to the priest. "And to this day, I don't know why he didn't listen to me, like, he, he went up there I guess the next day, or soon after, he come back crying."[448]

Students were particularly vulnerable when they were alone. **Flora Northwest** said that she was victimized by both staff and fellow students at the Hobbema, Alberta school. To protect herself, she

---

[447] TRC, *Statement*, 2011-2514.
[448] TRC, *Statement*, 2011-4391.

said, "I always tried to make sure that I was not alone. I'd try not to be alone."[449]

Aaron Leon said he was abused by supervisors at the Mission, British Columbia, school. The abuse generally took place on the weekends when there were fewer students and staff at the school.[450]

Certain dormitory supervisors used their authority to institute dormitory-wide systems of abuse. Arthur Plint was eventually convicted for abuses he committed while he was a dormitory supervisor at the Alberni, British Columbia school. **Richard Hall** was one of his victims. According to Hall, Plint coerced a group of older students into assisting him in imposing a regime of abuse upon the rest of the students in the dormitory. "And there's times when that, the bullies, I called them goons, I called them. They chased me, get me and bring me to that pedophile so he could molest me, have his way with me. And you would live in constant fear. You'd watch for these guys all the time. You'd be running all the time because I was in a group of boys that I was one of the smaller, a runt of the boys, I guess you would say but I was aggressive. And that's probably one of the reasons they moved me really quick because I was aggressive. I did learn to be aggressive. And times, at night, these boys under his thumb would get their ways and do things to the kids. I could hear

---

[449] TRC, *Statement*, SP124.
[450] TRC, *Statement*, 2011-3460.

the kids and those fears were also in me that you'd be urinated on and they had an ointment called Winter Green that they used to put, at night, used to reach under the blankets of the young boys and wipe it all over their genitals and it would burn. And if you added water it will burn even more, and they laughed about it. They got what they wanted. If the dorm was punished these boys got the food, they got to do what they want. And for some of the behaviours, Plint, I think also gave them alcohol. These boys would also in the night travel to other dorms. I know because they asked me to be part of it but it wasn't in my nature." The experience of abuse changed his life immediately. "I went home for the summer. I went home a different person back to Bella Coola for the summer. I was twelve years old. At twelve years old I began drinking alcohol to forget."[451]

Frances Tait was also sexually abused by staff and students at the Alberni school. In this case, several supervisors might have been involved in the abuse. "I was taken out night after night after night. And that went on until I was about twelve years old. And it was several of the male supervisors plus a female. And it was in the dorm; it was in their room; it was in the carport; it was in his car; it was in the gym; the back of the crummy that took us on road trips; the public school; the change room."[452]

---

[451] TRC, *Statement*, 2011-1852.
[452] TRC, *Statement*, 2011-3974.

Outright Abuse

Timothy Henderson, who attended school in Manitoba, said he recalled the tension he felt lying in bed. "I know nobody was sleeping, 'cause he hadn't picked anybody yet. So you'd be under your covers; I know I was. You know right under them. I could hear light footsteps."[453]

Students were particularly vulnerable to abusive staff members who sought to win their trust through what initially appeared to be simple kindness. **Marlene Kayseas** recalled that at the school she attended, the principal began focusing extra attention on her. "I don't remember if he did that to other kids, but he used to let me stay up when they used to have movies, sometimes, if the Sister was in a good mood, I guess. We watched a movie on tv and if the kids, some kids went to bed, if they didn't listen they were sent to bed." This favouritism, however, was the prelude to a sexual assault that left her scared and confused. "'Why is my friend doing this to me?' I trusted him. And I just started to feel really, not good."[454]

Fred Brass said that on one occasion at the Roman Catholic school at Kamsack, Saskatchewan, a nun, who he thought was consoling him after he had been beaten up by other students, "made me put my hands down her panties and made me feel her up and this went on for a long, long time. That was supposed to be the one that was supposed to

---

[453] TRC, *Statement*, 2011-0291.
[454] TRC, *Statement*, SP035.

comfort me and help me. But she used me in that way for her own self-gratitude."[455]

Elaine Durocher recalled that the staff at the same school took advantage of the children's simplest needs to coerce them into sexual activities. "And then after church, there was a little canteen in the church, and the priest would sell us candies. Well, after they got to know us, they started making us touch their penis for candy. So not only were we going to church to pray, and go to catechism, but we were also going to church 'cause they were giving us candy for touching them. We didn't have money."[456]

Shortly after **Ben Pratt** started attending the Gordon's, Saskatchewan school, the residence supervisor, William Starr, asked him if he wanted to work in the school canteen. He agreed, since it was a way of making some extra spending money. However, after a short time on the job, he was invited into Starr's office. "And I remember after that evening, he took me into his office, and there was about five or six of us boys in there, and he started touching us boys. Some would leave, and some would come back, some would leave and come back when we're watching tv in, in the back of his office. He had a couch in there, and a tv. And we'd all get ready to go to bed, and he made me stay back. And at that time, I didn't know what was gonna happen. I was sitting there, and I was wondering how come I

---
[455] TRC, *Statement*, SP039.
[456] TRC, *Statement*, 02-MB-16JU10-059.

had to stay back, and I was watching tv there, and then he start touching me, and between my legs, and he pulled my, my pajamas down. And the experience that I went through of him raping me, and I cried, and I yelled, but it didn't do any good, 'cause he shoved the rag in my mouth, and he was much stronger than me, he held me down, and the pain and the yelling that I was screaming why are you doing that to me, there was no one to help me. I felt helpless. And after he finished doing what he did to me, he sent me back to my room, and I was in so much pain I couldn't even hardly walk, and I could feel this warm feeling running down the back of my leg on my pajamas and on my shorts. And I went to the washroom. I tried to clean myself up. This was blood." Starr organized a variety of extracurricular clubs to justify taking students on field trips. According to Pratt: "We went all, all over, Saskatchewan, and dancing powwow, and going boxing, be different places, cadets, but it still continued to happen. As we were travelling in the vehicle, we always had big station wagons, or a van, and he fondled us boys. All of us boys knew what was happening, but none of us ever spoke about it, or shared anything what happened to us. We were too ashamed, too, too scared."[457]

Percy Isaac, who also lived in the Gordon's residence, recalled how Starr would first win the confidence of the students he intended to abuse. "Like paying us off, paying us off when we worked

---

[457] TRC, *Statement*, 2011-3318.

the canteen. Paying us off when we'd work the bingo. Paying us off to do any kind of things which he had. Like he had a boat, he had skidoos, he had all these different kind of gadgets, cars, let us drive cars when we were underage, we were driving a car." He too recalled how field trips were both rewards and opportunities for abuse. "Abused, abused in hotels, motels, all over the damn place. Toronto, Ottawa, you name it. Finland, went to Finland, got abused over there, you know. I was just constantly abused, sexually abused from this man. It was horrible."[458]

In 1993, Starr was convicted of ten counts of sexually assaulting the Gordon's residence students.

Many students thought they were the only children being abused. **Clara Quisess** said she was abused by a staff person at the Fort Albany school. "There was no support, no one to tell that this is all happening in this building. A lot of girls must have experienced it, what the priest was doing and you're not to tell anybody. I always hate that priest and then I had to live like that for two years, even though I didn't want to. It's like I had no choice, put myself in that situation. Him, putting his hand underneath my dress, feeling me up, I felt so disgusted. Even though I didn't have no words for what I was feeling."[459]

This confusion made it difficult for students to describe or report their abuse. **Lynda Pahpasay**

---

[458] TRC, *Statement*, SP035.
[459] TRC, *Statement*, 02-MB-17JU10-032.

McDonald said she was sexually molested by a staff member of the Roman Catholic school in Kenora. "And this woman, what she did to me, and how she molested me as a child, and I was wondering why I'll be the only one being taken to this room all the time, and to her bedroom and stuff like that. And I thought it was normal. I thought it was, you know, this is what happened, like, to everybody, so I never said nothing."[460]

Abusers often told their victims never to speak of what had happened. **Larry Roger Listener**, who was abused when he attended residential school in Alberta, said a priest told him that "'God's going to punish you if you say anything.' I always fear God. All these years I never said anything. I still kind of fear God because I never forgot what that priest told me. He going to punish me."[461]

Mary Vivier, who was abused at the Fort Frances school, was told she would "be in purgatory" for the rest of her life if she spoke of her abuse. The staff-member who sexually abused **Elisabeth Ashini**[462] at the Sept-Îles, Québec, school, told her she could never speak of what he had done to her. He said "'You have to keep it to yourself, because little Jesus will be angry, he won't be happy.'" As a result, she did not report the abuse.[463]

---

[460] TRC, *Statement*, 02-MB-16JU10-130.
[461] TRC, *Statement*, SP125.
[462] TRC, *Statement*, 2011-6139.
[463] TRC, *Statement*, SC110.

When he went home for the Christmas break, **Ivan George** told his father he was being abused at the Mission school. "And he'd say, 'What did he do? What he'd been doing to you?' And I told him, 'He was kind of drunk.' He says, 'No, you're going back. You're just making that up just to stay out of there.'" The following year, he ran away and refused to be sent back to the school. "I never did return ... and I was glad of it. I was put into foster homes, group homes after that. I didn't go back."

In **Ben Pratt's** case, a laundry worker at the Gordon's residence realized that something was wrong and asked him what had happened. Pratt initially resisted telling her, but then he explained how William Starr had abused him. "The look on her face she was angry, but she never said nothing." When he was an adult, Pratt told his mother about the abuse that he and other students were being subjected to at Gordon's. "And she screamed, and she started crying, and I continued telling her what was happening when I was there. And the look on her face, the anger and the rage that came out of her, she screamed and yelled, and she went quiet for a long time, and this is the first time I ever had talked to my mother. She went calm for about fifteen, twenty minutes. And she said, 'My boy,' she said, 'the school I went to, when I was a young girl,' she said, 'I, too, was sexually abused,' she said, 'by the Fathers.' And I asked her, 'What school did you go to, Mom?' She said, 'St. Philips.' I didn't know where it was. And the things she told me that happened to her as a girl, from the Fathers that run the school or

OUTRIGHT ABUSE

worked there, the anger that came up inside me was so painful. I bent over, and I couldn't sit up straight, how much anger and rage I had inside when she was telling me what happened. We talked for a good half-hour to an hour, me and my mother. Then it's the first time I ever heard my mom tell me 'I love you, my boy.'"[464]

Shortly after he was enrolled at the Sturgeon Lake school in Calais, Alberta, **Jimmy Cunningham** was sexually assaulted. When he told one of the nuns what had been done to him, he was strapped for lying. "I told the Sister what happened. She didn't believe me. She strapped me for lying. So, I went to see the priest, Father Superior ... and he says there's nothing he could do. Sent me back to the boys' hall and then the first thing you know the phone rang. The old crank phones. The Sister answered it and it was Father telling her that I had been there complaining about what happened. She immediately took me again and strapped me again for doing that without her permission."[465]

Others simply felt too ashamed to ever speak of the abuse. One of the supervisors at the Assiniboia school in Winnipeg attempted to rape **Violet Rupp Cook** in the school gymnasium. She was able to beat him back, but the event left her shaken. "I didn't know what to do. I was, I was afraid, I was just shaking, I went, I went back to the dorms. I didn't tell

---

[464] TRC, *Statement*, 2011-3472.
[465] TRC, *Statement*, SP207.

anybody I was so, I felt so ashamed. I didn't tell my supervisor, I didn't tell anyone. I didn't tell any of the girls that were there." From then on, she was always afraid and unable to concentrate on her school work.[466]

Elizabeth Good said she was abused during her years at the Alberni school. "I won't get into detail about the abuse, because it was so violent. I had three abusers, two men and one woman. I was also the youngest one in the residential school at the time." She wondered if that was one of the reasons she was targeted by one of the abusers. "There was a couple of occasions where he had mentioned that I was the baby in the residential school, and he always told me that I was gonna be a no good for nothing squaw. All I'll be good, good for is having babies, and they're gonna be worthless, and he is so wrong today."[467]

Some students ran away from school in an attempt to escape sexual abuse. **Hazel Mary Anderson** and her sister found the atmosphere so abusive at the Gordon's school that they ran away so often that they were transferred to the Lestock school.[468]

Wayne Reindeer was abused while attending the Roman Catholic hostel in Inuvik. He had been placed in residential school by his family because his

---

[466] TRC, *Statement*, 2011-2565.
[467] TRC, *Statement*, 2011-3469.
[468] TRC, *Statement*, 02-MB-18JU10-034.

Outright Abuse

mother was ill and his father could not care for all his children. He ran away from the school several times. On one occasion, he returned to the family home in Inuvik. "I hid under the house for two days and my sisters fed me, until the hostel contacted my father and he said, 'Wayne has been missing.' And my dad found out from my sisters and he dragged me back, kicking and screaming all the way. I wanted to stay home."[469]

Students also fought back. **Ken A. Littledeer** was sexually abused by Leonard Hands, a member of the staff of the Sioux Lookout school. Initially, he submitted to the abuse because he feared Hands "might get mad, and hit me, and spank me, or something like that, or punish me." But when Hands approached him a second time, Littledeer punched him and ran away.[470]

Sphenia Jones said that when a staff member attempted to abuse her one night, she fought back. "I grabbed her, and I, boom, I went like that to her, and she went flying, and then all the kids in the dormitory woke up when I started screaming. She crawled back out the door, and she didn't come back in the dormitory for, gee, for maybe a week or two after that, right, but she never bothered me again."[471]

---

[469] TRC, *Statement*, SP125
[470] TRC, *Statement*, 01-ON-24-NOV10-028.
[471] TRC, *Statement*, 2011-3300.

Many of those who fought back were overpowered. **Lawrence Waquan** said that he was sexually abused by male and female staff at a residential school in northern Alberta. He told the Commission that he eventually concluded, "Nothing you can do. You can say no, and the more you fight back, she'd slap you over and over again. Finally, you can't cry, you know, you are shaken, scared."[472]

In some cases, students fought back *en masse*. At the Edmonton, Alberta school, students deliberately barred the doors to the dormitory in order to stop the abuse during the nights. **Mel H. Buffalo** said he was one of the organizers of the protest. He told the Commission "... about how the students had backed up the, the ... dressers that were full of clothes and stuff, and put it against the entrance to the dorm, and at 4:30 in the morning the people were, I guess they were doing the checks, couldn't ... couldn't open the door. And this time they were really furious. They got the bigger boys from the other areas to come help them try to break down the door, but they couldn't. Eventually, he said, the police were called. We threw our shoes and stuff out at them, and yelled ... some guys knew how to swear, I didn't, they were swearing at everybody. We threw a list of demands down to the principal; we wrote on there that we wanted better food, we wanted certain staff people fired that we were suspicious of, and we wanted our clothes back that we came with when we, we got to school. Because

---

[472] TRC, *Statement*, SC111.

they confiscated all our clothes and gave us government-issued clothes ... we finally decided, well we better do, what needs to be done." When the protest ended, he was called into the principal's office. "I went down to see the principal, and to my surprise there was my grandfather, sitting there. And the principal said, 'Mr. Buffalo, your son is here ... we can't handle him, we'd appreciate it if you could take him back, and good luck in raising him.'"[473]

---

[473] TRC, *Statement*, SP124.

Student vs Student

The statements from former students from coast to coast indicate that other students could be just as much of a source of concern as the staff. The testimonies highlight the difficulties in getting staff to address bullying and help explain why other students did not raise the issue with staff. In the statements, it was often recalled how badly bullies contributed to the atmosphere of fear and violence that prevailed at many of the schools. Former students rarely referred to attempts to report episodes of bullying to the school administration. The statements of those who did make such reports suggest that they found it difficult to get staff to believe them or take them seriously. From robbery to rape this became yet another gigantic obstacle for a child with little to know support structure to take on. Bullying is never easy for any children to deal with, but the nature of the schools left the students especially exposed to ongoing, unfettered, abuse.

William Garson recalled that at the Elkhorn, Manitoba school, "we were always like hiding in the corners; you know away from any abusement. From other, older, from older, elder boys, students."[474]

Percy Thompson said that at the Hobbema, Alberta, school, "one bully used to come at me and he'd pretend he was going to talk to me and all of

---
[474] TRC, *Statement*, 2011-0122.

sudden hit me in the belly. And of course I gag, gag, and he'd laugh his head off and, you know, to see me in such a predicament."[475]

Alice Ruperthouse spoke of "the cruelty of the other children" at the Amos, Québec, school. "It was, you know, like in a jungle. Like in a jungle, you don't know what's going to come out but you know you had to watch out." [476]

Albert Elias felt that the classroom at the Anglican school in Aklavik "was the safest place to be in 'cause that's where nobody could beat me up. I dreaded recesses and lunches and after school, I dreaded those times."[477]

Bullying might start shortly after arrival. In some schools, all new male students were put through a hazing. **Denis Morrison** gave the following description of arrival at the Fort Frances school. "It's almost like every kid that came in, the new kid that came in, like, you almost had, that's like being a new, they call us new fish, eh, the new fish and coming into the tank. They used to initiate you, like, they would beat the hell out of you, the other kids would. It wasn't anybody else, it was the other kids, the older ones, eh. It's like they, it was like the normal thing to happen. You were the one that had to get

---

[475] TRC, *Statement*, SP125.
[476] TRC, *Statement*, SP100.
[477] TRC, *Statement*, SC092.

beat up now, eh, and so you, you went through the getting beat up."[478]

In some cases, the schools encouraged these fights. **Joseph Maud** recalled that at the school at Pine Creek, Manitoba, students were forced to fight one another. "It seems to me that there was also a lot of boxing, like, boxing matches between the boys. We had to box against another boy, and, you know, until one of us cried. So, I don't know if that's, like it just seemed like I, I picked up some of those habits from, from that supervisor. It seemed like he liked that. He got a kick out of watching another boy beat up another boy, just like that, you know that, there's a word they call that, like being kind of, like, sadistic, like enjoying pain, inflicting pain, and you know, like, you were the loser, you know, of course he would be crying. And I know I lost my, my share of, of boxing matches. And you know, like, and nobody could really help you. Like, sure, my brothers were there, and 'cause I know they were made to fight, too, other boys, so it was like a no-win situation. Even if you did win, just like, just like another boy would challenge you anyway, like, if you did win your fight, and just, like the supervisor liked that, and he enjoyed it, you know, watching boys pound each other, give each, give each other bleeding noses, or making each other cry. It almost seemed like that, that supervisor enjoyed that, and it almost seemed

---

[478] TRC, *Statement*, 02-MB-17JU10-028.

Student vs Student

like I picked up some of those habits later on in my life."[479]

Bob Baxter recalled that there were student gangs at the Sioux Lookout school. He was beaten up and knifed on one occasion. He had a vivid memory of people tying him to his bed and throwing hot water over him.[480]

Clara Quisess said that at the Fort Albany school in Ontario, older girls would threaten the younger ones with knives.[481]

Louisa Birote recalled that the girls at the La Tuque, Québec school all formed themselves into hostile groups. "We hated each other. So, this little gang didn't like the other gang. That's the way at the school, that's what we were taught, fears, and we were scared, and I went to hide in what we called the junk room, the junk closet."[482]

Such violence bred violence. **David Charleson** said that at the Christie, British Columbia school, the students were "learning how to hurt each other."[483]

Victoria McIntosh said the Fort Alexander school reminded her of a "prison yard". "If you didn't have older siblings to protect you, you're on your

---

[479] TRC, *Statement*, 02-MB-18JU10-081.
[480] TRC, *Statement*, 01-ON-24NOV10-012.
[481] TRC, *Statement*, 02-MB-17JU10-032.
[482] TRC, *Statement*, SP104.
[483] TRC, *Statement*, 2011-5043.

own, so you learned how to, to fight, anger, and not trusting anybody, and just being hard, you know, and you weren't gonna cry, and if you cried then that was not a good thing, and it was a sign of being weak. But I always felt, like, inside that I hated, I hated all of that. I never wanted to intentionally hurt anybody."[484]

To survive at schools in northern Ontario in the 1960s, one former student said she made herself "tough" and began "picking on those younger than me." She said she was "trying to look out for me since nobody else was."[485]

At school in Prince Albert, Saskatchewan, **Leona Bird** grew up fearful and angry. "They are girls from Manitoba, girls from different places. They weren't too friendly with me. I learned to fight. The hatred that built up in me, I learned to fight my way out of everything that I can, whether a beating or not, I didn't care, as long as I fought back. That's how hatred was building up so big there inside my whole body. I couldn't do nothing."[486]

Louise Large described herself as "the leader of the pack" at the Blue Quills school. "Nobody could bother the Crees, or ... they would have to deal with me. And so I ended up, I beat anybody. And it came to the point where the boys would try and, you know, even when we started playing with the boys

---

[484] TRC, *Statement*, 02-MB-16JU10-123.
[485] TRC, *Statement*, 02-MB-18JU10-062.
[486] TRC, *Statement*, 2011-4415.

Student vs Student

slowly, but even the boys would come fight with us, and I, and I would always beat them all up."[487]

Don Willie said that the Alert Bay school had a bully system. "It started out with the senior boys, and it just worked its way right down." He said he "used to get punched every day by one of them." Eventually, he fought back. "I end up fighting him back, and then he's saying, 'No, the only reason you're fighting is the girls are watching.' And so all the girls rushed to the window when we started fighting. But I said, 'Okay, well let's go upstairs and fight then.' So, we went upstairs, and he just backed right off, but he didn't bother me again after that, and I thought one of the other bullies were gonna come after me, but they didn't, so. But it was that system that, I don't know, kind of really bothered me after, and I know it bothered my brother."[488]

Janet Murray had a similar experience at the same school. "I thought here I would have an easy life but the kids picked on me and abused me. So where the little kids were between seven and five years old, that's where I was. That's where I was placed. And the supervisor was old, very old. He couldn't look after us, so he asked these two seniors to come look after us, help us out. Comb my hair and to teach us how to make our beds, I guess. And that's when the abuse started.... there were three of us, and things were always done to us. Seniors. These

---

[487] TRC, *Statement*, 01-AB-06JA11-012.
[488] TRC, *Statement*, 2011-3284.

girls—young women—were big that came there to look after us. They combed our hair. I don't know if it's a wire brush or something. They used to hit us on the head like this until we had scabs. We had to have a brush cut because we had scabs all over our heads. And when we went to school, the boys, young men laughed at us because we had bald heads. Sometimes they stabbed us in the face, and we had bruises but they say we were so clumsy they said we banged our face into the wall, that's what they said. And one time they came and woke us up in the middle of the night. They told us to take our panties off. They told us to spread our legs and they used that brush between our legs and they even put a cloth in our mouths so we couldn't yell or cry. For two weeks we couldn't go to school because we couldn't walk. There were scars all over there. Sometimes they would come to our bed and spread our legs just to see what damage they had done to us, and they'd laugh like if it's funny." When she tried to get help, she was punished again. "But that time I couldn't talk English. Even now. I was trying to speak for myself. Talking Cree I was trying to tell the supervisor. Instead I was hit for talking Cree."[489]

The most important source of protection against bullying was another family member. **Daniel Nanooch** was bullied and beaten by other students at the Wabasca, Alberta school. "Everybody was fighting me, beating me up because I was alone, I had no brothers … everybody else had their brothers with

---

[489] TRC, *Statement*, 2011-3881.

Student vs Student

them but I had nobody there to protect me. So I was fighting, I was getting beat up so when I think back as a little child in the mission, I remember all those crying for somebody to see they're getting beat up by the nuns, or by the other kids, because they knew I was there alone so they could hit me and there was nobody to protect me."[490]

When **Gordon Keewatin** attended the Portage la Prairie and Birtle schools in Manitoba, he depended on his brother to protect him from school bullies. He said that "the next thing I knew there were older boys there that used to, used to pick on the younger ones, and I was starting to get picked on. But I always ran to my brother, always looked for him, especially if somebody come and start poking me." In later years, he looked after his younger brother. He gave him the same advice his older brother had given him: "Not to ask questions, and to just go with the flow, to follow orders, do what he was told. I told him I'd protect him if he, somebody tried to fight him or whatever."[491]

Students could not always protect their siblings. In some cases, all they could do was watch them being bullied and humiliated. **Mary Rose Julian** remembered seeing her brother bullied at the Shubenacadie school. "And one time I was working in, in the refectory, I was cleaning up in there, and I saw my brother cornered. There was about four, four

---

[490] TRC, *Statement*, 2011-1868.
[491] TRC, *Statement*, 01-SK-18AU10-003.

or five boys, you know, that cornered him in there. There was the chapel and the, the refectory, and he was cornered, and I went like this, you know, I was gonna see him getting beat, he got, he was getting beaten up, and he was just cornered, and these guys were going after him. All of a sudden, I saw somebody grab those boys and throw them off one by one, and they scattered, and he went and picked up my brother, and when he turned around, I recognized him, it was Albert Marshall from Eskasoni. He was, like, friends from our same community, eh. And oh, my God, I was relieved, and I was there screaming, and I was going like this, you know, you know I was just screaming inside, I couldn't do nothing, helpless and everything. I didn't want my brother in, in that kind of situation."[492]

In some situations, students were obliged to punish their siblings. **Harvey Behn** recalled how students who ran away from the Lower Post, British Columbia, school were forced to run the 'gauntlet.' "He said that for you people that don't understand what the gauntlet is, it's a row of people standing with weapons in their hands, their fists clenched and the offending students were made to run through this group of people and get hit and get beat. And if they didn't participate, then they were forced to run through this gauntlet. So I, myself, was made to run through and was hit and beaten and my brother ran

---

[492] TRC, *Statement*, 2011-2880.

through it and I had to hit him and I had to beat him."[493]

At Stringer Hall, the Anglican residence in Inuvik, **Angus Havioyak** said he was physically abused by both fellow students and residents of Inuvik. He fought back. "At the same time, I was abused by an Indian for who I am. I'm an Inuk, and they're the Indians, and they go against me for some reason. They tease me, tease me for who I am. So, I tried my best, you know, not to be scared anymore, so I grabbed his neck. I was tired of his, his bullshit and that, and his buddy standing around us. I grabbed his neck and put him down, and I got a scar yet from that, I still have it right now."[494]

Alphonsine McNeely used to try to talk to the students from the Anglican school at Aklavik when those children went for walks near the Catholic school she attended. "The Sister used to tell me they're evil, they're no good, they're not Catholics, and they're no good. And, and then they used to get some of the girls to throw rocks or whatever at them. They taught us hate, to, to hate other religion."[495]

In some cases, students were able to overcome these barriers. **Martina Therese Fisher** went to the Assiniboia residence in Winnipeg in the 1970s. She was the only student from the Bloodvein Reserve at the school. "I was harassed by these

---

[493] TRC, *Statement*, SP021.
[494] TRC, *Statement*, 2011-0518.
[495] TRC, *Statement*, 01-NWT-JY10-002.

students from up north; they were from God's Lake. And they said, 'You're not going to, you won't be able to stay here one year.' And I said, 'Why?' And they said, 'We chased all the Saulteaux girls away before you came.' But because they said that to me I made up my mind, 'I'm going to stick it out here this year.'" She did and, eventually, she and the other girls became friends.[496]

Noel Starblanket said that at the Qu'Appelle school, he and his friends would have to "give this bully our bread, or our butter, or whatever, that, that was our payment to him for not bullying us, and, and then we'd eat whatever we had left then."[497]

Dorothy Ross said that at the Presbyterian school in Kenora in the 1960s, the older students "would take our candies, whatever you had, food, candies, chocolate bars. We weren't allowed. We had to pass them on to the bigger, the older. Or if you had money, they would take that money from you."[498]

Some bullies demanded money, rather than food. **Isaac Daniels** said that at the Prince Albert school, an older boy robbed him of money that was intended for his sick brother. "He said, 'You got any money?' I said, 'No.' 'Let me see it,' he said. 'No,' I said, 'I don't have no money.' Well, he beat the heck

---

[496] TRC, *Statement*, 2011-2564.
[497] TRC, *Statement*, 2011-3314.
[498] TRC, *Statement*, 01-ON-24NOV10-014.

out of me, threw me down right in the washroom there, took my wallet, took all my money."[499]

At the Beauval, Saskatchewan school, an older boy was assigned by the school to help **Albert Fiddler** adapt to the school. However, the boy soon insisted that Albert give him his dessert at dinner. "So, I had to go out there, and sneak, and give him my, my sweet stuff, yeah, that's how I was paying him for that. That's how they were, they were doing that, I guess. They had this little racket going on that they were, they get all the dessert from the small boys, or otherwise they will, like, it was more of a, they're gonna protect us, or whatever." In this case, bullying became increasingly sinister: eventually, the bully began to sexually abuse Fiddler. Fiddler was one of many students who were sexually abused by fellow students. Many more students reported such abuse in their statements.[500]

The assaults ranged from being forced to kiss someone, to being forced to simulate a sex act, to being raped. While, in some cases, victims were given small treats to encourage them to be silent, in other cases, they were told they would be killed if they reported the assault. **Agnes Moses** recalled being molested by older girls at a hostel in northern Canada. "I never quite understood it, and it really wrecked my life, it wrecked my life as a mother, a

---

[499] TRC, *Statement*, 2011-1779.
[500] TRC, *Statement*, 2011-1760.

wife, a woman, and sexuality was a real, it was a dirty word for us."[501]

The experience of being abused at a British Columbia school by a group of boys left **Don Willie** distrustful of most people. "The only, only friends I kept after that were my relatives."[502]

As with the case of Albert Fiddler, some new students were victimized by older students who had been assigned responsibility for initiating them into the life of the school. The younger students could also be confused or uncertain about what was being done to them. In describing the abuse she was subjected to by a fellow student, **Alphonsine McNeely** said, "I'm just a little girl. I didn't know what she was doing to me. She was touching my private parts, and used to push her hand way into me, and, and she used to tell me, 'Don't say anything.' And I don't know what is going on, I don't know, I don't, I didn't know that what she is doing is not a good thing."[503]

Wesley Keewatin said that when he attended the Qu'Appelle school, he found the routine strange at first, but soon adapted. But then older boys started coming into his bed at night. "And then they'd, they'd make me feel them and then they'd feel me, me up and then, it started, they started, oh how can I put this, is there any way to put

---

[501] TRC, *Statement*, SC090.
[502] TRC, *Statement*, 2011-3284.
[503] TRC, *Statement*, 01-NWT-JY10-002.

it? They started sexually molesting me. They were, screwing my bottom and when, when it started happening, you know like I'd, I'd, I was confused, I was confused there because, you know like I had older brothers there and I said, 'Okay, you know, I'm going to get these guys for doing that to me.' But they, they used to tell me ... 'Yeah, I know your brothers, you know, if you tell them, they'll get a licking too,' you know. You know it went on like that for a long time. And I used to tell and I used to tell the nuns that this was going on, this was happening to me. And what they'd tell me was, 'Go pray; just go pray.' And, and that, oh that, that really confused me even more you know. It's like they knew that it was going but they, like who would, who would they believe? You know, like would they believe me or, or whoever I was pointing my, my finger at? You know because these older boys, they could certainly, most certainly deny it." Keewatin told his parents of the abuse, but they continued to send him to the school. "It must have happened to them too because they'd always bring me back and, I figured, 'Okay, you know, this is normal.'"[504]

Gladys Prince recalled that her mother did not believe her when she told her of the sexual abuse of students at the Sandy Bay, Manitoba, school.

---

[504] TRC, *Statement*, 2011-3276.

Students who were seen as being different were often particularly vulnerable to bullying. [505]

Gordon James Pemmican said he was the subject of regular bullying when he was a student at the Sioux Lookout school. "So, they used to beat me up quite a bit, and they teased me because of my voice. I was born prematurely, and I sounded different. And I too, also as a result, I had, probably had bladder problems, like peeing the bed, and so I got teased for that. The kids were really mean there, and I never understood that, eh. And I got beaten up quite often, almost every day. It was hard for me to find moments, you know, where I can actually just relax and have fun with some, you know, some other, other little kids, eh. If we got too exposed, and the other kids seen me, then they came over and, you know, they would take me off and beat me up."[506]

One student was raped by three fellow students while living in Grollier Hall in the Northwest Territories in the 1970s. One of the staff members could see she was in distress. However, the student could not bring herself to tell her what had happened. "I felt so ashamed, you know, and I thought it was my fault. And then I quit school; and I went home, you know."[507]

---

[505] TRC, *Statement*, 2011-2498.
[506] TRC, *Statement*, 02-MB-18JU10-0069.
[507] TRC, *Statement*, 2011-2689.

STUDENT VS STUDENT

The younger siblings of abusive students reported that on some occasions, they were abused during the holiday period or when their sibling left school. Within a week of being placed in a Manitoba residential school, **Greg Murdock** was raped by a group of older boys. That assault represents a failure on the part of the residential school system to protect him. But the failure did not end there. Murdock told school officials about the assault the day after it occurred. "They said, 'Don't worry, Greg, we will look after it.' The next night it happened again, I got raped again. I remember getting beat, putting my hand up, 'Don't hit me, stop hitting me.' No, they did it again. The next day I went again, but this time, the second day I couldn't speak so loud, my voice was a little smaller now. 'They hurt me again,' I said. 'What did they do?' But at that time I was only seven, I didn't know what it was, so I just said, 'Well, they hurt me.' Well the next night it happened again. This time they said, 'You really going to get it if you speak, you are really going to get it.'" When school staff asked him the next day if anything had happened, he said, "No, nothing happened." His mother brought him home, where he told her: "'Don't send me back there no more.' She said, 'Greg, I have got to send you back.' I said, 'I don't want to go there, they are mean to me, Mom, don't send me back.' She sent me back. Again I was being beaten. Again I went home. This time I thought, no, I gotta do something different, I know what I'm going to do. I got up early in the morning on Sunday and I cleaned up the floors, I washed the floors, I washed the windows, I washed all of the dishes. I said, 'Mom, look what I did, I cleaned the house for you, don't send me back. If you, if you don't send me back, I will always look after the house, Mom. I will always keep it clean. They're mean to me. Don't send me there.' 'I gotta send you there my son,' she said. I said, 'No, Ma, don't, they are mean.' She sent me in the taxi and I remember I jumped out of that taxi and I ran away, I was running away down to the bush. And I could hear this man chasing me and he picked me up, put me under his arm and he carried me. I looked in the taxi and I could see my mom crying, and me too I was crying. But they took me."[508]

---

[508] TRC, *Statement*, SC111.

Warm memories

Although the overall descriptions of their residential school years were overwhelmingly negative, many students also pointed to benefits they received from their schooling, activities they enjoyed, or staff members they remembered with affection. It can't be left out that some of the students found a sense of safety and security they were unable to find in their homes, and others found the skills and the knowledge they needed to achieve success that would perhaps have been otherwise unachievable. As they say, even a stop clocked is right twice a day.

Paul Johnup said his two and a half years at the Stirland Lake, Ontario, school were both positive and negative. "I learned things there. I knew, I got to know people that are, people from other communities. I got to learn, I got to know some people from the States. That's where the staff was from, eh, mainly from the, from the States. And I learned some academic courses too, and I learned carpentry, mechanical, electrical."[509]

Monique Papatie, who attended the Amos school and went on to teach, was positive about much of her residential school experience. "I learned some fine things at the school. When I began working at the school, I was never late. It was very

---

[509] TRC, *Statement*, 02-MB-16JU10-147.

rare that I was late. This, that's what I learned in residential school and to be ready to teach. That's why this morning you see me walking with a book, I'm still that way today, I'm still an educator. That's what I learned in the residential school, and to tell the truth as well, that's what I learned."[510]

Although **Lillian Kennedy** had problems with academics in the higher grades of the Fort Alexander school, she said she enjoyed being at the residential school. "I think I learned lots from the nuns that were there. And I got along with everybody. I had lots of friends, and then I helped at the kitchen or wherever, whenever they did work, I did, I did, like housekeeping work, making bread, helping the old lady that made bread every day. And then we learned how to knit and sew embroidery. Whatever they had I enjoyed doing it. I, I helped with everything in the school."[511]

Jennie Thomas recalled a teacher at one of the schools she attended in British Columbia who encouraged her to read. "There was a whole set of those, I don't know, Spot and Jane books, and then little blue books that went up from there—read all of those books, went down to the grade-level books, read all of those; and then, there was, I think, there was a yellow colour, too. So, these are really old books, and they're school books. And I remember reading through all of those, and that's what kept me

---

[510] TRC, *Statement*, SP101.
[511] TRC, *Statement*, 2011-2563.

going. I don't know if those books are still around, but that just came back to me. And that was really ... I guess that's what kept me sane."[512]

Shirley Ida Moore had positive memories of a supervisor named Mrs. Saunders at the Norway House school. "She made these chocolate, Easter-nest type things. She took us down to the kitchen and she, we made them. That was my, my, my one food I liked."[513]

Geraldine Shingoose had positive memories of the Lestock school principal. "But one of the things I wanted to share about Father Desjarlais was that I really, I really liked him. He was, he treated us good. He was, he was the principal of the school and that, and I know that he, he meant it in his heart to take care of, of the kids, just the staff that were working there didn't."[514]

Jeanne Rioux found the Edmonton school to be a respite from an unpleasant family situation. "My mother didn't really seem to know how to show affection physically at all so there's a kind of cold atmosphere and my father was absent a lot and he was working. I mean I sort of understand that was necessary because there were so many of us and, but it was not really the most loving circumstance so anyway that's just kind of a bit of a framework. I went to ... I was sent to boarding school when I was

---

[512] TRC, *Statement*, 2011-3992.
[513] TRC, *Statement*, 2011-0089.
[514] TRC, *Statement*, 02-MB-19JU10-033.

fourteen. And that was 100 miles away from where we lived. I lived in Red Deer at the time. And I was sent to boarding school in Edmonton and for me that was a pleasure to be in boarding school. There were a lot of people in the school that were trying to run away constantly but I was happy to be there because it was less hurting and less anger and yeah."[515]

Martha Minoose had strong memories of the friendships she formed with some girls at the Roman Catholic school in Cardston. Like many others, she described her friends as her residential school 'family.' "I had three friends, they were my best friends and I was the fourth one and we hang around together. We became so close. I think we took each other as a family. We were so close so one day we said let's really try our best so we won't get punished so we can go to the show. We have to watch everything we do so we are really trying our best. Next thing we got our name again, for some little thing and we couldn't go to the show and … but we remained close and that has kept us going and in our little group we always laughed, we always shared stories, we always talk Blackfoot, that made us feel better."[516]

Alphonsine McNeely said that on the weekends, the students at the Roman Catholic school at Aklavik used to go for school picnics. "Then we'd

---

[515] TRC, *Statement*, 2011-3206.
[516] TRC, *Statement*, 2011-1748.

play outside. We go sliding. We play all kind of games on the lake, and, oh, we'll just have fun."[517]

According to **David Charleson**, the only time he had fun at the Christie school was when he was "out of the school building. When we were in the woods, we felt free, or we were down on the beach by the water, collecting food that we were used to eating."[518]

Like many other schools, the Spanish boys' school had regular movie nights. **William Antoine** said that "the best thing that we all liked was the movies. They had movies on Sunday, on Sunday night; and oh that was the one thing that we looked forward to, back then, it was the movies."[519]

At the Presbyterian school in Kenora in the 1960s, Saturday night was the highlight of the week. **Donald Copenace** recalled, "They'd bring a box of old comic books and the kids would all, we'd grab whatever comic book and read that and that was it."[520]

Even those students who were abused at school could identify certain, qualified benefits of their school experience. **Amelia Galligos-Thomas**, who was sexually assaulted at the two schools she attended in British Columbia, spoke of the trips that

---

[517] TRC, *Statement*, 01-NWT-JY10-002.
[518] TRC, *Statement*, 2011-5043.
[519] TRC, *Statement*, 2011-2002.
[520] TRC, *Statement*, 02-MB-17JU10-062.

the school organized for students. "The one thing I could say that came good out of boarding school is we got to travel. I got to learn to play different instruments. I got to meet Pierre Trudeau. The farthest I've travelled was Disneyland. I've met Bob Barker. I learned how to Scottish dance. I learned how to play "Star Wars" on an instrument."[521]

Robert Malcolm, who was sexually abused while attending the Sandy Bay school, said there were positive aspects to the residential school experience. "I guess it, it wasn't all, it wasn't all bad, like, even though I received an education, I actually did fairly well in, in my studies when I was there. Like, I'm thankful that I was able to be involved in sports, when those sports weren't part of my home environment before. I was able to play hockey, and baseball, and stuff like that, basketball."[522]

Mary Rose Julian valued what she learned at the Shubenacadie school. "I learned English. And that's why I want to make this statement, because so much negative came out of it, but I can see a lot of positives. I learned English; that was my objective for going there in the first place. My brother learned English; that was my second objective, for him to learn English. And, and then I learned more prayers. I learned Latin, and I, I learned, like, there was Sunday school every Sunday, so you learned your Bible. I know my Bible inside and out. I know my Latin. I can

---

[521] TRC, *Statement*, 2011-3975.
[522] TRC, *Statement*, 02-MB-16JU10-090.

read Latin. And, and I know, and another thing I learned was I learned how to take care of kids. I already knew how to take care of kids. I had a little bit of experience with my brothers and sisters, but over there I learned when I had a charge, I would look after my charge no problem at all. And then I learned to sew. Already I, I already knew, when I went to residential school, I already knew how to sew, and it was on those pedal machines. I could even thread the needle, I mean bobbins and stuff, and I could do all that." Julian said she never experienced physical abuse at the school. "I was there a year and a half; a nun never laid a hand on me. And lot of people that I've listened to, you know, talk about this ordeal every single night, or every single day, you know, they were being strapped, or something was happening to them. Nothing like that ever happened to me."[523]

For **Percy Tuesday**, who attended the Roman Catholic school in Kenora, the only positive memories of schooling came from when he stood up for himself. "This friend of mine and I used to play guitar a lot together. So, we used to play, jamming, you know. One day that, that boy's supervisor took my guitar away, took it from me, and I felt, I guess there was nothing I could do. So I went, I went storming up to the principal's office, and I told him, 'This guy took my guitar, I want it back now.' And I was, I was mad. I had it back within ten minutes. That's the only time that I remember standing up for

---

[523] TRC, *Statement*, 2011-2880.

myself, everything else, I did what I was told, 'cause obedience was the highest virtue, you know."[524]

---

[524] TRC, *Statement*, 02-MB-18JU10-083.

Graduation Days

Graduating from a residential school meant going home and never coming back. A day most of the students had dreamt about for up to a decade or more. While most students would leave residential school when they turned sixteen, some contrived to leave earlier, while others would be forced to stay longer at the principal's discretion.

At the end of one summer, **Roy Denny** hid in the woods so he would not be returned to school. When the Indian agent came to visit his grandmother, she told them he would rather be at home helping her. According to Roy, "They said, 'okay,' and jeez, I was real glad; real happy."[525]

Rebecca Many Grey Horses' parents successfully withdrew her from the Anglican school in Cardston after another student broke her collarbone. "I was taken to the hospital and spent a few days there, my parents came, and so, it was at that time that I asked that, you know, not to be put back in there."[526]

Many of the students in the hostels in northern Canada in the 1960s and 1970s were well over the official school-leaving age. But they had come from remote communities to finish high school

---
[525] TRC, *Statement*, 2011-2678.
[526] TRC, *Statement*, SP127.

or take vocational training. As they grew older, some found the curfews and limits on personal freedom difficult to accept. When she was in her late teens, **Lena McKay** snuck out of Breynat Hall, one of the Fort Smith residences in the Northwest Territories, to spend an evening with a friend. She was caught sneaking back in later that night. The event left her frustrated with the limits on her freedom. "I was just sick of it, so I said no, it's not for me. I can't stay. So, and I said, 'I'm not gonna sneak around, and yeah, I'm not gonna do that again.'" As a result, she left.[527]

Many students could remember their day of discharge. **Roy Johnson** was glad when the day came when he could leave the Carcross school. "And when I left, I was, you know, well, abused, psychological damage, illiterate. I was very happy the last day came along when I left Carcross. Jump on that bus, that's your angel is the bus driver, 'cause he'd be taking you home, really."[528]

William Francis Paul vividly recalled the day he was discharged from Shubenacadie. He said he was woken up in the middle of the night and informed that he was going home. He was driven to the local train station and placed on a train to his home community. While on the train, he befriended an Aboriginal woman with a son his age. Instead of continuing on to his home, he got on the train and lived with them for a while. Eventually, the Indian

---

[527] TRC, *Statement*, 2011-0382.
[528] TRC, *Statement*, 2011-0203.

agent located him and returned him to his family in Membertou, Nova Scotia.[529]

For some students, the last day of school was also the last day that the school itself was open. **Rose Marie Prosper** said she would never forget the day the students were told that the Shubenacadie school was going to be closed. One day in early 1967, her teacher, Sister Charles Marie, came into the classroom. "She went up to her, her desk there, and she just stood there, and she, she was looking at us, like we were all just talking among ourselves, and she was just standing there looking at us. And, we were like, 'Okay, she's going to flip out pretty soon. She's going to snap her yardstick on our desk and tell us to be quiet or something.' And she didn't say anything. And I was sitting at my desk, and I was looking at her. I wasn't talking because I, I get strapped for everything, so I kind of learned, not to talk. So, I was sitting there, and I was looking at her and she was standing there. She had her hands like this up to her mouth and she was looking at all of us. And, she said, 'Okay,' she said, 'I want everyone to quiet down.' So, we were sure we were all going to start our work. So she sat on her desk in the front there. She said, 'I have something to tell all of you.' And she said, 'After I tell you,' she said, 'I want you all to stay in your desks, stay in your chairs, and not to make any noise; to be very, very quiet.' So we didn't know what was going on or anything. And then she said, 'When you leave here in June, you're not coming back.' She said,

---

[529] TRC, *Statement*, 2011-2873.

'The doors are closing for good.' It was the happiest news; it was the happiest thing we ever heard. I mean, at the time you're not supposed to touch a boy or nothing, but we had boys in our classroom, and when she said that nobody was coming back in June, that you'll never see each other again; you'll never see any of the nuns again, you'll never see the school again, nothing. She goes, 'When you go home, you're staying home for good.' When she told us that, we all jumped out of our chairs, we banged our desks, our books went flying, we hugged each other, we grabbed the boys. And we were crying, we were laughing; it was the best thing we ever, ever heard."[530]

Dorene Bernard was also at the Shubenacadie school when it closed in 1967. "I remember my last day walking out of the residential school at the end of June 1967, and we were the last ones to leave because we were getting on a plane, so we had to be, we were the last ones to leave that school, me and my brother and my sisters. My mom was going to meet us at the airport in Boston. We were waiting for a drive to come take us to the airport. And it was just like an evil place, it was empty, you hear your echoes walking through and talking, like this place, you could hear your echo everywhere you went. And I could remember getting into the car, looking back, and Sister came running down the stairs, and she said, 'You forgot something. Dorene, you forgot something,' and she passed me

---

[530] TRC, *Statement*, 2011-2868.

that Bible missal. And I took it and I threw it, I threw it away and told her to keep it, 'I don't need it where I'm going.' And my sister was even scared when we were getting ready to leave. 'Don't do that. Don't say that,' she said. I said, 'What can they do to me? They're not going to do anything to us now. We're outta here.'"[531]

---

[531] TRC, *Statement*, SP029.

To conclude

For every story in this book, one thousand more are lost forever, never to be told. For over one hundred years and spanning 4 generations, stories just like these were lived out every day from coast to coast of Canada. The days of our lives that are meant to be the most carefree, stolen by institution in the name of the greater good. If hindsight is truly 20-20 it can now without a doubt be said that the residential school program was a failure. It was all for naught. In has become apparent that speaking English or French, as well as several other new skills would indeed need to be learned by the Indigenous populations to adapt to their new life alongside European settlers, but this could have been achieved without the destruction of the family structures, culture, and languages of said populations.

To this day we walk alongside the ruins of an amazing culture we can never hope to fully understand. So much has been lost over the century and a half that we can never hope to fully comprehend what came before us. Many of traditional languages are on the verge of going extinct, while still others are already gone. The real lesson of the residential school program will turn out to be how foolish and costly our hubris can be, and they will forever stand out as a blemish on the relations between the Indigenous and the Government of Canada, the Church, and the Crown. Hopefully, with enough passing of the talking stick, with enough speaking hard truths, and hearing them, it's a lesson that we will hopefully only need to learn once.

GRADUATION DAYS

Acknowledgements

This book is based on the interviews conducted by the Truth and Reconciliation Commission of Canada. It is with heartfelt appreciation and acknowledgement to both the survivors who dug into painful memories and made the effort to make sure their stories were not forgotten, and to officers tasked with tracking down, conducting, cataloging, and publishing the interviews and reports. Without the hard work and dedication of those mentioned above this book would not be possible.

Thank you again to John Edmunds for his continued efforts to inform the public and for his timeline, which I also used in my previous book. Without people like these we'll never be able to fully reconcile the mistakes of the past. John's 'Indian Residential Schools: A Chronology' has been used in several books since its original publication in 2014.

I would also like to take a moment to thank N.F. Davin and Monica Lamb-Yorski. Their work was also instrumental in the creation of this and previous projects.

Appendix

Indian Residential Schools – Chronology

1755 – Indian Department created as branch of British military to establish and maintain relations with Indians.

1820 – This decade sees Anglican and Methodist missionary schools established in Upper Canada and Red River settlement.

1842 – Governor General Sir Charles Bagot appoints Commission to report on "the Affairs of the Indians in Canada."

1844 – Bagot Commission finds reserve communities in a "half-civilized state"; recommends assimilationist policy, including establishment of boarding schools distant from child's community, to provide training in manual labour and agriculture; portends major shift away from Royal Proclamation of 1763 policy that Indians were autonomous entities under Crown protection.

1847 – Dr. Adolphus Egerton Ryerson, Methodist minister and educational reformer, commissioned by Assistant Superintendent General of Indian Affairs to study Native education, supports Bagot approach (as does Governor General Lord

Elgin); proposes model on which Indian Residential School system was built.

1856 – "Any hope of raising the Indians ... to the ... level of their white neighbours, is yet a ... distant spark": Governor General Sir Edmund Head's Commission "to Investigate Indian Affairs in Canada."

1857 – Gradual Civilization Act passed; males "sufficiently advanced in the elementary branches of education" could be enfranchised (they would no longer be "Indians," and could vote).

1861 – St. Mary's Mission Indian Residential School, Mission, and Presbyterian Coqualeetza Indian Residential School, Chilliwack, first residential schools in B.C., established.

1862 – What became Blue Quills Indian Residential School (Hospice of St. Joseph / Lac la Biche Boarding School) established at Lac la Biche, later Saddle Lake, then St. Paul, AB; first residential school on the Prairies.

1867 – Confederation: British North America Act (now Constitution Act, 1867) establishes federal jurisdiction over Indians. Thus, while education is under provincial jurisdiction, Indian matters including education are federal. Fort Providence and Fort Resolution Indian Residential Schools established; first residential schools north of 60º.

Appendix

1871 – Treaty No. 1 entered into at Lower Fort Garry: "Her Majesty agrees to maintain a school on each reserve ... whenever the Indians of the reserve should desire it." This promise, repeated in subsequent treaties (though hedged in Treaties No. 5 on), reflected desire of Indian leadership to ensure transition of their youth to demands of anticipated newcomer society.

1876 – Indian Act passed into law by Parliament.

1879 – Nicholas Flood Davin, journalist and defeated Tory candidate, commissioned by Prime Minister Macdonald, also Minister of the Interior, to produce proposal for Indian education; visits US industrial schools grounded in policy of "aggressive civilization"; produces Report on Industrial Schools for Indians and Half-Breeds. Four residential schools already operated in Ontario; "mission schools" planned for the west. This date generally taken to mark beginning of Indian Residential Schools, though the system had early predecessors in New France and New Brunswick, and several schools were already operating. Duncan Campbell Scott, best known later as a "Confederation poet," joins Indian Affairs at age 17 as "copying clerk," at direction of Macdonald.

1883 – First industrial school established, at Battleford, modelled on Davin Report.

APPENDIX

1885 – Residential schools necessary to remove children from influence of the home only way "of advancing the Indian in civilization": Lawrence Vankoughnet, Deputy Superintendent General, to Prime Minister Macdonald. Despite treaty promises, reserves lacked schools; removal, often forcible, of pupils to residential schools is option chosen by government.

1890 – Physician Dr. G. Orton reports to Indian Affairs that tuberculosis in the schools could be reduced by half; measures rejected as "too costly."

1892 – Regulations passed giving control over daily school administration to churches: Catholic, Anglican, Presbyterian, Methodist. (In 1925, Methodists joined most Presbyterians and others to form United Church, which continued to run schools.)

1896 – Programme of Studies issued; stresses importance of replacing "native tongue" with English. Children forbidden to speak their native language, even to each other, and punished for doing so. This continued to be the policy for life of the system.

1904 – Dr. Peter Bryce appointed "Medical Inspector" to the Departments of the Interior and Indian Affairs.

1904 – Minister Sir Clifford Sifton announces

closure of industrial schools – large urban institutions – in favour of boarding schools. They are closed over the next two decades.

1907 – Dr. Bryce visits 35 schools; reports appallingly unsanitary conditions, micro-organism-bearing ventilation, high death rates; "the almost invariable cause" is tuberculosis.

"The appalling number of deaths among the younger children ... brings the Department within unpleasant nearness to the charge of manslaughter": Hon. S.H. Blake, K.C., Chair of Advisory Board on Indian Education (partner in what is now national law firm Blake, Cassels & Graydon), to Minister Frank Oliver.

1908 – Indian Affairs Accountant F.H. Paget reports school buildings in bad condition.

1909 – Duncan Campbell Scott appointed Superintendent of Indian Education.

1910 – "I can safely say that barely half of the children in our Indian schools survive to take advantage of the education we are offering them": Scott to Major D.M. McKay, Indian Affairs Agent General in B.C.

The children "catch the disease ... in a building ... burdened with Tuberculosis Bacilli": Duck Lake Indian Agent MacArthur on the continuing prevalence of tuberculosis.

APPENDIX

1912 – "... in the early days of school administration ... [t]he well-known predisposition of Indians to tuberculosis resulted in a very large percentage of deaths among the pupils ... fifty percent of the children who passed through these schools did not live to benefit from the education which they had received therein": Scott, in an essay in the authoritative 22-volume Canada and its Provinces.

1913 – Scott appointed Deputy Superintendent General of Indian Affairs (deputy minister), reporting to Minister of the Interior and Superintendent General Dr. William A. Roche.

1919 – Position of Medical Inspector for Indian Agencies and Residential Schools abolished (in the year of the Spanish flu) by order in council on recommendation of Scott "for reasons of economy."

1920 – "I want to get rid of the Indian problem": D.C. Scott to Parliamentary Committee. A Scott-instigated amendment to the Indian Act, with church concurrence, compelled school attendance of all children aged seven to fifteen. Though no particular kind of school was stipulated, Scott favoured residential schooling to eliminate the influences of home and reserve and hasten assimilation.

"I am afraid I cannot give a very encouraging answer to the question. We are not convinced that it is increasing, but it is not decreasing": Prime Minister Arthur Meighen, former Minister of the Interior, on being asked whether tuberculosis was increasing or decreasing amongst the Indians.

1922 – Dr. Bryce publishes The Story of a National Crime: Being an Appeal for Justice to the Indians of Canada, the Wards of the Nation, Our Allies in the Revolutionary War, Our Brothers-in-Arms in the Great War. He charges that, for 1894-1908, within five years of entry 30% to 60% of students had died, an avoidable mortality rate had healthy children not been exposed to children with tuberculosis: A "trail of disease and death has gone on almost unchecked by any serious efforts on the part of the Department of Indian Affairs." His 1907 recommendations on tuberculosis control not given effect, he says, "owing to the active opposition of Mr. D.C. Scott."

1923 – "Residential Schools" adopted as official term, replacing "boarding" and "industrial," housing 5,347 children.

1932 – Scott retires as Deputy Superintendent General after more than 52 years in the department. The anthologist John Garvin writes that Scott's "policy of assimilating the Indians had been so much in keeping with the thinking of the time that he was widely praised for his capable administration." He embodied a fundamental contradiction: While a rigid and often heartless bureaucrat, "his sensibilities as a poet [were] saddened by the waning of an ancient culture" (Canadian Encyclopedia).

Appendix

1939 – 9,027 children are in 79 residential schools run by Catholic (60%), Anglican (25%), United and Presbyterian churches. "1939 [was] the approximate mid-point of the history of the system": John S. Milloy, A National Crime.

1944 – Consensus develops among senior Indian Affairs officials that integration into provincial systems should replace segregated Aboriginal education.

1951 – Indian Act of 1876, with many amendments, repealed; replaced with modernized Indian Act (today's Act, with amendments) conceptually similar to previous Act.

1955 – Jean Lesage, Minister of Northern Affairs and National Resources, department responsible for Inuit (then known as Eskimos), gets Cabinet approval for broad education policy in the North. General policy is to substitute settlements for nomadic life. A school is built at Chesterfield Inlet, followed by Coppermine, and ten "hostels." Some Inuit had formerly been sent south to Indian Affairs schools. "Destitute" Métis were sometimes also enrolled.

1969 – Indian Affairs takes over sole management of residential schools from churches.

1969 – Indian Affairs Minister Jean Chretien produces assimilationist "White Paper" to abolish

Appendix

Indian status; strongly opposed by Indian organizations. Alberta Indian Association produces Citizens Plus, known as "Red Paper," in response. White Paper retracted two years later.

1971 – Blue Quills School, St. Paul, AB, becomes first Indian-run school, following month-long contentious occupation by elders and others.

1972 – National Indian Brotherhood (predecessor of Assembly of First Nations) produces Indian Control of Indian Education, advocating greater band control of education on reserves; adopted next year by government.

1975 – Six residential schools close this year; 15 remain.

1976 – NIB proposes amendments to Indian Act to provide legal basis for Indian control of education; rejected by government.

1978 – National Film Board produces first film ever on residential schools: Wandering Spirit Survival School, about a non-traditional school organized by parents who had themselves survived residential schools.

1984 – 187 bands are operating own (day) schools, half in B.C.; the rest mainly on Prairies.

1993 – Archbishop Michael Peers, Primate of Anglican Church of Canada, apologizes to survivors of Indian residential schools on behalf of the Church.

1996 – Gordon Indian Residential School, Punnichy, Saskatchewan, closes; last of 139 Indian Residential Schools in Canada. The Report of the Royal Commission on Aboriginal Peoples recommends public investigation into violence and abuses at residential schools. Report brings these issues to national attention.

1998 – Minister of Indian Affairs Jane Stewart responds with "Statement of Reconciliation," acknowledging government's role, stating "sexual and physical abuse ... should never have happened. To those of you who suffered this tragedy at residential schools, we are deeply sorry." Established Aboriginal Healing Foundation to assist Aboriginal communities to build healing processes, with $350 million endowment. Express apology had to wait until 2008.

2001 – Federal Office of Indian Residential Schools Resolution Canada created to manage and resolve large number of abuse claims filed by former students, resulting in 17 court judgments.

2003 – National Resolution Framework launched, including Alternative Dispute Resolution process, an out of court process providing compensation and psychological support for former students who were physically or sexually abused or had been wrongfully confined.

2004 – Assembly of First Nations (AFN) Report on Canada's Dispute Resolution Plan to compensate for Abuses in Indian Residential Schools leads to resolution discussions. RCMP Commissioner Giuliano Zaccardelli expresses sorrow for the force's role in the residential school system.

2005 – $1.9 billion compensation package announced to benefit former residential school students.

2007 – Indian Residential Schools Settlement Agreement, largest class action settlement in Canadian history, negotiated and approved by parties, and Courts in nine jurisdictions, implemented. Of the 139 schools ultimately included in the settlement, 64 were Roman Catholic, 35 Anglican, 14 United Church, and the balance other or no denomination. The objective was reconciliation with the estimated 80,000 former students then still living, of over 150,000 enrolled since 1879.

Elements are,
•Common Experience Payment to be paid to all eligible former students who resided at a recognized Indian Residential School;
•Independent Assessment Process for claims of sexual or serious physical abuse;
•Establishment of a Truth and Reconciliation Commission;

- Commemoration Activities;
- Measures to support healing such as the Indian Residential Schools Resolution Health Support Program and an endowment to the Aboriginal Healing Foundation.

Survivors report harsh and cruel punishments, suicides of others, physical, psychological and sexual abuse, poor quality and meagre rations and shabby clothing in the schools, and inability on leaving to belong in either the Aboriginal or larger world. Posttraumatic stress disorder, major depression, anxiety disorder and borderline personality disorder have been diagnosed, and many have criminal records.

2008 – Prime Minister Harper offers formal apology in Parliament for the Indian Residential Schools, in presence of Aboriginal delegates and church leaders. Indian Residential Schools Truth and Reconciliation Commission (TRC) established June 1, with five-year mandate, later extended to 2015.

2009 – AFN Chief Phil Fontaine meets Pope Benedict XVI at Vatican. Pope Benedict expresses "sorrow" and "sympathy and prayerful solidarity," but avoids apologizing.

After a rocky start, with resignations of original Commissioners, Truth and Reconciliation Commission begins work under Justice Murray Sinclair, an Aboriginal Manitoba judge who became the province's Associate Chief Justice in 1988.

APPENDIX

2010 – Truth and Reconciliation Commission begins hearings in Winnipeg.

2011 – University of Manitoba president David Barnard apologizes to Truth and Reconciliation Commission of Canada for institution's role in educating people who operated the residential school system.

2012 – Truth and Reconciliation Commission releases Interim Report. Reviews progress, explains statement gathering and document collection process. Tells of degrading treatment, unwarranted punishments, and physical and sexual abuse by "loveless institutions." Makes numerous recommendations respecting public education about residential schools and about mental health and wellness programs, especially in the North, and that Canada and churches establish a cultural revival fund. Notes mandate to establish a National Research Centre.

Over 105,000 applications for Common Experience Payments were received by Canada by the September 19, 2012 deadline; over 79,000 were found eligible and paid, the average amount being $19,412.

2014 – Commission hearings in more than 300 communities wrap up. "National Events," in Winnipeg, Inuvik, Halifax, Saskatoon, Montreal, and Vancouver were held, as required by the Settlement

Agreement, the final one taking place March 27-30 in Edmonton.

2015 – Final year for the Truth and Reconciliation Commission; related events occur:

August 16: Dr. Peter Bryce (1853-1932), author of The Story of a National Crime, is honoured by the unveiling of a plaque in his honour at Ottawa's Beechwood Cemetery, the National Cemetery of Canada.

November 1: The plaque at Beechwood Cemetery honouring Scott as a poet modified to include mention of his role in residential schools.

December 15: The massive final six-volume, 3,231-page TRC report is released. The TRC also produced a summary and five other companion volumes, 2012-15.

December 18: The Truth and Reconciliation Commission closes its doors. As required by the Settlement Agreement, the National Centre for Truth and Reconciliation opens, with a mandate to hold and make accessible all of the materials gathered by the Commission throughout its mandate. It is located at 177 Dysart Road on the University of Manitoba Fort Garry Campus in south Winnipeg: nctr.ca.

The Report looks to the future: "Reconciliation is not about 'closing a sad chapter in Canada's past,' but about opening new healing pathways of reconciliation that are forged in truth and justice."

Assimilation policy was cultural genocide, "the destruction of those structures and practices that allow [a targeted] group to continue as a group."

APPENDIX

At the heart of the Report are 94 "Calls to Action," under two main headings, "Legacy" and "Reconciliation." Governments, educational, professional and sports bodies, media, churches (including the Pope), the arts, and the corporate sector are called to action. "Legacy" calls are to "redress the legacy of residential schools" in the areas of child welfare, education, language and culture, health, and justice. Under "Justice," an "Investigation into missing and murdered Aboriginal women and girls" is called for, and is underway. "Reconciliation" calls are more general, the most numerous calling for "full" adoption and implementation of the United Nations Declaration of the Rights of Indigenous Peoples "as the framework for reconciliation," and related matters. This is controversial, and the federal government is equivocal. Other calls are for a "Covenant of Reconciliation," a National Council for Reconciliation, church apologies, and a National Day for Truth and Reconciliation as a statutory holiday. Many non-governmental entities, including law societies, have acted in response to the Report.

2016 – The Supreme Court of Newfoundland and Labrador approves a $50 million settlement of five class action lawsuits on behalf of indigenous former students from Labrador who attended one of the residential schools at Cartwright (Lockwood), North West River (Yale), Makkovik and Nain (in Labrador) and St. Anthony (on the island of Newfoundland). The schools were established by the International Grenfell Association or by the Moravian

Mission well before 1949 when Newfoundland joined Canada, but subsequently received government support until the last one closed in 1980.

2017 – Prime Minister Trudeau apologizes, at Happy Valley-Goose Bay, NL, to the indigenous former students who attended residential schools in Newfoundland and Labrador, and to their "families, loved ones and communities impacted by these schools for the painful and sometimes tragic legacy these schools left behind." Residential school students were not included in Prime Minister Harper's 2008 apology, having been excluded from the 2007 Indian Residential Schools Settlement Agreement in the province.

Bibliography

Canada. Truth and Reconciliation Commission of Canada. *The Survivors Speak: A Report of the Truth and Reconciliation Commission of Canada*. Ottawa, 2015. Available at www.trc.ca

Davin, N. F. *Report on Industrial Schools for Indians and Half-Breeds*. Ottawa, 14 March 1879. https://www.canadiana.ca/view/oocihm.03651/3?r=0&s=1

Edmond, John. "Indian Residential Schools: A Chronology." LawNow, July 7, 2014. https://www.lawnow.org/indian-residential-schools-chronology/

Lamb-Yorski, Monica. "Orange Shirt Day Makes its Debut in Williams Lake Sept. 30." Williams Lake Tribune, 19 September 2013. http://www.wltribune.com/news/224499761.html.

Prime Minister Stephen Harper. *Statement of Apology – to former students of Indian Residential Schools.* 11 June 2008. https://www.rcaanc-cirnac.gc.ca/eng/1100100015644/1571589171655

TRC. AVS.[532] *Statement to the Truth and Reconciliation Commission of Canada,* Alfred Nolie. (Statement Number: 2011-3293). Alert Bay, British Columbia. 20 October 2011.

TRC. AVS. *Statement to the Truth and Reconciliation Commission of Canada,* [Name redacted]. (Statement Number: 02-MB-18JU10-055). Winnipeg, Manitoba, 18 June 2010.

---

[532] Audio/Video Statement (AVS) Database: The Audio/Video Statement database contains video and audio statements provided to the TRC at community hearings and regional and national events held by the TRC, as well as at other special events attended by the TRC.

BIBLIOGRAPHY

TRC. AVS. *Statement to the Truth and Reconciliation Commission of Canada,* [Name redacted]. (Statement Number: SP039). Key First Nation, Saskatchewan, 21 January 2012.

TRC. AVS. *Statement to the Truth and Reconciliation Commission of Canada,* [Name redacted]. (Statement Number: 2011-2681.). Eskasoni First Nation, Nova Scotia, 14 October 2011.

TRC. AVS. *Statement to the Truth and Reconciliation Commission of Canada,* [Name redacted]. (Statement Number: 2011-3879). Prince Albert, Saskatchewan, 1 February 2012. (Translated from Woodland Cree to English by Translation Bureau, Public Works and Government Services Canada).

TRC. AVS. *Statement to the Truth and Reconciliation Commission of Canada,* [Name redacted]. (Statement Number: SP039). Key First Nation, Saskatchewan, 21 January 2012.

TRC. AVS. *Statement to the Truth and Reconciliation Commission of Canada,* [Name redacted]. (Statement Number: 02-MB-18JU10-062). Winnipeg, Manitoba, 18 June 2010.

TRC. AVS. *Statement to the Truth and Reconciliation Commission of Canada,* [Name redacted]. (Statement Number: 2011-2012). Little Current, Ontario, 13 May 2011.

TRC. AVS. *Statement to the Truth and Reconciliation Commission of Canada,* [Name redacted]. (Statement Number: 2011-2689). 23 Fort Simpson, Northwest Territories, November 2011.

TRC. AVS. *Statement to the Truth and Reconciliation Commission of Canada.* [Name redacted]. (Statement Number: 2011-2689). Fort Simpson, Northwest Territories, 23 November 2011.

TRC. AVS. *Statement to the Truth and Reconciliation Commission of Canada,* [Name redacted]. (Statement Number: 2011-3279). Gambier Island, British Columbia, 29 July 2011.

TRC. AVS. *Statement to the Truth and Reconciliation Commission of Canada,* [Named redacted]. (Statement Number: SP039). Key First Nation, Saskatchewan, 21 January 2012.

BIBLIOGRAPHY

TRC. AVS. *Statement to the Truth and Reconciliation Commission of Canada, Aaron* Leon. (Statement Number: 2011-3460). Mission, British Columbia, 19 May 2011.

TRC. AVS. *Statement to the Truth and Reconciliation Commission of Canada, Adam* Highway. (Statement Number: 2011-1781). Pelican Narrows, Saskatchewan, 14 February 2012. (Translated from Woodland Cree to English by Translation Bureau, Public Works and Government Services Canada.)

TRC. AVS. *Statement to the Truth and Reconciliation Commission of Canada, Agnes* Moses. (Statement Number: SC090). Inuvik, Northwest Territories, 29 June 2011.

TRC. AVS. *Statement to the Truth and Reconciliation Commission of Canada, Alan* Knockwood. (Statement Number: SP029). Indian Brook, Nova Scotia, 12 October 2011.

TRC. AVS. *Statement to the Truth and Reconciliation Commission of Canada, Albert* Elias. (Statement Number: SC092). Inuvik, Northwest Territories, 1 July 2011.

TRC. AVS. *Statement to the Truth and Reconciliation Commission of Canada,* Albert Fiddler. (Statement Number: 2011-1760). Saskatoon, Saskatchewan, 24 June 2012.

TRC. AVS. *Statement to the Truth and Reconciliation Commission of Canada,* Albert Marshall. (Statement Number: 02-MB-17JU10-050). Winnipeg, Manitoba, 17 June 2010.

TRC. AVS. *Statement to the Truth and Reconciliation Commission of Canada,* Alex Alikashuak. (Statement Number: 02-MB-16JU10-137). Winnipeg, Manitoba, 16 June 2010.

TRC. AVS. *Statement to the Truth and Reconciliation Commission of Canada,* Alice Quinney. (Statement Number: 02-MB-18JU10-049). Winnipeg, Manitoba, 18 June 2010.

TRC. AVS. *Statement to the Truth and Reconciliation Commission of Canada,* Alice Ruperthouse. (Statement Number: SP100). Val d'Or, Québec, 5 February 2012.

Bibliography

TRC. AVS. *Statement to the Truth and Reconciliation Commission of Canada,* Allen Kagak. (Statement Number: SC090). Inuvik, Northwest Territories, 29 June 2011.

TRC. AVS. *Statement to the Truth and Reconciliation Commission of Canada,* Alma Scott. (Statement Number: 02-MB-16JU10-016). Winnipeg, Manitoba, 17 June 2010.

TRC. AVS. *Statement to the Truth and Reconciliation Commission of Canada,* Alphonsine McNeely. (Statement Number:01-NWT-JY10-002). Fort Good Hope, Northwest Territories, 13 July 2010.

TRC. AVS. *Statement to the Truth and Reconciliation Commission of Canada,* Amelia Galligos-Thomas. (Statement Number: 2011-3975). Victoria, British Columbia, 13 April 2012.

TRC. AVS. *Statement to the Truth and Reconciliation Commission of Canada,* Andrew Bull Calf. (Statement Number: 2011-0273). Lethbridge, Alberta, 10 October 2013.

TRC. AVS. *Statement to the Truth and Reconciliation Commission of Canada,* Andrew Paul. (Statement Number: SP067). Paulatuk, Northwest Territories, 17 April 2012.

TRC. AVS. *Statement to the Truth and Reconciliation Commission of Canada,* Andrew Speck. (Statement Number: 2011-3988). Victoria, British Columbia, 14 April 2012.

TRC. AVS. *Statement to the Truth and Reconciliation Commission of Canada,* Andy Norwegian. (Statement Number: SP033). Fort Simpson, Northwest Territories, 23 November 2011.

TRC. AVS. *Statement to the Truth and Reconciliation Commission of Canada,* Angus Havioyak. (Statement Number: 2011-0518). Kugluktuk, Nunavut, 13 April 2011.

TRC. AVS. *Statement to the Truth and Reconciliation Commission of Canada,* Anthony Henry. (Statement Number: 02-MB-17JU10-086). Winnipeg, Manitoba, 17 June 2010.

BIBLIOGRAPHY

TRC. AVS. *Statement to the Truth and Reconciliation Commission of Canada,* Antonette White. (Statement Number: 2011-3984). Victoria, British Columbia, 13 April 2012.

TRC. AVS. *Statement to the Truth and Reconciliation Commission of Canada,* Archie Hyacinthe. (Statement Number: 2011-0279). Kenora, Ontario, 15 March 2011.

TRC. AVS. *Statement to the Truth and Reconciliation Commission of Canada,* Arthur Ron McKay. (Statement Number: 02-MB-18JU10-044). Winnipeg, Manitoba, 18 June 2010.

TRC. AVS. *Statement to the Truth and Reconciliation Commission of Canada,* Ben Sylliboy. (Statement Number: SP030). Eskasoni First Nation, Nova Scotia, 14 October 2011.

TRC. AVS. *Statement to the Truth and Reconciliation Commission of Canada,* Benjamin Joseph Lafford. (Statement Number: SC075). Halifax, Nova Scotia, 28 October 2011.

TRC. AVS. *Statement to the Truth and Reconciliation Commission of Canada,* Bernadette Nadjiwan. (Statement Number: 2011-5029). Spanish, Ontario, 12 September 2009.

TRC. AVS. *Statement to the Truth and Reconciliation Commission of Canada,* Bernard Catcheway. (Statement Number: 2011-2510). Skownan First Nation, Manitoba, 12 October 2011.

TRC. AVS. *Statement to the Truth and Reconciliation Commission of Canada,* Bernard Sutherland. (Statement Number: 2011-3180). Fort Albany, Ontario, 29 January 2013. (Translated from Cree to English by Translation Bureau, Public Works and Government Services Canada).

TRC. AVS. *Statement to the Truth and Reconciliation Commission of Canada,* Bernice Jacks. (Statement Number: 2011-3971). Victoria, British Columbia, 13 April 2012.

TRC. AVS. *Statement to the Truth and Reconciliation Commission of Canada,* Betsy Annahatak. (Statement Number: 2011-2896). Halifax, Nova Scotia, 28 October 2011.

BIBLIOGRAPHY

TRC. AVS. *Statement to the Truth and Reconciliation Commission of Canada,* Betsy Olson. (Statement Number: 2011-4378). Saskatoon, Saskatchewan, 21 June 2012.

TRC. AVS. *Statement to the Truth and Reconciliation Commission of Canada,* Betty Smith-Titus. (Statement Number: 2011-1132). Whitehorse, Yukon, 27 May 2011.

TRC. AVS. *Statement to the Truth and Reconciliation Commission of Canada,* Beverley Anne Machelle. (Statement Number: 2011-1133). Whitehorse, Yukon, 27 May 2011.

TRC. AVS. *Statement to the Truth and Reconciliation Commission of Canada,* Bob Baxter. (Statement Number: 01-ON-24NOV10-012). Thunder Bay, Ontario, 24 November 2010.

TRC. AVS. *Statement to the Truth and Reconciliation Commission of Canada,* Bruce R. Dumont. (Statement Number: 01-SK-18-25JY10-013). Batoche, Saskatchewan, 23 July 2010.

TRC. AVS. *Statement to the Truth and Reconciliation Commission of Canada,* Calvin Myerion. (Statement Number: 02-MB-16JU10-122). Winnipeg, Manitoba, 16 June 2010.

TRC. AVS. *Statement to the Truth and Reconciliation Commission of Canada,* Campbell Papequash. (Statement Number: SP038). Key First Nation, Saskatchewan, 20 January 2012.

TRC. AVS. *Statement to the Truth and Reconciliation Commission of Canada,* Carmen Petiquay. (Statement Number: SP104). LaTuque, Québec, 5 March 2013.

TRC. AVS. *Statement to the Truth and Reconciliation Commission of Canada,* Cecilia Whitefield-Big George. (Statement Number: 02-MB-17JU10-030). Winnipeg, Manitoba, 17 June 2010.

TRC. AVS. *Statement to the Truth and Reconciliation Commission of Canada,* Chris Frenchman. (Statement Number: SP124). Hobbema, Alberta, 24 July 2013.

Bibliography

TRC. AVS. *Statement to the Truth and Reconciliation Commission of Canada,* Clara Quisess. (Statement Number: 02-MB-17JU10-032). Winnipeg, Manitoba, 17 June 2010.

TRC. AVS. *Statement to the Truth and Reconciliation Commission of Canada,* Connie McNab. (Statement Number: 2011-2715). Fort Simpson, Northwest Territories, 23 November 2011.

TRC. AVS. *Statement to the Truth and Reconciliation Commission of Canada,* Daniel Andre. (Statement Number: 2011-0202). Whitehorse, Yukon, 23 May 2011.

TRC. AVS. *Statement to the Truth and Reconciliation Commission of Canada,* Daniel Nanooch. (Statement Number: 2011-1868). High Level, Alberta, 4 July 2013.

TRC. AVS. *Statement to the Truth and Reconciliation Commission of Canada,* Darlene Thomas. (Statement Number: 2011-3200). Vancouver, British Columbia, 19 September 2013.

TRC. AVS. *Statement to the Truth and Reconciliation Commission of Canada,* Darlene Wilson. (Statement Number: 2011-4065). Port Alberni, British Columbia, 13 March 2012.

TRC. AVS. *Statement to the Truth and Reconciliation Commission of Canada,* Darryl Siah. (Statement Number: 2011-3473). St. Mary's Mission, British Columbia, 18 May 2011.

TRC. AVS. *Statement to the Truth and Reconciliation Commission of Canada,* David Charleson. (Statement Number: 2011-5043). Deroche, British Columbia, 20 January 2010.

TRC. AVS. *Statement to the Truth and Reconciliation Commission of Canada,* David Nevin. (Statement Number: SP029). Indian Brook, Nova Scotia, 12 October 2011.

TRC. AVS. *Statement to the Truth and Reconciliation Commission of Canada,* Delores Adolph. (Statement Number: 2011-3458). Mission, British Columbia, 19 May 2011.

BIBLIOGRAPHY

TRC. AVS. *Statement to the Truth and Reconciliation Commission of Canada,* Denis Morrison. (Statement Number: 02-MB-17JU10-028). Winnipeg, Manitoba, 17 June 2010.

TRC. AVS. *Statement to the Truth and Reconciliation Commission of Canada,* Diana Lariviere. (Statement Number: 2011-2011). Little Current, Ontario, 13 May 2011.

TRC. AVS. *Statement to the Truth and Reconciliation Commission of Canada,* Diane Bossum. (Statement Number: 2011-5079). La Tuque, Québec, 5 March 2013.

TRC. AVS. *Statement to the Truth and Reconciliation Commission of Canada,* Don Willie. (Statement Number: 2011-3284). Alert Bay, British Columbia, 3 August 2011.

TRC. AVS. *Statement to the Truth and Reconciliation Commission of Canada,* Donald Copenace. (Statement Number: 02-MB-17JU10-062). Winnipeg, Manitoba, 17 June 2010.

TRC. AVS. *Statement to the Truth and Reconciliation Commission of Canada,* Donna Antoine. (Statement Number: 2011-3287). Enderby, British Columbia, 13 October 2011.

TRC. AVS. *Statement to the Truth and Reconciliation Commission of Canada,* Dorene Bernard. (Statement Number: SP029.) Indian Brook, Nova Scotia, 12 October 2011.

TRC. AVS. *Statement to the Truth and Reconciliation Commission of Canada,* Doris Judy McKay. (Statement Number: 2011-2514). Rolling River First Nation, Manitoba, 23 November 2011.

TRC. AVS. *Statement to the Truth and Reconciliation Commission of Canada,* Doris Young. (Statement Number: 2011-3517). Saskatoon, Saskatchewan, 22 June 2012.

TRC. AVS. *Statement to the Truth and Reconciliation Commission of Canada,* Dorothy Jane Beaulieu. (Statement Number: 2011-0379). Fort Resolution, Northwest Territories, 28 April 2011.

BIBLIOGRAPHY

TRC. AVS. *Statement to the Truth and Reconciliation Commission of Canada*, Dorothy Nolie. (Statement Number: 2011-3294). Alert Bay, British Columbia, 20 October 2011.

TRC. AVS. *Statement to the Truth and Reconciliation Commission of Canada*, Dorothy Ross (Statement Number: 01-ON-24NOV10-014). Thunder Bay, Ontario, 25 November 2010.

TRC. AVS. *Statement to the Truth and Reconciliation Commission of Canada*, Earl Clarke. (Statement Number: 01-SK-JU10-002). Poundmaker First Nation, Saskatchewan, 30 June 2010.

TRC. AVS. *Statement to the Truth and Reconciliation Commission of Canada*, Edmund Metatawabin. (Statement Number: SP098). Fort Albany, Ontario, 28 January 2013.

TRC. AVS. *Statement to the Truth and Reconciliation Commission of Canada*, Elaine Durocher. (Statement Number: 02-MB-16JU10-059). Winnipeg, Manitoba, 16 June 2010.

TRC. AVS. *Statement to the Truth and Reconciliation Commission of Canada*, Eli Carpenter. (Statement Number: 02-MB-17JU10-018). Winnipeg, Manitoba, 17 June 2010.

TRC. AVS. *Statement to the Truth and Reconciliation Commission of Canada*, Elizabeth Good. (Statement Number: 2011-3469). Mission, British Columbia, 18 May 2011.

TRC. AVS. *Statement to the Truth and Reconciliation Commission of Canada*, Elizabeth Joyce Brass. (Statement Number: 02-MB-19JU10-005). Winnipeg, Manitoba, 19 June 2010.

TRC. AVS. *Statement to the Truth and Reconciliation Commission of Canada*, Elizabeth Papatie. (Statement Number: SP101). Val d'Or, Québec, 6 February 2012.

TRC. AVS. *Statement to the Truth and Reconciliation Commission of Canada*, Elizabeth Tapiatic Chiskamish. (Statement Number: 2011-3363). Chisasibi, Québec, 20 March 2013. (Translated from Cree to English by Translation Bureau, Public Works and Government Services Canada.)

BIBLIOGRAPHY

TRC. AVS. *Statement to the Truth and Reconciliation Commission of Canada*, Ellen Smith. (Statement Number: 2011-0346). Fort McPherson, Northwest Territories, 14 September 2011.

TRC. AVS. *Statement to the Truth and Reconciliation Commission of Canada*, Emily Kematch. (Statement Number: 02-MB-18JU10-063). Winnipeg, Manitoba, 18 June 2010.

TRC. AVS. *Statement to the Truth and Reconciliation Commission of Canada*, Ernest Barkman. (Statement Number: 2011-0123). Garden Hill First Nation, Manitoba, 30 March 2011. (Translated from Oji-Cree to English by Translation Bureau, Public Works and Government Services Canada).

TRC. AVS. *Statement to the Truth and Reconciliation Commission of Canada*, Ethel Johnson. (Statement Number: 2011-2680). Eskasoni First Nation, Nova Scotia, 14 October 2011.

TRC. AVS. *Statement to the Truth and Reconciliation Commission of Canada*, Eugene Tetreault. (Statement Number: 01-BC-20DE10-001). Williams Lake, British Columbia, 20 December 2010.

TRC. AVS. *Statement to the Truth and Reconciliation Commission of Canada*, Evelyn Kelman. (Statement Number: SP128). Lethbridge, Alberta, 10 October 2013.

TRC. AVS. *Statement to the Truth and Reconciliation Commission of Canada*, Faron Fontaine. (Statement Number: 01-MB-26JY10-009). Long Plain First Nation, Manitoba, 27 July 2010.

TRC. AVS. *Statement to the Truth and Reconciliation Commission of Canada*, Flora Northwest. (Statement Number: SP124). Hobbema, Alberta, 24 July 2013.

TRC. AVS. *Statement to the Truth and Reconciliation Commission of Canada*, Florence Horassi. (Statement Number: 2011-0394). Tulita, Northwest Territories, 10 May 2011.

TRC. AVS. *Statement to the Truth and Reconciliation Commission of Canada,* Frances Tait. (Statement Number: 2011-3974). Victoria, British Columbia, 13 April 2012.

TRC. AVS. *Statement to the Truth and Reconciliation Commission of Canada,* Frank Tomkins. (Statement Number: 01-SK-18-25JY10-009). Batoche, Saskatchewan, 21 July 2010.

TRC. AVS. *Statement to the Truth and Reconciliation Commission of Canada,* Fred Brass. (Statement Number: SP039). Key First Nation, Saskatchewan, 21 January 2012.

TRC. AVS. *Statement to the Truth and Reconciliation Commission of Canada,* Fred Kistabish. (Statement Number: SP101). Val d'Or, Québec, 6 February 2012.

TRC. AVS. *Statement to the Truth and Reconciliation Commission of Canada,* Frederick Ernest Koe. (Statement Number: SC091.). Inuvik, Northwest Territories, 30 June 2011.

TRC. AVS. *Statement to the Truth and Reconciliation Commission of Canada,* Gerald McLeod. (Statement Number: 2011-1130). Whitehorse, Yukon, 27 May 2011.

TRC. AVS. *Statement to the Truth and Reconciliation Commission of Canada,* Geraldine Archie. (Statement Number: SC110). Winnipeg, Manitoba, 18 June 2010.

TRC. AVS. *Statement to the Truth and Reconciliation Commission of Canada,* Geraldine Bob. (Statement Number: 2011-2685). Fort Simpson, Northwest Territories, 23 November 2011.

TRC. AVS. *Statement to the Truth and Reconciliation Commission of Canada,* Gilles Petiquay. (Statement Number: 2011-6001). La Tuque, Québec, 6 March 2013. (Translated from French).

TRC. AVS. *Statement to the Truth and Reconciliation Commission of Canada,* Gladys Prince. (Statement Number: 2011-2498). Brandon, Manitoba, 13 October 2011. (Translated from Ojibway to English by Translation Bureau, Public Works and Government Services Canada)

BIBLIOGRAPHY

TRC. AVS. *Statement to the Truth and Reconciliation Commission of Canada,* Gordon James Pemmican. (Statement Number: 02-MB-18JU10-069). Winnipeg, Manitoba, 18 June 2010.

TRC. AVS. *Statement to the Truth and Reconciliation Commission of Canada,* Gordon Keewatin. (Statement Number: 01-SK-18AU10-003). Regina, Saskatchewan, 18 August 2010.

TRC. AVS. *Statement to the Truth and Reconciliation Commission of Canada,* Greg Murdock. (Statement Number: SC111). Winnipeg, Manitoba, 18 June 2010.

TRC. AVS. *Statement to the Truth and Reconciliation Commission of Canada,* Greg Rainville. (Statement Number: 2011-1752). Saskatoon, Saskatchewan, 22 June 2012.

TRC. AVS. *Statement to the Truth and Reconciliation Commission of Canada,* Harvey Behn. (Statement Number: SP021). Watson Lake, Yukon, 25 May 2011.

TRC. AVS. *Statement to the Truth and Reconciliation Commission of Canada,* Hazel Bitternose. (Statement Number: SP036). Regina, Saskatchewan, 17 January 2012.

TRC. AVS. *Statement to the Truth and Reconciliation Commission of Canada,* Hazel Mary Anderson. (Statement Number: 02-MB-18JU10-034). Winnipeg, Manitoba, 18 June 2010.

TRC. AVS. *Statement to the Truth and Reconciliation Commission of Canada,* Helen Hanson. (Statement Number: 2011-5045). Deroche, British Columbia, 20 January 2010.

TRC. AVS. *Statement to the Truth and Reconciliation Commission of Canada,* Helen Harry. (Statement Number: 2011-3203). Vancouver, British Columbia, 20 September 2013.

TRC. AVS. *Statement to the Truth and Reconciliation Commission of Canada,* Howard Stacy Jones. (Statement Number: 01-BC-03DE10-001). Victoria, British Columbia, 4 December 2010.

BIBLIOGRAPHY

TRC. AVS. *Statement to the Truth and Reconciliation Commission of Canada,* Ida Ralph Quisess. (Statement Number: 01-ON-24NOV10-002). Thunder Bay, Ontario, 24 November 2010.

TRC. AVS. *Statement to the Truth and Reconciliation Commission of Canada,* Ilene Nepoose. (Statement Number: 2011-2380). Hobbema, Alberta, 25 July 2013.

TRC. AVS. *Statement to the Truth and Reconciliation Commission of Canada,* Inez Dieter. (Statement Number: SP035). Regina, Saskatchewan, 16 January 2012.

TRC. AVS. *Statement to the Truth and Reconciliation Commission of Canada,* Isaac Daniels. (Statement Number: 2011-1779). Saskatoon, Saskatchewan, 22 June 2012.

TRC. AVS. *Statement to the Truth and Reconciliation Commission of Canada,* Isabelle Whitford. (Statement Number: S-KFN-MB-01-004). 28 May 2010. Keeseekoowenin First Nation, Manitoba, 28 May 2010.

TRC. AVS. *Statement to the Truth and Reconciliation Commission of Canada,* Ivan George. (Statement Number: 2011-3472). Mission, British Columbia, 18 May 2011.

TRC. AVS. *Statement to the Truth and Reconciliation Commission of Canada,* J. G. Michel Sutherland. (Statement Number: SP099). Fort Albany, Ontario, 29 January 2013.

TRC. AVS. *Statement to the Truth and Reconciliation Commission of Canada,* Jack Anawak. (Statement Number: NNE202). Inuvik, Northwest Territories, 30 June 2011.

TRC. AVS. *Statement to the Truth and Reconciliation Commission of Canada,* Jaco Anaviapik (Statement Number: SP044). Pond Inlet, Nunavut, 7 February 2014. (Translated from Inuktitut).

TRC. AVS. *Statement to the Truth and Reconciliation Commission of Canada,* Jeanette Basile Laloche. (Statement Number: 2011-6136). Montreal, Québec, 27 April 2013. (Translated from French)

BIBLIOGRAPHY

TRC. AVS. *Statement to the Truth and Reconciliation Commission of Canada,* Jeanne Paul. (Statement Number: 2011-3464). Mission, British Columbia, 18 May 2011.

TRC. AVS. *Statement to the Truth and Reconciliation Commission of Canada,* Jeannette Coo Coo. (Statement Number: SP105). La Tuque, Québec, 6 March 2013.

TRC. AVS. *Statement to the Truth and Reconciliation Commission of Canada,* Jennie Thomas. (Statement Number: 2011-3992). Victoria, British Columbia, 14 April 2012.

TRC. AVS. *Statement to the Truth and Reconciliation Commission of Canada,* Jimmy Cunningham. (Statement Number: SP207). Edmonton, Alberta, 30 March 2014.

TRC. AVS. *Statement to the Truth and Reconciliation Commission of Canada,* Joanne Morrison Methot. (Statement Number: 2011-2875.) Halifax, Nova Scotia. 28 October 2011.

TRC. AVS. *Statement to the Truth and Reconciliation Commission of Canada,* Joe Krimmerdjuar. (Statement Number: SC091). Inuvik, Northwest Territories, 30 June 2011.

TRC. AVS. *Statement to the Truth and Reconciliation Commission of Canada,* John B. Custer. (Statement Number: 02-MB-19JU10-057). Winnipeg, Manitoba, 19 June 2010.

TRC. AVS. *Statement to the Truth and Reconciliation Commission of Canada,* John Edwards. (Statement Number: 2011-0328). Inuvik, Northwest Territories, 5 August 2011.

TRC. AVS. *Statement to the Truth and Reconciliation Commission of Canada,* John Kistabish. (Statement Number: 2011-6135). Montreal, Québec, 26 April 2013.

TRC. AVS. *Statement to the Truth and Reconciliation Commission of Canada,* Joseph Martin Larocque. (Statement Number: 2011-4386). Saskatoon, Saskatchewan, 21 June 2012.

TRC. AVS. Joseph Maud. *Statement to the Truth and Reconciliation Commission of Canada,* (Statement Number: 02-MB-18JU10-081). Winnipeg, Manitoba, 19 June 2010.

TRC. AVS. *Statement to the Truth and Reconciliation Commission of Canada,* Josephine Eshkibok. (Statement Number: 2011-2014). Little Current, Ontario, 13 May 2011.

TRC. AVS. *Statement to the Truth and Reconciliation Commission of Canada,* Josephine Sutherland. (Statement Number: 01-ON4-6NOV10-013). Timmins, Ontario, 8 November 2010.

TRC. AVS. *Statement to the Truth and Reconciliation Commission of Canada,* Josiah Fiddler. (Statement Number: SC111). Winnipeg, Manitoba, 18 June 2010.

TRC. AVS. *Statement to the Truth and Reconciliation Commission of Canada,* Julianna Alexander. (Statement Number: 2011-3286). Enderby, British Columbia, 12 October 2011.

TRC. AVS. *Statement to the Truth and Reconciliation Commission of Canada,* Ken A. Littledeer. (Statement Number: 01-ON-24-NOV10-028). Thunder Bay, Ontario, 26 November 2010.

TRC. AVS. *Statement to the Truth and Reconciliation Commission of Canada,* Kiatch Nahanni. (Statement Number: 2011-2684). Fort Simpson, Northwest Territories, 23 November 2011.

TRC. AVS. *Statement to the Truth and Reconciliation Commission of Canada,* Larry Beardy. (Statement Number: SP082). Thompson, Manitoba, 25 September 2012.

TRC. AVS. *Statement to the Truth and Reconciliation Commission of Canada,* Larry Roger Listener. (Statement Number: SP125). Hobbema, Alberta, 25 July 2013.

TRC. AVS. *Statement to the Truth and Reconciliation Commission of Canada,* Lawrence Wanakamik. (Statement Number: 01-ON-06JA11-002). Thunder Bay, Ontario, 6 January 2011.

BIBLIOGRAPHY

TRC. AVS. *Statement to the Truth and Reconciliation Commission of Canada,* Lawrence Waquan. (Statement Number: SC111). Winnipeg, Manitoba, 18 June 2010.

TRC. AVS. *Statement to the Truth and Reconciliation Commission of Canada,* Lena McKay. (Statement Number: 2011-0382). Fort Resolution, Northwest Territories, 28 April 2011.

TRC. AVS. *Statement to the Truth and Reconciliation Commission of Canada,* Lena Small. (Statement Number: SP124). Hobbema, Alberta, 24 July 2013.

TRC. AVS. *Statement to the Truth and Reconciliation Commission of Canada,* Leon Wyallon. (Statement Number: 2011-0244). Behchoko, Northwest Territories, 15 April 2011.

TRC. AVS. *Statement to the Truth and Reconciliation Commission of Canada,* Leona Agawa. (Statement Number: 01-ON-4-6 NOV10-006). Sault Ste. Marie, Ontario, 6 November 2010.

TRC. AVS. *Statement to the Truth and Reconciliation Commission of Canada,* Leona Bird. (Statement Number: 2011-4415). Saskatoon, Saskatchewan, 21 June 2012.

TRC. AVS. *Statement to the Truth and Reconciliation Commission of Canada,* Leonard Peter Alexcee. (Statement Number: 2011-3228). Vancouver, British Columbia, 18 September 2013.

TRC. AVS. *Statement to the Truth and Reconciliation Commission of Canada,* Lillian Kennedy. (Statement Number: 2011-2563). Bloodvein First Nation, Manitoba, 25 January 2012.

TRC. AVS. *Statement to the Truth and Reconciliation Commission of Canada,* Lily Bruce. (Statement Number: 2011-3285). Alert Bay, British Columbia, 4 August 2011.

TRC. AVS. *Statement to the Truth and Reconciliation Commission of Canada,* Linda Head. (Statement Number: 2011-4442). Saskatoon, Saskatchewan, 24 June 2012.

BIBLIOGRAPHY

TRC. AVS. *Statement to the Truth and Reconciliation Commission of Canada,* Lizette Olson. (Statement Number: 2011-3878). Prince Albert, Saskatchewan, 1 February 2012. (Translated from Woodland Cree to English by Translation Bureau, Public Works and Government Services Canada).

TRC. AVS. *Statement to the Truth and Reconciliation Commission of Canada,* Loretta Mainville. (Statement Number: 02-MB-16JU10-089). Winnipeg, Manitoba, 16 June 2010.

TRC. AVS. *Statement to the Truth and Reconciliation Commission of Canada,* Lorna Morgan. (Statement Number: 02-MB-16JU10-041). Winnipeg, Manitoba, 17 June 2010.

TRC. AVS. *Statement to the Truth and Reconciliation Commission of Canada,* Louisa Birote. (Statement Number: SP104). La Tuque, Québec, 5 March 2013.

TRC. AVS. *Statement to the Truth and Reconciliation Commission of Canada,* Louise Bossum. (Statement Number: SP105). La Tuque, Québec, 6 March 2013.

TRC. AVS. *Statement to the Truth and Reconciliation Commission of Canada,* Louise Large. (Statement Number: 01-AB-06JA11-012). St. Paul, Alberta, 7 January 2011.

TRC. AVS. *Statement to the Truth and Reconciliation Commission of Canada,* Lydia Ross. (Statement Number: 02-MB-16JU10-029). Winnipeg, Manitoba, 16 June 2010.

TRC. AVS. *Statement to the Truth and Reconciliation Commission of Canada,* Lynda Pahpasay McDonald. (Statement Number: 02-MB-16JU10-130). Winnipeg, Manitoba, 16 June 2010.

TRC. AVS. *Statement to the Truth and Reconciliation Commission of Canada,* Mabel Brown. (Statement Number: 2011-0325) Inuvik, Northwest Territories, 28 September 2011.

TRC. AVS. *Statement to the Truth and Reconciliation Commission of Canada,* Madeleine Dion Stout. (Statement Number: 02-MB-18JU10-059). Winnipeg, Manitoba, 18 June 2010.

TRC. AVS. *Statement to the Truth and Reconciliation Commission of Canada,* Marcel Guiboche. (Statement Number: 02-MB-19JU10-034). Winnipeg, Manitoba, 19 June 2010.

TRC. AVS. *Statement to the Truth and Reconciliation Commission of Canada,* Margaret Plamondon. (Statement Number: 2011-0387). Fort Smith, Northwest Territories, 6 May 2011.

TRC. AVS. *Statement to the Truth and Reconciliation Commission of Canada,* Margaret Simpson. (Statement Number: 02-MB-18JU10-051). Winnipeg, Manitoba, 18 June 2010.

TRC. AVS. *Statement to the Truth and Reconciliation Commission of Canada,* Margo Wylde. (Statement Number SP100). Val d'Or, Québec, 5 February 2012.

TRC. AVS. *Statement to the Truth and Reconciliation Commission of Canada,* Marilyn Buffalo. (Statement Number: SP125). Hobbema, Alberta, 25 July 2013.

TRC. AVS. *Statement to the Truth and Reconciliation Commission of Canada.* Marlene Kayseas. (Statement Number: SP035). Regina, Saskatchewan, 16 January 2012.

TRC. AVS. *Statement to the Truth and Reconciliation Commission of Canada,* Martha Loon. (Statement Number 01-ON-24NOV10-021). Thunder Bay, Ontario, 25 November 2010.

TRC. AVS. *Statement to the Truth and Reconciliation Commission of Canada,* Martha Minoose. (Statement Number: 2011-1748). Lethbridge, Alberta, 10 October 2013.

TRC. AVS. *Statement to the Truth and Reconciliation Commission of Canada,* Marthe Basile-Coocoo. (Translated from French. Statement Number: 2011-6103). Montreal, Québec, 26 April 2013.

TRC. AVS. *Statement to the Truth and Reconciliation Commission of Canada,* Martin Nicholas. (Statement Number: 07-MB-24FB10-001). Manitoba, Grand Rapids, 24 February 2010.

BIBLIOGRAPHY

TRC. AVS. *Statement to the Truth and Reconciliation Commission of Canada,* Martina Therese Fisher. (Statement Number: 2011-2564). Bloodvein First Nation, Manitoba, 26 January 2012.

TRC. AVS. *Statement to the Truth and Reconciliation Commission of Canada,* Mary Beatrice Talley. (Statement Number: 2011-3197). High Level, Alberta, 3 July 2013.

TRC. AVS. *Statement to the Truth and Reconciliation Commission of Canada.* Mary Courchene. (Statement Number: 2011-2515). Pine Creek First Nation, Manitoba, 28 November 2011.

TRC. AVS. *Statement to the Truth and Reconciliation Commission of Canada,* Mary Lou Iahtail. (Statement Number: 01-ON-05FE11-005). Ottawa, Ontario, 5 February 2011.

TRC. AVS. *Statement to the Truth and Reconciliation Commission of Canada,* Mary Olibuk Tatty. (Statement Number: 2011-0156). Rankin Inlet, Nunavut, 21 March 2011.

TRC. AVS. *Statement to the Truth and Reconciliation Commission of Canada,* Mary Rose Julian. (Statement Number: 2011-2880). Halifax, Nova Scotia, 27 October 2011.

TRC. AVS. *Statement to the Truth and Reconciliation Commission of Canada,* Mary Stoney. (Statement Number: SP124). Hobbema, Alberta, 24 July 2013.

TRC. AVS. *Statement to the Truth and Reconciliation Commission of Canada,* Mary Teya. (Statement Number: SP019). Aklavik, Northwest Territories, 12 May 2011.

TRC. AVS. *Statement to the Truth and Reconciliation Commission of Canada,* Mary Vivier. (Statement Number: 02-MB-18JU10-082). Winnipeg, Manitoba, 18 June 2010.

TRC. AVS. *Statement to the Truth and Reconciliation Commission of Canada,* Maureen Gloria Johnson. (Statement Number: 2011-1126). Whitehorse, Yukon, 26 May 2011.

BIBLIOGRAPHY

TRC. AVS. *Statement to the Truth and Reconciliation Commission of Canada,* Meeka Alivaktuk. (Statement Number: SP045). Pangnirtung, Nunavut, 13 February 2012. (Translated from Inuktitut)

TRC. AVS. *Statement to the Truth and Reconciliation Commission of Canada,* Megan Molaluk. (Statement Number: SC090). Inuvik, Northwest Territories, 29 June 2011.

TRC. AVS. *Statement to the Truth and Reconciliation Commission of Canada,* Mel H. Buffalo. (Statement Number: SP124). Hobbema, Alberta, 24 July 2013.

TRC. AVS. *Statement to the Truth and Reconciliation Commission of Canada,* Mervin Mirasty. (Statement Number: 2011-4391). Saskatoon, Saskatchewan, 21 June 2012.

TRC. AVS. *Statement to the Truth and Reconciliation Commission of Canada,* Mollie Roy. (Statement Number: 2011-1129). Whitehorse, Yukon, 26 May 2011.

TRC. AVS. *Statement to the Truth and Reconciliation Commission of Canada,* Monique Papatie. (Statement Number: SP101). Val d'Or, Québec, 6 February 2012.

TRC. AVS. *Statement to the Truth and Reconciliation Commission of Canada,* Muriel Morrisseau. (Statement Number: 02-MB-18JU10-057). Winnipeg, Manitoba, 18 June 2010.

TRC. AVS. *Statement to the Truth and Reconciliation Commission of Canada,* Murray Crowe. (Statement Number: 2011-0306). Sault Ste. Marie, Ontario, 1 July 2011.

TRC. AVS. *Statement to the Truth and Reconciliation Commission of Canada,* Nellie Ningewance. (Statement Number: 2011-0305). Sault Ste. Marie, Ontario, 1 July 2011.

TRC. AVS. *Statement to the Truth and Reconciliation Commission of Canada,* Nellie Trapper. (Statement Number: 02-MB-16JU10-086). Winnipeg, Manitoba, 18 June 2010.

BIBLIOGRAPHY

TRC. AVS. *Statement to the Truth and Reconciliation Commission of Canada,* Nick Sibbeston. (Statement Number: NNE202). Inuvik, Northwest Territories, 30 June 2011.

TRC. AVS. *Statement to the Truth and Reconciliation Commission of Canada,* Noel Knockwood. (Statement Number: 2011-2922). Halifax, Nova Scotia, 29 October 2011.

TRC. AVS. *Statement to the Truth and Reconciliation Commission of Canada,* Noel Starblanket. (Statement Number: 2011-3314). Regina, Saskatchewan, 16 January 2012.

TRC. AVS. *Statement to the Truth and Reconciliation Commission of Canada,* Nora Abou-Tibbett. (Statement Number: 2011-0205). Watson Lake, Yukon, 25 May 2011.

TRC. AVS. *Statement to the Truth and Reconciliation Commission of Canada,* Patrick Bruyere. (Statement Number: 02-MB-16JU10-157). Winnipeg, Manitoba, 16 June 2010.

TRC. AVS. *Statement to the Truth and Reconciliation Commission of Canada,* Patrick James Hall. (Statement Number: 03-001-10-036). Winnipeg, Manitoba, 21 December 2010.

TRC. AVS. *Statement to the Truth and Reconciliation Commission of Canada,* Paul Dixon. (Statement Number: SP101). Val d'Or, Québec, 6 February 2012.

TRC. AVS. *Statement to the Truth and Reconciliation Commission of Canada,* Paul Johnup. (Statement Number: 02-MB-16JU10-147). Winnipeg, Manitoba, 16 June 2010.

TRC. AVS. *Statement to the Truth and Reconciliation Commission of Canada,* Percy Thompson. (Statement Number: SP125). Hobbema, Alberta, 25 July 2013.

TRC. AVS. *Statement to the Truth and Reconciliation Commission of Canada,* Percy Tuesday. (Statement Number: 02-MB-18JU10-083). Winnipeg, Manitoba, 18 June 2010.

TRC, AVS. *Statement to the Truth and Reconciliation Commission of Canada,* Peter Nakogee. (Statement Number: 01-ON-4-6NOV10-023). Timmins, Ontario, 9 November 2010. (Translated from Swampy Cree to English by Translation Bureau, Public Works and Government Services Canada.)

TRC. AVS. *Statement to the Truth and Reconciliation Commission of Canada,* Peter Ross. (Statement Number: 2011-0340). Tsiigehtchic, Northwest Territories, 8 September 2011.

TRC. AVS. *Statement to the Truth and Reconciliation Commission of Canada*, Phyllis Webstad. (Statement Number: SP111). Williams Lake, British Columbia, 16 May 2013.

TRC. AVS. *Statement to the Truth and Reconciliation Commission of Canada,* Pierrette Benjamin. (Statement Number: SP105). La Tuque, Québec, 6 March 2013.

TRC. AVS. *Statement to the Truth and Reconciliation Commission of Canada,* Piita Irniq. (Statement Number: 2011-2905). Halifax, Nova Scotia, 27 October 2011.

TRC. AVS. *Statement to the Truth and Reconciliation Commission of Canada,* Rachel Chakasim. (Statement Number: 01-ON-4-6NOV10-019). Timmins, Ontario, 9 November 2010.

TRC. AVS. *Statement to the Truth and Reconciliation Commission of Canada,* Raphael Victor Paul. (Statement Number: 02-MB-19JU10-051). Winnipeg, Manitoba, 19 June 2010.

TRC. AVS. *Statement to the Truth and Reconciliation Commission of Canada,* Ray Silver. (Statement Number: 2011-3467). Mission, British Columbia, 17 May 2011.

TRC. AVS. *Statement to the Truth and Reconciliation Commission of Canada,* Raymond Cutknife. (Statement Number: SP125). Hobbema, Alberta, 25 July 2013.

TRC. AVS. *Statement to the Truth and Reconciliation Commission of Canada,* Raynie Tuckanow. (Statement Number: SP036). Regina, Saskatchewan, 17 January 2012.

BIBLIOGRAPHY

TRC. AVS. *Statement to the Truth and Reconciliation Commission of Canada,* Rebecca Many Grey Horses. (Statement Number: SP127). Lethbridge, Alberta, 9 October 2013.

TRC. AVS. *Statement to the Truth and Reconciliation Commission of Canada,* Richard Hall. (Statement Number: 2011-1852). Vancouver, British Columbia, 18 September 2013.

TRC. AVS. *Statement to the Truth and Reconciliation Commission of Canada,* Richard Kaiyogan. (Statement Number: SC091). Inuvik, Northwest Territories, 30 June 2011.

TRC. AVS. *Statement to the Truth and Reconciliation Commission of Canada,* Richard Morrison. (Statement Number: 02-MB-17JU10-080). Winnipeg, Manitoba, 17 June 2010.

TRC. AVS. *Statement to the Truth and Reconciliation Commission of Canada,* Rick Gilbert. (Statement Number: 2011-2389). Vancouver, British Columbia, 20 September 2013.

TRC. AVS. *Statement to the Truth and Reconciliation Commission of Canada,* Ricky Kakekagumick. (Statement Number: 2011-4200). Thunder Bay, Ontario, 15 December 2011.

TRC. AVS. *Statement to the Truth and Reconciliation Commission of Canada,* Rita Carpenter. (Statement Number: 2011-0339). Tsiigehtchic, Northwest Territories, 8 September 2011.

TRC. AVS. *Statement to the Truth and Reconciliation Commission of Canada,* Robert Joseph. (Statement Number: SC093). Winnipeg, Manitoba, 16 June 2010.

TRC. AVS. *Statement to the Truth and Reconciliation Commission of Canada,* Robert Malcolm. (Statement Number: 02-MB-16JU10-090). Winnipeg, Manitoba, 17 June 2010.

TRC. AVS. *Statement to the Truth and Reconciliation Commission of Canada,* Roddy Soosay. (Statement Number: 2011-2379). Hobbema, Alberta, 25 July 2013.

BIBLIOGRAPHY

TRC. AVS. *Statement to the Truth and Reconciliation Commission of Canada,* Roger Cromarty. (Statement Number: 02-MB-16JU10-132). Winnipeg, Manitoba, 17 June 2010.

TRC. AVS. *Statement to the Truth and Reconciliation Commission of Canada,* Ronalee Lavallee. (Statement Number: 2011-1776). Saskatoon, Saskatchewan, 24 June 2012.

TRC. AVS. *Statement to the Truth and Reconciliation Commission of Canada,* Rosalie Webber. (Statement Number: 2011-2891). Halifax, Nova Scotia, 26 October 2011.

TRC. AVS. *Statement to the Truth and Reconciliation Commission of Canada,* Rose Dorothy Charlie. (Statement Number: 2011-1134). Whitehorse, Yukon, 27 May 2011.

TRC. AVS. *Statement to the Truth and Reconciliation Commission of Canada,* Rose Marie Prosper. (Statement Number: 2011-2868). Halifax, Nova Scotia, 28 October 2011.

TRC. AVS. *Statement to the Truth and Reconciliation Commission of Canada,* Rosie Kagak. (Statement Number: SC090). Inuvik, Northwest Territories, 29 June 2011.

TRC. AVS. *Statement to the Truth and Reconciliation Commission of Canada,* Roy Denny. (Statement Number: 2011-2678). Eskasoni, Nova Scotia, 14 October 2011.

TRC. AVS. Russell Bone. *Statement to the Truth and Reconciliation Commission of Canada,* (Statement Number: S-KFN-MB-01-001). Keeseekoowenin First Nation, Manitoba, 28 May 2010.

TRC. AVS. *Statement to the Truth and Reconciliation Commission of Canada,* Sam Kautainuk (Statement Number: SP044). Pond Inlet, Nunavut, 7 February 2012. (Translated from Inuktitut).

TRC. AVS. *Statement to the Truth and Reconciliation Commission of Canada,* Sam Ross. (Statement Number: 2011-0294). Opaskwayak Cree Nation, Manitoba, 17 January 2012.

BIBLIOGRAPHY

TRC. AVS. *Statement to the Truth and Reconciliation Commission of Canada,* Sarah McLeod. (Statement Number: 2011-5009). Kamloops, British Columbia, 8 August 2009.

TRC. AVS. *Statement to the Truth and Reconciliation Commission of Canada,* Sheila Gunderson. (Statement Number: 2011-2687). 2 Fort Simpson, Northwest Territories, 3 November 2011.

TRC. AVS. *Statement to the Truth and Reconciliation Commission of Canada,* Shirley Ida Moore. (Statement Number: 2011-0089). Winnipeg, Manitoba, 2 March 2011.

TRC. AVS. *Statement to the Truth and Reconciliation Commission of Canada,* Shirley Leon. (Statement Number: 2011-5048). Deroche, British Columbia, 19 January 2010.

TRC. AVS. *Statement to the Truth and Reconciliation Commission of Canada,* Shirley M. Villeneuve. (Statement Number: 2011-2691). Fort Simpson, Northwest Territories, 23 February 2011.

TRC. AVS. *Statement to the Truth and Reconciliation Commission of Canada,* Shirley Waskewitch. (Statement Number: 2011-3521). Saskatoon, Saskatchewan, 24 June 2012.

TRC. AVS. *Statement to the Truth and Reconciliation Commission of Canada,* Shirley Williams. (Statement Number: 2011-5040). Spanish, Ontario, 12 September 2009.

TRC. AVS. *Statement to the Truth and Reconciliation Commission of Canada,* Simeon Nakoochee. (Statement Number: 2011-4316). Fort Albany, Ontario, 28 January 2013.

TRC. AVS. *Statement to the Truth and Reconciliation Commission of Canada,* Stella August. (Statement Number: 02-MB-16JU10-005). Winnipeg, Manitoba, 16 June 2010.

TRC. AVS. *Statement to the Truth and Reconciliation Commission of Canada,* Stella Bone. (Statement Number: S-KFN-MB-01-006). Keeseekoowenin First Nation, Manitoba, 29 May 2010.

BIBLIOGRAPHY

TRC. AVS. *Statement to the Truth and Reconciliation Commission of Canada,* Stephen Kakfwi. (Statement Number: NNE202). Inuvik, Northwest Territories, 30 June 2011.

TRC. AVS. *Statement to the Truth and Reconciliation Commission of Canada,* Thérèse Niquay. (Statement Number: SP105). La Tuque, Québec, 6 March 2013.

TRC. AVS. *Statement to the Truth and Reconciliation Commission of Canada,* Thomas Keesick. (Statement Number: 02-MB-16JU10-156). Winnipeg, Manitoba, 16 June 2010.

TRC. AVS. *Statement to the Truth and Reconciliation Commission of Canada,* Timothy Henderson. (Statement Number: 2011-0291). Winnipeg, Manitoba, 28 June 2011.

TRC. AVS. *Statement to the Truth and Reconciliation Commission of Canada,* Tina Duguay. (Statement Number: 2011-5002). Kamloops, British Columbia, 9 August 2009.

TRC. AVS. *Statement to the Truth and Reconciliation Commission of Canada,* Ula Hotonami. (Statement Number: 2011-2654). Winnipeg, Manitoba, 5 January 2012.

TRC. AVS. *Statement to the Truth and Reconciliation Commission of Canada,* Verna Kirkness. (Statement Number: 02-MB-18JU10-033). Winnipeg, Manitoba, 18 June 2010.

TRC. AVS. *Statement to the Truth and Reconciliation Commission of Canada,* Victoria Boucher-Grant. (Statement Number: 01-ON-05FE11-004). Ottawa, Ontario, 5 February 2011.

TRC. AVS. *Statement to the Truth and Reconciliation Commission of Canada,* Victoria McIntosh. (Statement Number: 02-MB-16JU10-123). Winnipeg, Manitoba, 16 June 2010.

TRC. AVS. *Statement to the Truth and Reconciliation Commission of Canada,* Violet Beaulieu. (Statement Number: 2011-0377). Fort Resolution, Northwest Territories, 28 April 2011.

BIBLIOGRAPHY

TRC. AVS. *Statement to the Truth and Reconciliation Commission of Canada,* Violet Rupp Cook. (Statement Number: 2011-2565). Bloodvein First Nation, Manitoba, 25 January 2012.

TRC. AVS. *Statement to the Truth and Reconciliation Commission of Canada,* Vitaline Elsie Jenner. (Statement Number: 02-MB-16JU10-131). Winnipeg, Manitoba, 16 June 2010.

TRC. AVS. *Statement to the Truth and Reconciliation Commission of Canada,* Walter Jones. (Statement Number: 2011-4008). Victoria, British Columbia, 14 April 2012.

TRC. AVS. *Statement to the Truth and Reconciliation Commission of Canada,* Wesley Keewatin. (Statement Number: 2011-3276). Gambier Island, British Columbia, 28 July 2011.

TRC. AVS. *Statement to the Truth and Reconciliation Commission of Canada,* Wilbur Abrahams. (Statement Number: 2011-3301). Terrace, British Columbia, 30 November 2011.

TRC. AVS. *Statement to the Truth and Reconciliation Commission of Canada,* William Antoine. (Statement Number: 2011-2002). Little Current, Ontario, 12 May 2011.

TRC. AVS. *Statement to the Truth and Reconciliation Commission of Canada,* William Francis Paul. (Statement Number: 2011-2873). Halifax, Nova Scotia, 28 October 2011.

TRC. AVS. *Statement to the Truth and Reconciliation Commission of Canada,* William Garson. (Statement Number: 2011-0122). Split Lake First Nation, Manitoba, 24 March 2011.

TRC. AVS. *Statement to the Truth and Reconciliation Commission of Canada,* William Herney. (Statement Number: 2011-2923). Halifax, Nova Scotia, 29 October 2011.

TRC. AVS. *Statement to the Truth and Reconciliation Commission of Canada,* Woodie Elias. (Statement Number: 2011-0343). Fort McPherson, Northwest Territories, 12 September 2012.

BIBLIOGRAPHY

www.ingramcontent.com/pod-product-compliance
Lightning Source LLC
Chambersburg PA
CBHW070419010526
44118CB00014B/1819